For Jan —
Bon voyage and
best regards,
Marty Jackson
10/1/80

TROUBLE-FREE TRAVEL

Marty Leshner appears regularly as "The Travel Advisor" on the internationally syndicated Dinah Shore Show, DINAH!, and, in that capacity, reports each month on current travel news, destinations throughout the world, tips for travelers...and shares with viewers highlights of his trips at home and abroad. Chances are you may have read of Marty's travels if you've picked up a copy of *Carte Blanche, Westways, Travel/Holiday, The Travel Advisor, Diversion,* and *Airfair* magazines...or any of a dozen newspapers across the country which have published his travel features.

When he is not traveling his average 100,000 miles a year, Marty is a writer/producer in television, having worked with Joey Bishop, David Frost, Jack Paar, Alan King, Howard Cosell, and Dinah Shore...all of whom have happily encouraged his globetrotting instincts.

TROUBLE-FREE TRAVEL

WHAT TO KNOW BEFORE YOU GO

BY MARTY LESHNER

Franklin Watts
New York/London/Toronto/Sydney
1980

Library of Congress Cataloging in Publication Data

Leshner, Marty.
Trouble-free travel.

Includes index.
1. Travel. I. Title.
G151.L47   910′.2′02   80-10460
ISBN 0-531-09926-1
ISBN 0-531-09924-5 pbk.

Copyright © 1980 by Marty Leshner

Printed in the United States of America

5 4 3 2 1

CONTENTS_____

For Mom and Aunt Syl

FOREWORD

by Dinah Shore

In the three years that Marty Leshner has been associated with our show in a creative consultant capacity, I have noticed two very distinctive traits: (1) he disappears a lot on exotic trips, and (2) he has a persistent tan. Once I asked him how he managed these two things—he has never given me a satisfactory explanation for the tan but as to the disappearance for these exotic trips, he simply answered, "I have this terrific relationship with the star." And he does.

Early in 1978, "Marty Travel" (as we call him at the show) was encouraged to share his love of travel with our viewers. On a regularly scheduled basis, he appeared on Dinah! and talked about his adventures in Mexico, Poland, New England, and Sri Lanka filling us, as he spoke, with the wonder and joy that travel should be—and is—when Marty is talking about it. When he wasn't doing dream destination pieces, Marty showed us how to pack, how to stay healthy overseas, and how to fight the war with an elastic clothesline and survive. While we laughed a good deal, the responses from our viewers suggest that Marty is also providing a valuable service by removing some of the intimidating aspects of travel from the trips you and I have always wanted to take.

This book, like Marty, is good to have around, and because it is terrific and useful, it will no doubt help Marty embark on a new career which he deserves. Still, we'll count on his regular visits to the show and the vicarious pleasures he affords us with his adventures.

Bon voyage, Marty, and love.

INTRODUCTION_____

Travel is such a big business that it generates $126 billion a year in revenues, but that doesn't mean a thing to you if the tour package you bought fails to deliver all the features it promised. Something like twenty-six million Americans traveled overseas in 1978, but you could care less if the "deluxe" hotel room you reserved turns out to look like a reconverted jail cell.

This very personal experience called travel is as good to you as you are to it: a trip takes planning, thought, know-how, and a sense of humor. Most of all a sense of humor. During the past five years, I've traveled an average of 100,000 miles each year and—in that time—I have twice lost luggage (once I even lost a travel companion), contracted three common and two completely unknown diseases, have been made a tribal chief in Fiji and named principal dancer with a folk group in Dubrovnik, have flown in supersonic aircraft and hot-air balloons, have eaten anything placed before me which wasn't moving, and have the distinction of bringing home more overexposed photographs than any other returning tourist. And all of this has provided me with incredible learning experiences: I've met fascinating people throughout the world and—in genuinely warm encounters—have reached out to learn about them; I've brought back libraries of memories filled with visual images of South Pacific sunsets and Dalmatian autumns, religious rites and village weddings, presidential palaces and thatched-roof huts, sumptuous feasts and a grab bag from a roadside fruit stand. From *every* trip, I learned something that filled out my colors as a person . . . and that sense of personal growth is one of the unmistakable joys of travel.

For two years, I have been sharing my adventures and travel tips on Dinah Shore's television show where I serve as Dinah's on-the-air "travel advisor." Every three of four weeks, I appear on the show and either report on a specific destination or simply give practical tips of interest and (I hope) value to travelers. This experience has in many ways changed my life, affording me, as it does, visibility as a "performer" and the opportunity to establish a very personal contact with the millions of viewers who watch, and love, Dinah. (And, yes, she is that nice in person.) After each appearance, I get mail from viewers who want to know more about where I've been, what I've seen and done, and how they can get more information so they can do it too. More often than not, however, the mail deals with basic travel questions (many are reproduced in this book) that have nothing whatever to do with specific destinations: "Should I travel alone or with a group?" "How do I get a new passport?" "How much should I pack for a three-week trip?" "Where do I find a travel agent, and how much will he or she charge?" "Should I plan on drinking just bottled water?" "How much can I buy overseas and bring back home without paying duty?" "Do you think I'm the kind of person who would enjoy an ocean cruise?" "How can I be sure that I'll have a good time?"

This last question is the most persistent and ethereal of all and the answer is difficult because there are so many variables involved. Still, I'm certain you will increase the chances of your having a good time if you give the trip the attention and planning it, *you*, deserve. Even a vacation requires a little bit of hard work. This book, then, focuses on the various elements that could calm your vacation waters and help ensure that you enjoy trouble-free travel. If you know what you need to know, chances are you'll have a better time once you get there.

Since a vacation reflects the person who is taking it, I hope you will be asking yourself some penetrating questions about what you want to accomplish with your getaway. I suspect as many people are disappointed by having selected the wrong kind of trip as are disgusted by inept service or shoddy hotel rooms. Once you have decided on what it is you want, the pre-trip chores are easily negotiated. I promise.

In writing this book I have drawn not only on personal experiences but on the resourceful guidance of fellow travelers as well. When appropriate, I have mentioned references throughout the book that will provide you with additional information on specific subjects; some of these materials are yours for the asking—absolutely free. I'd like to acknowledge and recommend three books for the traveler: *Time Off, a Psychological Guide to Vacations* (Doubleday, $5.95); *The Year-' Round Travelers' Health Guide* by Drs. Patrick J. Doyle and James E. Banta (Acropolis Books, $4.95); and *The Complete Handbook for Travelers* (Simon and Schuster, $6.95).* Airlines produce an astonishing quantity of readable, free material on numerous subjects; in this regard, I found TWA's *Climates and Clothes* and *Tipping in Europe, the Middle East, and the United States* especially helpful. So will you.

Finally, I believe that travel is fun and so should books be that are written about it. Admittedly, it's difficult to be amusing in a book that recommends shops for opal in the Orient or the best trout amandine in Provence; fortunately, this is *not* that kind of book. Here, I've tried to organize essential information and trip-tested tips for the beginning traveler while providing some useful notions for the seasoned old hand. The goal for both audiences is, quite simply, to make the next trip the best one yet. It would please me very much to hear that you read this book and had a laugh while you learned. It would please me even more to find my lost luggage, to discover bathrooms that work, to eat croissants that do not crack caps, to be on an on-time flight, to find a tour guide who does not do Henny Youngman's jokes, and to have the last laugh on Montezuma. And that is a traveler's prayer.

Marty Leshner

Los Angeles, Calif.

---

* Prices noted are current as of publication date.

1

KNOWING WHO YOU ARE AND WHAT YOU WANT

Until I was twenty-four years old, travel seemed to be a book I was never destined to read. My family lived in Philadelphia and, for me, the only exotic destination I knew was Atlantic City; the most foreign of my confrontations was saying hello to the contestant from Puerto Rico at the Miss America Pageant. I hardly came from roots in the Lewis and Clark tradition of exploration. And yet all around me there were stimuli to set me off on some beaten path. I saw *Three Coins in the Fountain* and wondered when it would be my turn to throw a coin in the Fountain of Trevi; I was exhilarated by *Zorba the Greek* and began to read about the Greek isles while secretly sipping ouzo; and compassionate though I was in watching Elizabeth Taylor nearly being trampled to death by stampeding elephants in *Elephant Walk*, I envied her the adventure of a trip to Sri Lanka where the movie was filmed. Atlantic City might have Bert Parks, but it was no Sri Lanka.

When I graduated from college, I received a generous gift which had implications for that summer and, so it seems, for my life: I was given a trip to Europe. It was one of those whirlwind France, Belgium, Italy, Germany tours, and then, after breakfast, we got to see England, Portugal, and Spain. At least it seemed that hectic. Now, fifteen years later, when my alarm goes off in the morning, I still jump out of bed and automatically put my suitcase in the hall. I traveled with thirty-six truly diverse people bound by three goals: (1) to see all of Europe in twenty-eight days, (2) to accomplish this adventure as cheaply as possible (the tour was less than $1000 all-inclusive), and (3) to bump off our group leader once this odyssey was over. It's difficult to love a man who ends each day with, "breakfast at six thirty sharp." I learned a great deal about myself on that "If it's Tuesday, this must be Belgium" adventure. For instance, I discovered that I was equally at home in the English countryside (where I could speak the language) as I was in the streets of Portugal where I could not. I seemed at ease, content, and fascinated with strange hotels, exotic foods, sight-seeing, and—most of all—with the opportunity to meet the people of the world on their own turf.

Born without a silver passport in my mouth, I candidly confess that I was not the debonair bon vivant I would like to have been on that first European trip. In quaint Heidelberg, I had a beautiful evening at an old German inn as violinists coddled me into thinking that I, in fact, was "The Student Prince." After one too many steins of beer, I quietly retreated to use the hotel's facilities. The bathroom fixtures looked like a Cuisinart with a thyroid condition, and I had no idea which lever to pull. In desperation, I pulled several at the same time and instantly knew in my heart I had done something wrong. Screams and shouts echoed throughout the hotel, and I quickly discovered why: one of the levers had activated all the fountains . . . and there was an outdoor wedding in progress at the time. This incident gave several hundred Germans a new appreciation of the song "Singing in the Rain."

On successive trips, I became more familiar with the respective countries and the people who were my hosts; hopefully, I also became more successful as a diplomat. There have been no reruns of the fountain incident, though I still believe European bathrooms are really unused props from *Star Wars*. Most of all, however, the sheer excitement, bombardment of the senses, and, yes, exhaustion of travel remain. The secret to this continuing affair with new places and different people lies, I believe, within all of us: it comes from wishing to reach out to others in an attempt to know more about ourselves. Long after I have forgotten that beautiful sailfish I caught in Baja, or the fire walkers of Fiji, or the bounties of "bargains" stuffed into gasping suitcases, I will remember the simple, kindly Polish farmer who begged me to take his photograph and then, patting my arm, said, "Take my picture and my heart to America." And that, my friends, beats a good buy on a gold chain any day.

WHO ARE YOU, ANYWAY?

Travel brings out the best in us, and the worst. You will be amazed on trips with your own ambition and courage: you, who can't stand the unctuous look of your kid's turtles will don scuba equipment, descend to new depths, and gawk at sea anemones and trumpet fish. Your husband who, on your marriage day, took a holy vow never to dance again, will be the first to volunteer to shake his booty at a Tahitian tamaaraa. Your teenage daughter, whose room at home truly looks like a close encounter of the third kind, will become acutely sensitive to being neat and orderly in foreign hotel rooms. Your best friend, among whose many virtues cannot be numbered patience, will stand by your side forever smiling as you bargain for the leather case you must have as a remembrance of Florence.

Travel, alas, allows the Hyde to surface as well as the Jekyll. Your husband, the personification of punctuality at home, will lose all track of time and cause you to miss the once-weekly flight from Paris to Colombo. Your mother, a woman so shy that she can barely bring herself to say "good morning" to the man who has delivered her milk for twenty-three years, will suddenly vanish down a dimly lit street in the casbah with a suspicious character who sells "discount djellabas." And you, keeper of the family checkbook, comparison shopper extraordinaire, and pincher-of-pennies, will pay $9 for a magazine in London because you have not bothered to learn the local currency.

Travel is a very personal experience, one only you will have no matter how many other people have made the same trip. In beginning to assemble your thoughts concerning a future trip, it might be helpful to ask yourself a few soul-searching questions which could give you a tip or two about your own, unique "travelability."

1. Are you intimidated by anything, anyplace, or anyone different from what you are used to?

2. Do you believe that most people are out to make a buck largely at your expense?

3. Does the notion of trying to communicate in a foreign language turn you off?

4. Are you easily upset by delays, substitutions, or changes in plans?

5. Are you bugged by regimentation or even a minimal adherence to schedules?

6. Do you feel you can only get a good night's sleep in your own bed?

7. Do you believe that, away from home, you are much more susceptible to illness?

8. Do you tend to feel guilty about any time spent away from your family, home, or job?

9. Is a vacation, for you, a *total* escape?

10. Are you neurotic about every penny you spend on a trip?

Now you need not have experienced extensive psychoanalysis, est weekends, or sensitizing retreats to recognize that these ten characteristics answered yes could reduce your "travelability." It will be difficult to enjoy any experience against which you have built so many defenses, prejudices, and unrealistic expectations. Here's why:

1. If you are easily intimidated by the unknown and retreat from new, strange persons, places, or things, your trip will boast of few exposures to the wonders that make travel worthwhile. Extending yourself, risking a bit, and *experiencing* will encourage you to sail on a raft down a river's rapids, to drink viniak or eat octopus, to attend the rites of a primitive religious sect, and to wear a sarong. Let yourself live a little.

2. Travelers intent upon proving that they are suckers always about to be taken probably will be. It has been my

experience, as I travel at home and overseas, that I have generally been treated fairly and squarely. Sure, there is the occasional horror story of the $37 taxi ride from JFK Airport to Manhattan (because the cabdriver found a "shortcut" which added nine miles to the trip), and I have purchased "sterling silver" which was neither sterling nor silver, and—because of my own ignorance—I have overtipped porters, maids, and waiters throughout the world, but the fault, dear traveler, is in we ourselves. For one thing, the more you know about the object you are buying (leather, cameras, gems) the less likely the chance you will be taken. And—this is a cardinal rule of travel—it is incumbent upon you, the tourist, to know the currency and tipping customs of your host country. This newly acquired expertise probably would not have spared me the expensive taxi ride in New York, but I should have distinguished "sterling silver" from iron in Acapulco, known what to tip a porter in Athens, and realized that my extravagantly generous tip at a sidewalk café in Rome was big enough to entitle me to part ownership. Most people are out to make a living and you, the traveler, contribute to their livelihood. Indeed for the millions of service people in the tourism industry, *you are their livelihood*; but you don't have to be defensive about it. Know the rules everyone is playing by, and then go on about enjoying the game.

3. A foreign language divides travelers into three camps: (a) those who speak it fluently, (b) those who took a year of it in college, and (c) those who shout, "Doesn't anyone here speak English?" I have studied several languages in school (thereby falling into camp (b) and I still take refresher courses before any major trip overseas. It may seem a cliché, but I earnestly believe that my feeble attempts to make small talk and to undertake minor transactions in my host country's native tongue break down a few international barriers between me and the waiter, me and the shopkeeper, me and the customs official at the airport. I rush to add that I have never been awarded the Berlitz Oak Leaf Cluster, but I try.

At least I tried.... Recently, I found a charming, truly

ethnic restaurant in Mazatlán (Mexico). With a great flourish and in a voice that could be heard in Acapulco, I used my college Spanish to order the entire meal. My waiter waited until I finished my speech and quietly said, "Señor, you have just ordered 'credit cards not accepted.'" But I made friends of everyone in the restaurant, many of whom helped me with pronunciation and offered to share their sangria as well. At least learn how to deal with the basic expressions and travel amenities ("Good morning," "Where is...?" "Thank you," etc.) The natives will like you for it and, more importantly, you will like yourself.

4. You and your trusted travel agent may have planned your itinerary, reconfirmed reservations, and scrutinized schedules with a precision General MacArthur might have envied, but you must still expect the unexpected. Tour operators will substitute hotels (but the substitution better be equal to, or better in grade than, the one you were promised or you should start a riot and a lawsuit), airlines will have equipment failures or cancel flights, and sight-seeing tours frequently will be late in departing. It is impossible to foresee (yet alone predict) these quirks in your travel plans, but they will occur. You should simply plan carefully, document all arrangements in writing, and call the tour operator or airline as soon as you and your great expectations arrive in town. You may be lucky and experience a snag-free vacation run like a Swiss-made watch. But if your train from Florence to Rome leaves three hours late, if your ticket is for a flight that hasn't operated since VJ Day, if no one at the hotel ever heard of you—relax, explain, bribe, cajole, and smile—and remember that this is supposed to be a vacation.

5. No matter how independently you travel, you will have to adhere to certain schedules to get you from one place to another. Should you be traveling as a member of an organized tour group, regimentation becomes a way of life, and you are expected to accept the bad with the good. The major lesson here is that as soon as you leave your home, you will become a student of a whole new world of information: airline schedules,

sight-seeing tours, checkout times, business hours, visa expiration dates, curfews, and the "correct" hours during which to dine. Obviously, some regulations and hours are more stringent than others, but you need at least to be aware of a time frame in which your host country expects you to operate. On an organized tour, as we will examine later, all twenty-four, thirty-two, or forty of you function according to a predesigned, carefully timed itinerary so you will need to fit your plans within the group's program. An undisciplined traveler on a carefully orchestrated trip will be miserable and, at the other extreme, the old drill sergeant in you will be frustrated and outraged if you discover you're on a trip where nothing runs according to schedule. Since many people travel in order to escape life's daily time clock, it's important to appreciate that every trip has a time clock all its own.

6. You own and sleep in the world's most comfortable bed, you are used to drinking the country's preeminent cup of coffee, and your pillow is the only one ever designed that cradles and coddles your head. All of this is undeniably true, but it is unlikely that you will be taking your bed, brew, percolator, and pillow with you. Don't travel with the attitude that you will be able to duplicate the comforts of home; you can't, and if you could why would you spend all of that money to leave home in the first place? Some beds will be better than the heirloom in your bedroom; many will be worse. Coffee will be excellent, or potent, or taste like a can of STP. As for pillows, in Austria your head will be transported on downy clouds while elsewhere you might as well be sleeping on your kid's bike. Don't compare; enjoy . . . or at least be tolerant.

7. It is perfectly natural to feel a heightened vulnerability away from home—a sense of impending doom. For some people, this anxiety is transmitted as a fear of bodily harm ("Don't dare walk in the Borghese Gardens at night"), or a fear of theft ("You'll certainly get mugged in Central Park") or a fear of illness ("You could die in Mexico if you drink the water"). I have walked in the Borghese Gardens, skipped through Central Park at 4:00 A.M., and drunk the water in

Mexico and I'm still here. But make no joke about it, all of us feel less protected physically away from our family doctor and an all-night drugstore. There are ways (discussed later in this book) to reinforce good health prior to and during the trip, remembering—all the while—that worry about becoming sick sometimes can cause the sickness itself.

8. Guilt, or at least feelings of guilt, can make us crazy...especially on a trip. The "what am I doing here, I don't deserve this, why am I taking so much time and spending all this money?" syndrome is a potent destroyer of vacations. It's best to get at the root of the guilt-generating feelings before you pack your bags or else they will be likely to surface each time you buy a souvenir, select a bottle of wine, or spring for the hotel room with a view. You don't need to deserve a trip in order to take one, and while the existing work ethic suggests you must toil fifty weeks a year to play for two, that formula should not be your motivation for travel. Generally, unless you work for Ebenezer Scrooge, employers do not begrudge you your vacation. No guilt there. Your kids might prefer to accompany you, but they do have a garage full of toys, a competent baby-sitter, Little League teams, and television. They will be taller when you return, but there will be no other measurable changes. No guilt there either. Money? A trip can be an investment in your physical and/or emotional well-being or it can simply be fun; in either case, it is not inherently guilt-provoking. If you have the money, spend it; if you don't, evaluate the meaningfulness that a vacation could have for you at that particular time in your life. If you can borrow money for a car, a television, or Shirley's root-canal work, who is to say that skiing in Switzerland isn't equally important to your well-being?

9. To insist that your vacation become "a total escape" is like asking Raquel Welch to play a boy: it's a physiological impossibility. For one thing, total escapism places an unreasonable burden on the vacation, setting you up, as it does, for a letdown based upon disappointment and jarring reminders of problems you left at home. By traveling, we

merely relocate our minds and bodies—what's stored in both is merely transported to a new location. Do not ask of your Alaskan cruise that it make you forget problems with your business partner, do not expect a shopping spree on the Via Condotti to resolve your daughter's problems with grades, and do not count on a "romantic" trip with your spouse as the ultimate solution for extended spats and silences at home. A trip can be a wonderful, renewing adventure, but it cannot be guidance counselor, lawyer, tutor, doctor and shrink. Be realistic about what you hope to get from your travels and don't be disconcerted if you are carrying a suitcase marked "concerns" with you. The best vacation is one in which the traveler is neither running away from pressure nor racing toward it.

10. Some people save a lifetime in order to take an extended, round-the-world cruise; others go on skiing trips almost every other weekend in season. No matter what our destination, mode of transportation, and class of accommodations, as soon as we leave home all trips cost money. There are airlines, bus, or train tickets to buy, hotel rooms and rental cars to pay for, meals to eat, sights to see, and souvenirs to shop for. Whether we are in India or Indiana, Fort Worth or Port-au-Prince—all of these travel staples keep us poised with credit cards in one hand and traveler's checks in the other. To plan trip expenses you can rely on the expert guidance of a travel agent (who has access to current rates for all travel-related goods and services), but you must still allow for a "slush fund." One can only *estimate* expenses, and you will be both foolhardy and miserable if you try to balance your "projected" and "actual" budgets. By counting pennies you could miss Picassos. Still, if you plan carefully and remain fairly disciplined, you won't spend yourself into bankruptcy.

Even if you answered yes to all of the items on the "travelability quiz," there is still hope for you. It is important both to you and your traveling partners that you examine aspects of your personality as these apply to trips in the works. Wouldn't it be sad (to say nothing of expensive) to travel to nearby New Orleans or faraway Kuala Lumpur only to discover that you have carried with you some of the anxieties or concerns that could wreck your trip? Before plunking down that deposit, ask yourself about yourself in an effort to determine what the person you are wants for the traveler-to-be. The stakes are rather high: if you don't buy a house or car, chances are your vacation will represent your single greatest expense this year. And if you can spend twenty minutes at the supermarket picking out cantaloupes, can't you afford at least that much time finding out how happily and well you might travel?

WHAT DO YOU WANT FROM YOUR TRIP?

As friends disembark from airplanes returning them from the vacations of their dreams, they begin an almost involuntary dissection of what happened. "We never got to shop," "I'm exhausted . . . what I really need now is some rest." "I met lots of interesting people, but no one *special*," "The hotel was not nearly as elegant as we had hoped," "I don't ever want to see another museum as long as I live," and "Mexico City is interesting, but it's no Machu Picchu." These critiques are repeated long after we have modeled our newly purchased caftans and huaraches, and projected on any available screen pictures of what it was all really like. Many vacation disappointments occur because we failed to decide exactly what it was we wanted from that two weeks away, anyway. You know what you want from a new dishwasher, you have an excellent notion of your needs in a new car, and you even make certain demands of your butcher when selecting pot roast for that night's dinner. If you have thought a bit about who you are, it will follow that—in vacation planning—you should also consider what you want.

Keeping Up with the Joneses: Status
It doesn't matter how you refer to it: snob appeal, superiority complex, keeping up with the Joneses, dilettantism, or name-

dropping, the pursuit of status is a very potent force in selecting a vacation destination. I have a friend whose drive for status reaches such bizarre proportions that the only possible cure is exorcism. She knows the name of every restaurant (and its maître d') in the south of France, she seeks out and skis at next year's ski resort *this* year, and she is given to seizures of name-dropping that arrest any conversation in midstream (i.e., "You have never seen elephants until you go to the November roundup in Surin," "The most dazzling Buddhas are at Polonnaruwa," and, "The only place to find good rock lobsters is at Estrella del Mar in La Paz.") Her recommendations are valid, so why do I want to kill her every time she opens her mouth?

Status, if not pursued with a passion bordering on the psychotic, is a very healthy and even desirable goal. Each of us wants to enjoy a sense of pride and achievement, and the feeling that we have experienced a vacation truly special if not altogether unique. Though we are less assertive than my bragging friend (who has the subtlety of Shamu the whale), most of us seek status on other levels. Have you ever heard yourself saying, "Honolulu is for tourists—we go to the big island"; "Aspen is so crowded, but there's this lovely lodge no one has ever heard of"; "That restaurant is good, but superb food can't be found in that town"; and "We went there last year and would like to go somewhere a bit more unusual for our next vacation."? Don't be so smug; even if these aren't your exact words, most of us have had parallel thoughts.

Status is fine; as a matter of fact the moment you begin your trip you have achieved a certain measure of it simply by virtue of the fact that you are getting away. Some people can neither afford the time nor the money for a vacation and, in some circles, that distinction carries a certain status all its own.

If you recognize in yourself the need for a status-fulfilling vacation, you will possibly gravitate toward unusual, largely unknown destinations, expensive resorts, elegant cruises of some duration, custom-made tours for handpicked groups, and an itinerary that will get you to your destinations when all the other "tourists" have gone home. Status can be expensive (and humbling) as reflected in the conversation of two ladies sitting in an elegant dining room in Paris.

> First Lady: For my birthday last month, my husband gave me a trip around the world.
>
> Second Lady: Really, where will he send you next year?

Companionship and Sex

A trip can provide us with good company for the life of our vacation, friends who last, kindred spirits who also appreciate Mayan sculpture and sacher tortes, romantic interludes, or—wonder of wonders—that "someone special" who could matter in our lives. I haven't commissioned a field survey of the ratio of romantic interludes to enduring relationships, but I suspect that Bette Davis's encounter with Paul Henreid (in *Now Voyager*) is not characteristic of most holiday travel.

Be realistic about the important role companionship and sex (there I've said it) play in your vacation schedule. If you are seeking the company (intellectual, physical, and/or emotional) of the opposite sex, you need to ask your travel agent some pointed questions about prospective destinations and people who go there: "What is the typical age range of tourists?" "What is the ratio of men to women?" "What percentage of the guests are single?" "What is the ratio of American to foreign tourists?" "Is there a season or time of year most popular with single travelers?" If romance is on your mind and in your heart, you have every right to question and probe in an effort to find out if what you want will be waiting for you. Naturally, neither your travel agent nor the tour operator can guarantee that you will fall in love, throw open your French doors, and burst into "You Light Up My Life" immediately upon arrival, but he or she *can* tell you that the place is filled with families in August, and that the average age of your cruise mates will be sixty years and older.

How you and your erogenous zones can find happiness on holidays I leave to sex behaviorists and the world's social directors, but I can suggest that you be totally honest with yourself about this motivation for your travels. Be available rather than desperate, and try to keep your expectations rational and realistic so that a casual drink with a stranger (rather than an offer of marriage) does not throw you into despair.

Rest and Rehabilitation

Most travelers look upon their weekend, two-week, or three-month getaway as a chance to rejuvenate their sagging bodies, to renew their sapped spirits, or to recharge their mushy minds. We all need R and R, not only because of the new stimuli it provides, but for the sabbatical from old, persistent, tiring stimuli as well. We want to be free of driving the kids to school, writing reports, shopping, bosses, mothers-in-law, alarm clocks, doing laundry, and committee meetings. We want to replace the mandatory and programmed with the voluntary and self-indulgent; "I want to be lazy!" becomes the battle cry of our getaway. Suddenly we are seeking a brief interlude filled with sleep-in mornings, cocktails made when we want them and precisely to taste, luscious afternoon naps, new clothes draped over bodies renewed by the sun (and not sapped by 7:00 A.M. wake-ups to walk the dogs), and leisurely gourmet dinners unpunctuated by battling kids. The rest and rehabilitation can mean an absence of planned activities but, for some of us, R and R can mean a whirlwind social life which—because it is different from our usual schedule—can be equally rejuvenating.

When deciding what it is that you want, ask yourself how much you need to relax, unwind, indulge yourself, to be deprogrammed, and to do something for *you*. On every trip, however ambitious, carefully orchestrated, and expensive, there must be time for the body to renew itself and that, after all, is one of the reasons you might have chosen a vacation anyway. Exhausted from yesterday's tour?—then sleep in today (the museum has been there for a hundred years; it will be there for you tomorrow morning when you are rested, more responsive, and more appreciative).

For several of my friends, rest and rehabilitation is the preeminent motivation of any excursion outside their homes. If there is a sun to bake under, a pool to swim in, a martini to languish over, a band to dance to, and a clock to ignore—they are happy. For others of us, however, the magnetic appeal of a totally R and R vacation quickly dissipates, and after two days we begin to make dates, take lessons, and schedule tours in order to fill our time. Rest on a trip is important, but often it is not enough; try to maintain a reasonable ratio between being on the run and being by the pool.

The Quests: Mind and Body

Though we don't read much anymore about "affinity fares" (which permitted groups of people joined by a common interest or hobby other than travel to fly together at reduced charter rates), that era in travel encouraged many bird watchers, wine tasters, stamp collectors, and skin divers to explore the world in pursuit of their interests and to improve their skills.

The culture quest has a dizzying list of converts: the lady who last year happily walked the boardwalk of Atlantic City is this year touring and sampling the vineyards of France; the teenager who took spills off a surfboard in Malibu is now linking hands with the pharaohs by sailing the Nile; the family who last year "blew it all on a swimming pool" is this year driving the Americana Trail, tracing America's pioneering past in New England.

To know more is to be more interesting; and so we dabble a bit in art and architecture, choose destinations in conjunction with important music festivals and events in the theater, and select tour groups whose cultural interests are compatible with our own. In these ways we become "more cultured" from exposures to people, places, and events that reinforce our awareness of the arts. Certainly, you can visit museums in Philadelphia, there are dozens of weekly concerts in Atlanta, and New York boasts of more excellent dance companies than any city in the world—but the quest for culture implies a tracking to sources. The man who wouldn't wait in line for a theater ticket is now digging in Jordanian ruins, the woman who won't walk into a museum at home is analyzing every stone at the Acropolis, the teenagers who couldn't be seduced into an art course are now staring transfixed at the Mona Lisa. Why? Perhaps to tell their friends (status again), or because they are experiencing a sense of cultural awareness, or maybe it's simply because it is there and so are they.

Self-improvement is a force (or a goal) that guides us into several different types of trips. The body and the wondrous things we get it to do can variously be explored at tennis camps, dude ranches, sensitivity training retreats, ski resorts, "fat farms," and "jogathons." The body, which for fifty weeks of the year has done nothing more vigorous than turn a TV dial or take out the garbage, is now being coaxed into jogging along the beach, braced for cold morning mudpacks, and splashed in the sauna after a schuss on the slopes. The effort is noble, but the body had better be carefully conditioned and well-prepared for the self-improvement onslaught or it will let you down badly; maybe even worse.

Certainly it is valuable to do something for your mind and/or body on a vacation; frankly, it's difficult to imagine any trip which doesn't minister in some way to both. But, again, be reasonable. If your body tone would frighten a visiting Martian, don't expect miracles at the spa. If your tennis game would turn Chris Evert to social work, don't plan on emerging from your one-week tennis camp a pro. And if you ski an occasional weekend in Mammoth, be prepared for a more rigorous indoctrination if you sign on for an Alpine Holiday in Switzerland. If you are realistic about the quality and degree of the improvement you can logically expect, you will develop reasonable goals and reduce disappointment. Get the body in shape before you go, and before, during, and after the trip enjoy the warm good feeling of knowing that you are allowing yourself to do something for *you*.

Pioneer or Prince: The Style to Which You Are Accustomed
In today's travel world, it is quite possible to go virtually anywhere you'd like in any style you choose. In France, you may pitch a tent at a campsite for a few francs a night or you may stay at a five-star hotel at a cost equal to Ecuador's annual budget. The style in which you travel in terms of airline class, hotel, sight-seeing, meals, and shopping is determined by your personal preferences and the extent to which your checking account can indulge them. You may fly first-class, coach, or standby; luxuriate in a great hotel or be content in a youth hostel; you may tour in a sight-seeing bus with forty travelers or pursue the scenery in an air-conditioned limousine by yourself; you may grab a hot dog on the street for a quarter or dine on a six-course epicurean fantasy for substantially more; and you may limit your shopping to a few inexpensive souvenirs or go footloose and fancy-free, thereby making yet another adjustment in our balance of payments.

Beyond the question of how you want to go and the indulgences to which your pocketbook makes you privy, you had better think, too, about your disposition regarding formality and informality. If you like jeans, a torn sweat shirt, and the world's most comfortable sneakers and loathe the notion of dressing up while on vacation, ask your travel agent some specific questions regarding dress codes for men and women: "Will a tie and jacket be required for dinner?" "Does the tour include any formal events, receptions, or parties?" "Are slacks and shorts permitted?" "Will I feel comfortable wearing jeans in these hotels?" Maybe, all things considered, you really want a rustic adventure that links body and mind to nature; if so, the Gourmet's Tour of Italy might provide you with several kinds of indigestion.

Much has been written recently about our efforts as a nation to preserve our environment and to return to nature.

River rafting, camping, and the mushrooming use of recreational vehicles suggest that we are trying to find our way back to Walden Pond . . . to the simple, unencumbered world of nature. Bodies and minds can appreciate this kind of holiday too, but it is important to understand that tranquillity and untouched simplicity in nature (if you are lucky enough to find them) do not often come next door to duck à l'orange, boutiques, and discos blaring Donna Summer's latest hit. You can be a pioneer or a prince, and you can even plan a trip that allows you to be both. Just be sure you have come to terms with the style of vacation you want, and the kind of trip you can afford.

As you begin to search yourself about yourself and the joys you'd like your trip to bring you, perhaps it's time to decide who (if anyone) will be sharing this great adventure.

2

WHO SHOULD YOU GO WITH: ALONE? FAMILY? FRIENDS?

On my first frenetic fling through Europe, during which time I saw more countries than the Gabors had husbands, I traveled with a very good friend. At least we got on the plane at JFK in New York as good friends. When we concluded the trip we knew much more about ourselves, each other, and our friendship. We should have known better: the fact that we both loved good food and durable luggage in no way gave us passing grades in the litmus test for travel compatibility.

We spent hours in those days and nights before the trip discussing hotels, sight-seeing, history, the sheer adventure of the impending departure; we discussed everything except the important idiosyncrasies, personal preferences, and special motivations and goals that make people travel together in the first place. We allegedly knew each other but, in truth, we had never shared a hotel room, discussed personal finances, or tried a break-in weekend getaway to test our compatibility not as friends but as *travel mates*. There is, I assure you, an enormous difference between these two categories and a gold star in one doesn't assure you of a place of honor in the other.

ALONE AGAIN, NATURALLY?

It is reported that President John F. Kennedy once entered a room at the White House where a dinner was being held for the Nobel prize winners of the Western Hemisphere. Kennedy gazed about the room and said, "I have not seen so much wit and intelligence in one room since Thomas Jefferson dined alone." For many people, no one can provide the requisite camaraderie and intellectual stimulation that they can furnish themselves. The lone (not necessarily "lonely") traveler will be absolutely content to ride a narrow-gauge railroad in Costa Rica, bargain in Petticoat Lane, dine at Le Train Bleu, or photograph the temple at Sounion. Lone travelers treasure their independence and freedom as well as the responsibility that comes with solitary trips. Before deciding to affix your name to the scroll of "travelers who travel alone," you might wish to run through this quick personal inventory:

1. Do you want to do exactly what *you* want to do on the trip when *you* want to do it?

2. Do you regard yourself as self-confident, unintimidated by strange places and possibly stranger people?

3. Are you able to take charge of arrangements, reservations, and your daily needs, negotiating—if necessary—in a foreign language?

4. Are you content to be alone even if you might know no one in the city you are visiting?

5. Are you comfortable dining alone, if necessary, in a restaurant?

6. Would you venture out on your own to sight-see or shop in a foreign city?

7. Are you gregarious, or at least sufficiently extroverted to reach out and make acquaintances when you feel the need to?

8. Can you arrive in a foreign country exhilarated, rather than exasperated, at the notion that no one will be guiding you through customs, immigration, and on to your hotel?

9. Are you able to discover events and experience adventures without being led to them by another person?

10. Is the time you spend with you generally the most satisfying time you spend?

While there is no scientific foundation to this "test," I suspect that if you answer all ten questions yes, you are well on your way to out-Garboing Garbo. Still, aloneness in the comfort of your own home with the security of your neighbors nearby and a telephone to link you to voices you want to hear *is different* from sitting alone in a train station in Bombay or a bar in Belgrade.

In return for sacrificing the company provided by a travel companion (and the not insignificant fact that said travel companion would be sharing expenses so that the cost, per person, would be about half), you secure for yourself freedom of travel, freedom of choice, the opportunity to juggle itineraries, to get up for a drink of water six times during the night, to gargle loudly in the morning, to hang your socks over the mirror, to approach a stranger not-at-all-self-consciously in a local bar, and to tip the waiter exactly what you think his service is worth.

If, however, you are considering traveling with someone other than your spouse (who presumably has auditioned for the part as companion and has landed the role), it is really important that you both discuss your idiosyncrasies as they apply to a travel situation. For instance, have you considered:

1. *What do you each expect of the trip?*

This sounds much easier than it is, for it implies a no-holds-barred discussion of the ways in which each of you wishes to spend your days and nights while traveling.

——How much time will you want to be alone?

——How much emphasis are you placing on sight-seeing, shopping, and socializing?

——If one of you is the spontaneous "let's go to Vienna in the morning" type, and the other is the plodding planner who will not deviate from itineraries and schedules, how will you reconcile your different styles and make necessary accommodations for each other?

——How similar are your interests? If one of you wants to go to Europe to sight-see and shop and the other wants to socialize in lovely restaurants and drink in local cafés, your diverse goals and interests will have yet another effect on your travel schedule: the sight-seer–shopper will no doubt wish to arise early and hit the museums and shops; the socialite will be out late at night and might wish to sleep in every morning.

Sound insignificant? Wait until you have your first argument that starts with, "If I wanted to sleep late, I didn't have to come to Venice to do it," etc. As a general rule, I have experienced much more fulfilling, confrontation-free trips with companions whose interests were closest to my own with a good balance of time together and time alone.

2. *How will you handle finances?*

It is best to resolve this issue before the trip begins. In the first place, the two (or more) travel companions need to discuss how much they can afford to spend (fixed costs *and* variables) for the time period the trip covers. If one of you wishes to travel as a prince, and the other as a pauper—you are courting disaster by casting your lots together. Assuming you both have roughly equivalent budgets and seek similar experiences, set aside an agreed-upon amount for tips, extra meals, wine with dinner, etc., and take turns (perhaps a week each at a time) handling expenses. This will eliminate the need to "square away" debts after every glass of wine or tip to a porter. And trust each other...after all, you are friends and this is a vacation, isn't it?

3. *What do you know about each other's personal habits?*

There are few more shocking revelations in life than discovering on a trip that your friend is a weirdo. Who else smokes three packs of cigarettes a day and follows each cigarette with a blast of breath freshener, sleeps with the window wide open when it's winter in Russia, derives some bizarre amusement from a trail of toothpaste across the sink and onto the floor, gargles with a ferocity that registers a 6.5 on the Richter scale, hangs wet underwear to dry over your silk bathrobe, insists upon talking in his or her sleep about people you do not know, unpacks on *your* bed, uses the last remaining bar of soap without getting the maid to replenish the supply, and greets you each day with an incandescent "good morning" that would put Florence Henderson to shame. All of these may seem trivial idiosyncrasies when you are laughing about them at home, but in Cairo, Casablanca, and Cuernavaca, they are justifiable causes for murder.

We are all different from each other and that can be a

source of genuine amusement both in life and in travel. So much for philosophy. As a practical matter, the most realistic way in which to orient yourself to a prospective traveling partner is to take a weekend trip together. For starters, this out-of-town-break-in will serve as a subtle audition during which time each of you tests the other in the part of traveling companion. Here, during a fall weekend in New England or a three-day skiing vacation in Vail, you can begin to detect and discover the peculiarities about each other which will help you make a decision about your travel compatibility. Most importantly, the stakes on this trial run are not as high (in terms of the investment of time and money) as they would be on a six-week tour of the Orient or a three-week Mediterranean cruise. If the two of you don't jell as travelers during a weekend in Maine, chances are you will have problems on a more ambitious and elaborate trip later . . . but wasn't it valuable to find that out before you got to Madrid?

Spouses, it's worth mentioning, automatically assume that they will travel together and so they should. But it is perfectly acceptable for husband and wife (or live-er and live-ee) to take separate vacations if each wants a totally different experience or simply the breathing space away from the other that a vacation provides. Just remember that if one wants to fish and the other wants to shop, both are possible on the same trip. Trips, like marriages, are fifty-fifty propositions.

Sharing, in the context of travel, can be a truly memorable bonus to your trip but—as is usually the case—the quality of the experience depends on the chemistry of the people.

INDEPENDENT TRAVEL VERSUS ESCORTED TOUR GROUPS

I have taken trips alone, with a member of my family, with a friend, with a group of friends, and with a group of strangers on an escorted tour package. Independent travel, that is, a trip where you travel according to your own itinerary only in the company of the person(s) with whom you have chosen to make the trip, suits people who especially value freedom of movement and are deeply agitated by the "herding" instinct often associated with tour groups. There are other differences in the two travel experiences as the list below suggests.

INDEPENDENT TRAVEL versus	ESCORTED TOUR GROUPS
Itinerary You travel in accordance with your own itinerary.	You follow the tour company's itinerary for the group.
Freedom You may make spontaneous decisions about adding to, or excluding, destinations along the way.	There are rarely any deviations from the schedules and stops listed in the tour brochure.
Rates Air fare and hotel rates normally are higher for the independent traveler.	Tour groups benefit from the lowest available group air fares and hotel rates (because tour operators commit to a large block of airplane seats and hotel rooms at the minimum rate).
Extras The independent traveler pays for each service of the trip as it is provided (air fare, hotel, sight-seeing, etc.).	Most tour packages include air fare, hotel accommodations, airport transfers, some sight-seeing, many meals, and the services of a tour guide. Extras would be gratuities, taxes, laundry, alcoholic beverages, etc.

INDEPENDENT TRAVEL *versus*	ESCORTED TOUR GROUPS
Leisure time You may have as much leisure time as you wish to build into your schedule.	Leisure time for a group on a package tour is generally at a minimum. There is strict adherence to the schedule though an occasional "free afternoon" is provided for.
Companions You travel with the person (or persons) you have selected to make the trip with you.	You travel with a group of sixteen to forty strangers (unless, of course, you have friends who are taking the tour with you).
Pace You may establish your own pace both on a daily basis and for the duration of the trip.	The pace is established by the tour leader and normally includes early-morning departures.
Individual responsibility As an independent traveler, you assume *total* responsibility for negotiating customs formalities, communicating (in the language of the land) with locals, and handling all daily necessities from ordering breakfast to getting to the airport.	All travel arrangements, formalities, and negotiations with locals are the responsibility of the tour leader whose company provides a network of local contacts to facilitate these arrangements.
Safety and security You are on your own.	You will rarely be separated from the entire group and can count on spending even leisure time with some of its members.

INDEPENDENT TRAVEL	versus	ESCORTED TOUR GROUPS

Getting to know the country
You can chart your own course in terms of exploring the city, state, or country and its people. This flexibility may prove serendipitous and you might have truly unique adventures, or it might be hit and miss so that you exert a great deal of energy, time, and money still failing to get a feel for the people and their homeland.

The schedule on escorted tours is whirlwind, compact, and typically exhausting. You will see a great many things superficially and your exposure to a given country will be through the traditional (often cliché) tourist venues. Still, if you want to see a good deal in a short time, there is nothing hit or miss about a tour group's itinerary.

As a three-time member of escorted tour groups, I can report that I appreciated the group leader's total assumption of responsibility for all of our travel arrangements, and for the speed and efficiency with which he handled all the formalities associated with entering and leaving foreign countries. As a first-time traveler, I was intimidated by foreign languages and currencies and strange customs procedures, so the group leader assumed a burden I didn't want. But I soon grew annoyed at the peculiarities of a group of strangers who travel together and, perhaps because they are strangers, have little regard for the rest of the people on the bus. On my first European tour, in a group of thirty-six, five people were invariably late in the morning, six insisted upon singing "Row, Row, Row Your Boat" every afternoon, and two people asked our driver to stop every few miles so they could attend to requisite bodily functions. These are superficial irritations, but I was more frequently annoyed (and embarrassed) by the tendency of group members to be rude, arrogant, and vulgar. You can't pick the members of your group (unless you and friends charter a plane and buy a tour package together) and so you must take your chances. There are stories of lifelong friendships developed during tours of the South Pacific and the Orient, *and* there are horror stories of individuals who leave tours midway because they can't deal with the creeps who comprise their group. Before signing up with a group, at least get your travel agent to acquire some statistics (if available) on the age range, sex, and marital status of former participants. And if he has recommended the trip to other clients previously, ask for their names and phone numbers so that you can ask some pertinent questions of your own.

If you're up to the demanding schedule, and are adventurous enough to chance the group you get, an escorted tour package can be an excellent and economical introduction to travel—particularly for the person who cannot afford, is afraid, or does not wish to travel alone.

A LIST OF TOUR OPERATORS*

AAA World-Wide Travel, 8111 Gatehouse, Rd., Falls Church, VA 22042
Abbott Tours, Inc., 234 Loyola Bldg., New Orleans, LA 70112
Adventure Holidays International, 337 Merrick Rd., Lynbrook, NY 11563
Adventure Tours, 9118 Liberty Rd., Randallstown, MD 21133
A.I.T.S., 210 Boylston St., Boston, MA 02167
Aloha Hawaii Travel Ltd., 400 N. Michigan Ave., Chicago, IL 60611
American Express Company, American Express Plaza, New York, NY 10004
American Grand Circle, 555 Madison Ave., New York, NY 10022
American Sightseeing International, 420 Lexington Ave., New York, NY 10017
American Travel Abroad, Inc., 250 W. 57th St., New York, NY 10019
Ameropa Travel, Inc., 26 Court St., Brooklyn, NY 11242
Asensio Tours, 501 Fifth Avenue, New York, NY 10017
Ask Mr. Foster, 16055 Ventura Blvd., Encino, CA 91316
Asti Tours, 21 E. 40th St., New York, NY 10016
A.T.E.S.A., 501 Madison Ave., New York, NY 10022

*This list (and subsequent lists in this book) is not necessarily comprehensive; inclusion in the list is for the reader's reference use and does not imply any endorsement.

Atlas International Tours, 580 Fifth Ave., New York, NY 10036
Atpac Tours, 136 E. 57th St., New York, NY 10022
Auto Europe, 1270 Second Ave., New York, NY 10021
Aventura Travel, 2962A Aventura Blvd., N. Miami Beach, FL 33160
Bachelor Party Tours, Inc., 444 Madison Ave., New York, NY 10022
Bahama Island Tours, 255 Alhambra Circle, Coral Gables, FL 33134
Bamaco House, 58-33 College Point Blvd., New York, NY 11355
Barjet Services, Inc., 187 Park Ave. S., New York, NY 10016
Bennett Tours, Inc., 270 Madison Ave., New York, NY 10016
Betanzos OK Tours International, 35 Wisconsin Circle, Washington, DC 20015
Book-Couzens Travel Service, 1 Northland Plaza, Southfield, MI 48075
Breakaway Travel, Inc., 1938 Williamsbridge Rd., Bronx, NY 10461
Brendan Tours, 510 W. 6th St., Los Angeles, CA 90001
Brownell Tours, P.O. Box 2087, Birmingham, AL 35201
Bruwal Tours, Ltd., 212-29 Jamaica Ave., Queens Village, NY 11428
California Parlor Car Tours, Jack Tar Hotel, San Francisco, CA 94101
Carvavan Tours, Inc., 401 N. Michigan Ave., Chicago, IL 60611
Caribbean Holidays, 711 Third Ave., New York, NY 10017
Cartan Travel Bureau, One Crossroads of Commerce, Rolling Meadows, IL 60008
Casser Tours, 201 W. 41st St., New York, NY 10036
Cavalcade Tours, Inc., 254 W. 31st St., New York, NY 10001
Charter Travel Corp., 134 N. LaSalle St., Chicago, IL 60602
C.I.E. Tours International, 564 Fifth Ave., New York, NY 10036
CIT Travel Service, Inc., 500 Fifth Ave., New York, N.Y. 10036
Clara Laughlin Travel Services, Inc., 36 E. 57th St., New York, NY 10022
Club Mediterranee, 40 W. 57th St., New York, NY 10019
Columbia Tours, Inc. 535 Fifth Ave., New York, NY 10017
Compass Tours, Inc., 70 W. 40th St., New York, NY 10018
Continental Express, 144 Beverly Dr., Beverly Hills, CA 90212
Thomas Cook, 587 Fifth Avenue, New York, NY 10017
Creative World Travel, 1 Market Plaza, San Francisco, CA 94105
Crown Peters Wholesale Tour Operators, 555 Fifth Ave., New York, NY 10017
Daphna Tours, Inc., 444 Madison Ave., New York, NY 10022
David Travels, Inc., 1175 N.E. 125th St., N. Miami, FL 33161
Del Webb World Travel, P.O. Box 15313, Las Vegas, NV 89114
Destination France, 521 Fifth Ave., New York, NY 10017
DiCarlo Travel Bureau, 151 W. 40th St., New York, NY 10018
Discovery Tours, 1075 Central Ave., Scarsdale, NY 10583
Eastours, Inc.,1140 Avenue of the Americas, New York, NY 10036
Elkin Tours, P.O. Box 986, Southfield, MI 48037

Empire Tours, 605 Market St., San Francisco, CA 94105
Empress Travel, 293 Madison Ave., New York, NY 10017
Etsia, Inc., 576 Fifth Ave., New York, NY 10036
Europabus (Overseas), Inc., 11 E. 44th St., New York, NY 10017
Europacar Tours, Inc., 136 E. 57th St., New York, NY 10022
Europe by Car, 45 Rockefeller Plaza, New York, NY 10020
European Holidays, 500 Fifth Ave., New York, NY 10036
Europe on Skis, Inc., 49 W. 57th St., New York, NY 10019
Exprinter International, 500 Fifth Ave., New York, NY 10036
Finlay Fun-Time Tours, 11306 Burbank Blvd., North Hollywood, CA 91601
Flyfaire, Inc., 300 E. 42nd St., New York, NY 10017
Foreign Tours, Inc., 1140 Avenue of the Americas, New York, NY 10036
Foremost International Tours, 1255 Post St., San Francisco, CA 94109
Forlow Tours, 716 S. Main St., South Bend, IN 46618
Fourways Travel Ltd., 950 Third Ave., New York, NY 10021
Four Winds Travel, Inc., 175 Fifth Ave., New York NY 10010
Frames' Tours N.Y. Ltd., 185 Madison Ave., New York, NY 10016
French Caribbean Adventures, 475 Fifth Ave., New York, NY 10017
Arthur Frommer International, 380 Madison Ave., New York, NY 10017
Fun in the Sun Tours, 1 E. 57th St., New York, NY 10022
Funway Holidays, 152 W. Wisconsin Ave., Milwaukee, WI 53203
Garza Tours, 4256 N. Milwaukee Ave., Chicago, IL 60641
Gateway Holidays, 8 S. Michigan Ave., Chicago, IL 60603
General Tours, Inc. 49 W. 57th St., New York, NY 10019
Gibson Travel, 3258 Wilshire Blvd., Los Angeles, CA 90010
Globus Tours, 8 S. Michigan Ave., Chicago IL 60603
Go-Go Tours, Inc., 15 E. 40th St., New York, NY 10016
Gramercy Travel System, 444 Madison Ave., New York, NY 10022
Green Carpet Tours, 4 N. Broadway, Billings, MT 59101
Group Journeys, Inc., 5550 Main St., Buffalo, NY 14221
Groups Unlimited, 15 Central Park West, New York, NY 10023
GWV Travel, Inc., 161 Highland Ave., Needham Heights, MA 02194
Haley Corporation, 711 Third Ave., New York, NY 10017
Hawaiian Holidays, Inc., 500 Fifth Ave., New York, NY 10036
Hemphill Travel Corp., 1910 W. Sunset Blvd., Los Angeles, CA 90026
Henderson Tours, 931 Hunter St., NW, Atlanta, GA 30314
Hill Tours, P.O. Box 413, St. Petersburg, FL 33731
Holyland Tours, Inc., 952 Fifth Ave., New York, NY 10021
Inclusive Travel Corp., 685 Fifth Ave., New York, NY 10022
Intercontinental Tours, 609 S. Grand, Los Angeles, CA 90017
International Incentives, 10600 W. Higgins Rd., Rosemont, IL 60018
International Travel Service, 104 S. Michigan Ave., Chicago, IL 60603
Intourist (USSR), 45 E. 49th St., New York, NY 10017

Island Holiday Tours of Hawaii, 2222 Kalakaua Ave., Honolulu, HI 96815
Islands in the Sun, 2400 West Coast Hwy., Newport Beach, CA 92660
Japan & Orient Tours, Inc., 250 E. 1st St., Los Angeles, CA 90012
Japan Travel Bureau International, Inc., 45 Rockefeller Plaza, New York,
    NY 10020
Jet & Cruise, 32-03 Broadway, Astoria, L.I., NY 11106
Johansen Royal Tours, 1410 Vance Bldg., Seattle, WA 98101
Kneisel Travel, Inc., 348 N.E. 8th Ave., Portland, OR 97232
Kompas, 630 Fifth Ave., New York, NY 10020
Kuoni Travel, Inc., 11 E. 44th St., New York, NY 10017
Le Beau Tours, Inc., 6 E. 43rd St., New York, NY 10017
Lindblad Travel, Inc., 133 E. 55th St., New York, NY 10022
Lislind International, 5 World Trade Center, New York, NY 10048
Lotus Orient Tours Ltd., 244 E. 46th St., New York, NY 10017
Loyal Travel, Greyhound Tower, Phoenix, AZ 85077
Lynnot Tours, Inc., 117 E. 36th St., New York, NY 10016
MacKenzie Tours, Hawaii, P.O. Box 2561, Honolulu, HI 96804
MacPherson Travel Bureau, 500 Fifth Ave., New York, NY 10036
Magic Carpet Tours, 1406 Beacon St., Brookline, MA 02146
Maritz, Inc., 1325 N. Highway Dr., Fenton, MO 63026
Marriott World Travel, 1651 Old Meadow Rd., McLean, VA 22101
Martin Empire Tours, 711 Third Ave., New York, NY 10017
Maupintour, Inc., 900 Massachusetts St., Lawrence, KS 66044
Melia Tours, Inc., 580 Fifth Ave., New York, NY 10036
Mercator Tours, 720 Fifth Ave., New York, NY 10019
Mexico Travel Advisors, 25 W. 43rd St., New York, NY 10036
Miller Tours, Inc., 1100 Jorie Blvd., Oak Brook, IL 60521
Murray's Tours, 740 W. Santa Barbara Ave., Los Angeles, CA 90027
Nationwide Leisure Corp., 1 Huntington Quadrangle, Melville, L.I., NY
    11746
Nawas International Travel Service, 20 E. 46th St., New York, NY 10017
New Orient Express, Inc., 375 Park Ave., New York, NY 10022
Nilestar Tours, 9720 Wilshire Blvd., Beverly Hills, CA 90212
Nili Tours, 380 Madison Ave., New York, NY 10017
Olson-Travelworld Organization, 6922 Hollywood Blvd., Los Angeles, CA
    90028
Orbis Polish Travel Office, 500 Fifth Ave., New York, NY 10036
Orbitair International, Inc., 20 E. 46th St., New York, NY 10017
Osborne Travel Service, Inc., 3379 Peachtree Rd. NE, Atlanta, GA 30326
Overseas Charter a Coach, Inc., 10 Rockefeller Plaza, New York, NY 10020
Overseas Travel Company, 2 W. 45th St., New York, NY 10036
Pacific Delight Tours, 3 Pell St., New York, NY 10013
Pacific International Tours, Inc., 560 Sutter St., San Francisco, CA 94102

Pacific Pathways, 442 Post St., San Francisco, CA 94102
Paragon Tours, 678 Pleasant St., New Bedford, MA 02741
Park East Tours, 1841 Broadway, New York, NY 10023
Passport Holidays Ltd., 40 E. 49th St., New York, NY 10017
Peltours, Inc., 70 W. 40th St., New York, NY 10018
Percival Tours, Inc., 5820 Wilshire Blvd., Los Angeles, CA 90036
Perillo Tours, 4545 Third Ave., Bronx, NY 10458
Persepolis Travel Ltd., 667 Madison Ave., New York, NY 10021
Pink Holidays, 2630 Flossmoor Rd., Flossmoor, IL 60422
Pleasant Hawaiian Holiday, 960 Westlake Blvd., Ste. 260, Westlake Village,
    CA 91361
Pleasant Scandinavia Tours, 444 Madison Ave., New York, NY 10022
Pleasure Break Travel, 104 S. Michigan Ave., Chicago, IL 60603
Portuguese Tours, Inc., 321 Rahway Ave., Elizabeth, NJ 07202
Princess Tours, 1325 Fourth Ave., Seattle, WA 98101
Que Pasa Tours, 1290 Avenue of the Americas, New York, NY 10019
Questers Tours and Travel, 257 Park Ave., New York, NY 10010
Rogal Associates, 97 Union St., Newton Center, MA 02159
Russian Adventure Tours, Inc., 20 E. 46th St., New York, NY 10017
Sartours, 610 Fifth Ave., New York, NY 10020
Scandinavia Overseas Service, Inc., 444 Madison Ave., New York, NY 10022
Sharon Travel Associates, Inc., 18 E. 48th St., New York, NY 10017
Simba Safaris, 1113 Union Blvd., Allentown, PA 18103
Simmons Group Journeys, 205 E. 42nd St., New York, NY 10017
Sita World Travel, Inc., 2960 Wilshire Blvd., Los Angeles, CA 90010
Ski-America Tours, 8 S. Michigan Ave., Chicago, IL 60603
Ski Trails, 134 N. LaSalle St., Chicago, IL 60602
Skyline Tours, Inc., 574 Fifth Ave., New York, NY 10036
Spacific Tours, Inc., 4029 Westerly Place, Newport Beach, CA 92660
Sunny Land Tours, Inc., 166 Main St., Hackensack, NJ 07601
Talmage Tours, Inc., 1223 Walnut St., Philadelphia, PA 19107
Tauck Tours, Inc., 11 Wilton Rd., Westport, CT 06880
Thru the Lens Tours, Inc., 5301 Laurel Canyon Blvd., North Hollywood, CA
    91607
Top Flight Tours, 132 State St., Albany, NY 12207
Total Travel Ltd., 800 E. Northwest Highway, Palatine, IL 60067
Tour Arrangements, Inc., 82 Washington St., Marblehead, MA 01945
Touropa, 40 E. 49th St., New York, NY 10017
Tourstars, 300 W. 45th St., New York, NY 10036
Tower Travel Corp., 444 Madison Ave., New York, NY 10022
Trade Wind Tours of Hawaii, P.O. Box 2198, Honolulu, HI 96805
Trafalgar Tours USA, Inc., 745 Fifth Ave., New York, NY 10022
Travcoa World Tours, 875 N. Michigan Ave., Chicago, IL 60611

Travel America Corp., 551 Fifth Ave., New York, NY 10017
Travel and Transport, 3104 Farnam St., Omaha, NB 68131
Travel Arrangements, 435 N. Michigan Ave., Chicago, IL 60611
Travelcade Tours, 201 W. 41st St., New York, NY 10036
Travel Dynamics, Inc., 964 Third Ave., New York, NY 10022
Travel-Go-Round, 516 Fifth Ave., New York, NY 10036
Travel Guide, 3660 Wilshire Blvd., Los Angeles, CA 90010
Traveline, Inc., 680 Fifth Ave., New York, NY 10019
Travelpower, 108 W. Wells St., Milwaukee, WI 53203
Travel Systems International, 2652 Butterfield Rd., Oak Brook, IL 60521
Travel Tours, Inc., 25 W. 43rd St., New York, NY 10036
Travel World, Inc., 6922 Hollywood Blvd., Los Angeles, CA 90028
Travtour Ltd., 444 Madison Ave., New York, NY 10022
T.V. Travel, Inc., 3085 Woodman Dr., Dayton, OH 45420
United Touring Company, 350 Fifth Ave., New York, NY 10001
Unitours, Inc., 1671 Wilshire Blvd., Los Angeles, CA 90017
Universal/Sky Tours, Inc., 60 E. 42nd St., New York, NY 10017
U.S. Student Travel Service, 801 Second Ave., New York, NY 10017
Vacation Ventures, 55 E. Monroe St., Chicago, IL 60603
Venture Tours, 6007 Eighteenth Ave. South, Minneapolis, MN 55423
Western Ski Vacations, 3 W. 57th St., New York, NY 10019
Westours, 100 W. Harrison Plaza, Seattle, WA 98119

SHOULD YOU TAKE THE KIDS?

Depending on your destination, in most cases the answer is yes, provided, of course, that your kids are curious, healthy, intelligent, reasonably well behaved, and deserve the special reward that a trip can bring. You would have to be a real dingdong if you failed to appreciate the inherent benefits your children can derive from travel: if nothing else, you could help them to breathe life into their classes and textbooks and that is no small achievement. Whether you take them to the pioneer whaling village of New Bedford, Massachusetts, or through the Civil War battlefields of Gettysburg, or on a comprehensive tour of Scandinavia, you are helping them to link hands with the peoples of the world, their history, languages, customs, dress, food, and traditions. Trust me, a well-planned trip can be as much fun for your kids as *Star Wars* or *Laverne and Shirley*.

But decide first if your children are mature enough, chronologically *and* emotionally, to appreciate the difference between St. Louis and Saint-Tropez. Personally, I would prefer not to see very young children (say preschool age) traveling, especially to far off and even exotic destinations. I worry about their health and the possible toll that jet lag, missed meals, and strange climates will take on their still-fragile systems. Otherwise, I think age has very little to do with a child's candidacy for travel. I have watched destructive, disrespectful teenagers romp through the Smithsonian Institution while an eight-year-old little girl, mesmerized by the displays, listened to the guide as if she were waiting to be quizzed on the spiel. The child's interest in the trip usually will determine what he or she brings to it and takes from it. And here, *you* are an important catalyst.

If you are considering taking your kids along, prepare them for the trip by providing them with information about the city, state, and country you will be visiting. Better yet, encourage them to go to the library and find the background information themselves; in this way they'll help build the foundation for a trip that is more than just a sabbatical from school.

In deciding whether this getaway will be en famille, carefully consider if you need time to renew yourself away from the kids. Don't feel guilty if you and your husband want a romantic interlude without car pools, four daily laundry loads, and yet another critique of *The Incredible Hulk*. If you do decide that the vacation will be for the entire family, however, be sure you allow ample time to spend with the kids and have access to sitters or other kindly souls who will function in loco parentis.

And, where children are involved in travel, there are other preparations and considerations as well. For instance:

1. Prior to any major trip, children should have a complete physical examination by both their doctor and

dentist. This precaution can save you and the kids unexpected and unwanted grief away from home.

2. Carry with you whatever medication, first-aid items, and vitamins the children will need for the duration of the trip (every drugstore in the world does not carry what you need; some will never have even heard of it).

3. When making airline, train, or bus reservations, indicate you are traveling with children and inquire about discount fares and any available family plans. On most airlines, children under two (carried by the parent) travel free; children up to eleven pay 50 percent to 66⅔ percent, and those over eleven are considered adults (they should live so long) and pay full fare. On Amtrak trains and on Greyhound and Trailway buses, children under five traveling with an adult ride for free, while children from five to twelve travel for half fare.

4. If you are flying with an infant, be sure to apprise the airline of this fact when you make your reservation. Most jet aircraft are equipped with wall or bulkhead attachments for portable bassinets normally located in the first row of the coach section. Once you have boarded the plane and you and your baby have simultaneously announced your arrival, the stewardess will be happy to warm your formula for you. Do not, however, expect any in-flight personnel to function as a baby-sitter or diaper changer. Baby (and his or her ears) will appreciate a bottle during ascent and descent of the aircraft.

5. In flight, kids seem especially sensitive to changes in cabin pressure. Get them to chew gum, especially during landing and takeoff, and to yawn as often as possible during the flight.

6. Airlines generally supply flying children with a variety of pins (steward or stewardess "wings"), puzzles, playing cards, and games to occupy them throughout their flights and well into puberty. Ask the flight attendant for these happy distractions as soon as you board the aircraft.

7. Whether traveling with children by airplane, train, bus, or car, be sure to carry with you at least one or two items designed to occupy them during the trip. For younger children,

this item might well be a favorite toy; for older children, have them select a favorite game or several books.

8. Airlines normally accommodate young people's taste buds by providing a meal that could put a gleam in the most tearful of eyes. Imagine: hot dogs, potato chips, and ice cream at 37,000 feet! No matter what your mode of transportation, you'll discover that little Gary and bigger Gail still like to snack. As a precaution (and to maintain their satiated silence and your own sanity), carry a box of their favorite cookies or other snack foods. This practice, perhaps unnecessary in flight, can prove invaluable during long car trips when you simply can't stop every time a voice in the rear yells, "Mommy, I'm hungry."

9. When selecting hotels and motels, ask your travel agent to determine policies regarding additional costs for children. For instance, some hotels will permit children under a specified age to share the same room as their parents at no additional cost, or for a very nominal charge of perhaps $3 to $4 per night. Securing this information *in advance* can save you a sizable amount of money, since you may choose hotels and motels across the country that provide the most economical plan for traveling children.

10. If the kids are coming along, you or your travel agent should correspond directly with the resort hotels, lodges, or tourist boards to determine what facilities, activities, and supervision will be available for children: Is there a day camp? Are there counselors? Are baby-sitters available and on call? What kinds of daily activities have been planned with young people in mind? Obviously, brochures from prospective destinations will give you a clue as to the general emphasis (or lack of it) on family vacations and activities for children. Moreover, if you have any doubts as to the likelihood that your children will find other kids there with whom to play, write or call in advance. The only thing worse than a kid who is miserable at home is one who's miserable on vacation.

11. When you travel with children, of almost any vintage, you are unconsciously changing the world's ecology by moving

so many dirty clothes around. Select clothing that travels well, is comfortable, looks neat, stays fresh, is durable, and requires a minimum of care. Hotel laundry and dry-cleaning services are almost universally available, but such services are very expensive particularly if you need same-day service. Be prepared: carry packets of soap suds (enough to do each day's laundry each night) and a traveler's clothesline so you won't have to depend on shower bars and bureau drawers for drying.

Some Tips on Trips Kids Will Like

Most trips with children invariably begin with "Get into the car and don't hit your sister"; still—given the proper incentive and preparation—a trip with kids can be educational and it should be fun. Out there are countless opportunities to share with children a wealth of historical, wilderness, cultural, recreational, and *pleasurable* experiences which require some planning, a bit more money, and lots of patience.

If they have the proper maturity and motivation, your kids might be suitable candidates for overseas travel. For a variety of reasons, not the least of which being the considerable investment involved, all of you need to become students of the countries you plan to visit prior to your trip. Read voraciously, discuss your destinations, listen to ethnic music, do everything possible to heighten your expectations and to get into the mood. More and more families are traveling abroad to explore the "Valley of the Kings" in Egypt, to ruminate among the ruins in Rome, and to meet the islanders of Polynesia. If your kids are ready for such experiences and you can afford to underwrite them, by all means forgo the summer cottage at the beach or the cabin in the mountains for the sake of some new and fascinating travel adventures. But before you race out for passports and shots, consider some unexplored options that await you and your kids at home.

1. *National Parks.* There are twenty-seven million acres of national park land in America where families may encounter the unique thrill of breathing clean air. Beyond this, there are opportunities to hike, camp out, take pictures, go horseback riding, fish, go river rafting, and to discover what nature is all about. All thirty-five national parks are designed to preserve the natural beauty of our country, and I assure you that the adventure of the mile ride down the Grand Canyon on muleback will bring a smile to your child's face that Disneyland would envy. The parks are as diverse as the places in which you find them (for instance: Shenandoah National Park in Virginia, Everglades National Park in Florida, Carlsbad Caverns in New Mexico, Redwoods National Park in California), but all are inherently fun-filled playgrounds where your family and nature can get together. Incidentally, the National Park Service has initiated a Golden Eagle Passport (currently $10) which is an annual permit that allows free entry to the holder (and all persons accompanying him or her in a private vehicle) to all parks in the system. Since the Golden Eagle Passport expires on December 31, it's best to buy it early in the year. For additional information, write to:

> The National Park Service
> U.S. Department of the Interior
> Washington, DC 20240

2. *National Monuments.* Depending upon where you live and how far you are willing to travel, you also have access to an incredible variety of historical parks, national seashores, and national recreational areas. Having no children of my own, I have frequently "borrowed" kids from friends (who fall prostrate to their knees with gratitude) in order to share such fascinating national monuments as: Gettysburg Battlefield (Pennsylvania), Fort Sumter (South Carolina), Gila Cliff Dwellings (New Mexico), Statue of Liberty (New York), and Cape Cod (Massachusetts). After almost all of these adventures, the borrowed kids asked to be adopted. For details on our national monuments, contact The National Park Service.

3. *Indian Reservations.* No matter where you live, you and your family are within reach of America's unique Indian culture. There are six nations of Iroquois in Upstate New York, Penobscots in Maine, Chippewas in Michigan, Hopi and

Navajo in Arizona, and Nez Percé in Idaho. Most of the existing reservations have powwows, tribal dances, and specialized handicrafts to introduce you to their proud heritage. If you think your kids consider you the Big Chief now, wait until you've taken them to a genuine reservation. For some inventive suggestions along these lines, you may wish to consult *Fodor's Indian America* ($10.95).

4. *Cowboys, Pioneers, Rodeos, and Dude Ranches.* When foreign visitors come to the United States, their primary target is most likely to be the West. Languages, currencies, and customs may be nationalistic, but John Wayne is universal. The world of shoot-outs, ranches, marshals, covered wagons, and rodeos is alive and well and there are even a few places where the buffalo still roam. Dude ranches provide a unique opportunity, especially for the city kid, to ride a horse, feed cattle, and assume other chores that will make you wonder why you can't get him or her to wash the dishes at home. And, if your kids know Bat Masterson better than they know their cousins, can you imagine the thrill awaiting them in Tombstone, Arizona, where they can visit the O.K. Corral, the Wells Fargo Museum, and Boot Hill? Rodeos (about which the respective state tourist boards provide full information) are typically held in many cities in the West and Southwest; they truly embody the vigorous cowboy spirit: stoic, heroic, and competitive. And you and your kids can't be assured of a better bang-up time than at the Cheyenne Frontier Days in Wyoming.

5. *National Military Academies.* Ever since I saw Tyrone Power in *The Long Gray Line*, the U.S. Military Academy at West Point has held a special fascination for me, centering upon its tradition, discipline, authority, and spectacle. A visit to West Point not only conjures up magic names like Eisenhower, MacArthur, and Patton... but it provides battalion reviews, military bands, and drill teams as well. If you want your children to learn that McDonald's is not America's only tradition, you might consider a trip to picturesque West Point or to the equally impressive Coast Guard Academy at

New London, Connecticut, the U.S. Naval Academy at Annapolis, Maryland, or the U.S. Air Force Academy at Colorado Springs, Colorado. Contact the public information officer at the respective academy for a list of seasonal events, tours, and visiting hours.

6. *Riverboats.* The Nile is mysterious, the Thames is hectic, the Rhine is enchanting, and the Mississippi is everything. Here is an opportunity for a family vacation in which a modern riverboat provides you with transportation, accommodations, meals, entertainment, and sight-seeing as you ply your way along that famous river that just keeps rolling along. Your boat will have considerably more amenities than Captain Andy's *Show Boat*, but the essence of the old stern-wheel river steamboat, packed with cargo and blasting a proud calliope, remains. And whether you travel from Cincinnati upriver or downriver, you'll get a firsthand, up-close view of towns, cities, farms, plantations, and of what life along the river is all about. To get your dose of "river fever," write to:

> Delta Queen Steamboat Co.
> 511 Main Street
> Cincinnati, OH 45202

All of this may seem like a great deal of preparation for a trip that is supposed to be "spontaneous" and "fun," but children have expectations about travel, too, and they are much more likely to participate in, benefit from, and *enjoy* the entire adventure if all of you have given some thought to what needs to be done. And, when the trip is over, think of the reservoir of material they will have for the next five years of show and tell.

TRAVELING WITH, AND BY, THE HANDICAPPED

There was a time, and it wasn't that long ago, when individuals with handicaps found it virtually impossible to travel: the physically disabled could not get to see Diamond Head in Hawaii, the blind could not experience the magic of fall in New England, and the deaf could not 'hear" of the wonders of Jerusalem. Thanks to the resourceful leadership of organizations representing the handicapped and the cooperation of the travel industry, much of that has changed and the prognosis for greater access is better. Travel for the thirty-six million handicapped Americans is still neither easy nor necessarily affordable, but at least there are available and attractive options.

Disability comes in varieties and degrees: there are the blind, deaf, retarded, diabetic, infirmed, and arthritic, as well as amputees, paraplegics, individuals suffering with acute cardiovascular or lung disease, and travelers returning from Aspen with a broken leg from a skiing mishap. Your family doctor should be the ultimate authority regarding a handicapped person's candidacy for travel: he or she will know the history and extent of the disability and you will know the nature and demands of the proposed trip; together, you can deal with getting you where you want to go. Your final collaborator, of course, will be a tour operator or travel agent who specializes in travel for the handicapped. These inventive professionals have most recently arranged for disabled travelers to do a seven-day wheelchair tour in Hawaii, for the blind to spend eight days touring George Washington Country, and for deaf travelers to enjoy a special Caribbean cruise. In addition, there are a variety of trips for various disabled persons to Scandinavia, South America, California, Disney World, Nashville, the Pocono Mountains, and Israel...with guarantees, all along the way, that the handicapped traveler will find buses with lifts, ramps for wheelchairs, Braille menus, accessible bathrooms, and sign-language guides. Just like travel for the fully abled, trips by the handicapped require a certain amount of consideration and preparation.

1. *How do I find out which travel agencies and tour operators specifically cater to the needs of the handicapped?*

—Write to the Society for the Advancement of Travel for the Handicapped (SATH), 26 Court St., Brooklyn, NY 11242. This organization, which maintains a current file of cooperating, concerned travel agencies and tour operators, has been created to serve handicapped travelers better and to obtain for them the services they have a right to expect.

2. *What provisions does an airline make for the handicapped traveler?*

—Though airlines differ in their ardor and efforts in behalf of the disabled, the handicapped traveler has a right to expect pre-boarding and delayed deplaning (the handicapped normally are the first on, and the last off, an aircraft); seat selection in smoking or nonsmoking sections, as well as special consideration for easy access to lavatories or exits; availability of a forklift (or "Handicapped Lift," as TWA calls it) which is an enclosed, elevator-type vehicle which eliminates the need for carrying wheelchair passengers up and down aircraft steps at locations that do not yet have jetway facilities; the use of a regular wheelchair at the airport *and* a special narrow wheelchair to facilitate movement down the aisle of the aircraft to and from your seat; and the transportation of your own wheelchair free of charge.

3. *What special arrangements do I need to make with an airline for a handicapped person who plans to fly?*

—Inform the travel agent or the airline reservations clerk of all your special needs *at the time the flight is booked* (i.e., special meal, seat requirements, need for a wheelchair, etc.).

—Check whether the disabled person can travel alone or will require an attendant.

—Ensure that you have obtained any necessary medical clearance.

—Ask for details concerning accessibility of airport facilities. If the airline doesn't know, better get a copy of *Access Travel: Airports*, Airport Operators Council, International Consumer Information Center, Dept. 619-F, Pueblo, CO 81009.

—If the handicapped person travels with a Seeing Eye

guide dog and is flying overseas, it is imperative that restrictions governing importation of animals be checked (see chapter 3).

—Arrive at the airport at least one hour prior to flight time.

—Read *Air Travel for the Handicapped,* an informative brochure available from TWA (call TWA locally, or write: TWA, 605 Third Ave., New York, NY 10016).

4. *What special considerations are afforded to handicapped travelers by interstate bus companies?*

—Greyhound pioneered in assisting the handicapped to "get in touch with America" by instituting its Helping Hand service in 1975. The plan allows both handicapped persons and their companion to travel on a single ticket (the handicapped persons must present a written statement from a doctor stating that they need a companion for physical assistance in bus travel). In addition, the companion must be capable of assisting the disabled person in boarding and exiting during the trip and the pair must travel together for the complete trip.

—While many interstate buses are lavatory-equipped, it's important to remember that bus aisles are only fourteen inches wide so the disabled traveler should gauge times between rest and meal stops.

—When making bus reservations for a handicapped traveler, always inquire as to provisions in the terminal for such conveniences as handrails, ramps, rest rooms, and food service designed with the disabled traveler in mind.

5. *What about access for the handicapped in other modes of transportation such as rental cars, trains, and ships?*

—The major rental car companies, Avis, Hertz, and National, normally can offer hand controls (for brakes and accelerators) in large metropolitan areas. Make such special requests well in advance and always specify right- or left-hand controls.

—Amtrak's newest equipment incorporates some design features to respond to the needs of the handicapped. When making a train reservation, ask if provisions for the handicapped have been made in the lavatories, sleeping compartments and seats, and, when applicable, ask if a wheelchair can be accommodated.

—Most ships, with rare exceptions, have not been designed with the handicapped traveler in mind. If you are disabled and are determined to take an ocean voyage, communicate your specific needs to the steamship company well in advance of your departure.

6. *Are there hotels and motels which have special accommodations for the handicapped?*

—Yes, and here again it's important that you communicate any disability-related needs to your travel agent so that he or she can ensure in advance that you will find what you need once you get there.

—Though not a comprehensive list, the following hotel and motel chains generally make available accommodations specifically designed for the handicapped: Ramada Inns, Holiday Inns, Marriott Hotels, Hilton Hotels, Western International Hotels, and Sheraton Hotels and Motor Inns.

Opportunities for travel with, and by, the handicapped have increased dramatically in recent years so that the disabled can experience the adventure of travel often on tours offered to the general public. The philosophy of "mainstreaming" suggests that if handicapped persons can interact with able-bodied people in everyday life, there is no reason why they can't interact on vacation. Lois Reamy, whose book *Travel/ Ability* (New York: Macmillan, $9.95) is the major work in the field of travel for the handicapped, provides a reasonable criterion: "if you don't need buses with lifts, medical assistants, and the like, you can probably save money by taking a conventional tour, especially if you are traveling with an able-bodied companion."

No matter who we are, whatever the nature and degree of our disability, or whomever we want along as companions, a trip takes planning.

3

WHAT ABOUT FIDO? TRAVELING WITH YOUR PET

Pets, as far as we can tell, enjoy new places and new people as much as the rest of us, but their potential happiness en route carries with it an important set of prerequisites. For many travelers, the most commanding reason for taking their pets on trips is—quite simply—they can't bear to be without them. And that, perhaps, is justification enough. But as you anticipate that cool nose and excited tongue assaulting your face's landscape each morning, and as you rejoice in the cozy, cuddly, furry friend who will give you love each night, also carefully consider the important precautions you must take to make the trip for Fido happy and healthy, and the extent to which your own freedom, spontaneity, and pleasure may be compromised by having him along. Even away from home, Fido still needs attention...and to be fed, watched, walked, and entertained. Are you willing to deal with all of that while you're traveling?

GETTING YOUR PET READY TO TRAVEL

Just as we can sometimes be negligent about our own bodies, so can we also be careless (even reckless) about the experiences to which we subject our traveling pets. You are tense, anxious, and weary during a trip; so is Fido. You worry about strange noises (especially in an airplane), react cautiously to new people, and feel a certain sense of alienation as soon as you leave the comfortable, secure place that is home. . . . Don t you think your dog feels the same way? For your pet to have a secure, healthy trip—even when it is away from its favorite pillow, tree, and pals—you need to be aware of a number of pretrip preparations and considerations:

1. Before any trip, your pet should be given a thorough examination by its veterinarian. People need a clean bill of health before traveling and so do pets. At the time of examination, check on the status of your dog's protection against rabies since its shots must be current and valid. This is an excellent opportunity to discuss your pet's need for tranquilizers or sedatives during the journey; your vet will base this decision upon such considerations as your pet's health, temperament, and the length of the trip. In terms of a pet's health, it will come as no surprise to you that sick or pregnant animals are not considered good candidates for travel.

2. Pets, like people, travel best at certain times. When possible, travel with your dog or cat in the spring or fall when it is less likely to be irritated by extremes of hot and cold. Similarly, the early-morning and early-evening hours are far more pleasant for travel than summer trips made in the heat of the noonday sun (and we know from Noël Coward that only mad dogs and Englishmen go out in that).

3. On the day of your departure, feed your pet a very light meal. Its stomach, like yours, is subject to nervousness both before the trip and during.

4. Select a portable kennel for your pet well before any trip and give it the opportunity to become accustomed to it. Some friends of mine put their dog in her portable kennel, place her in the back seat of their car, and take little Lizzy for a long drive before she is about to embark on any cross-country flight. This "out-of-town tryout" makes perfectly good sense since it gives Lizzy a preconditioning to confinement and a feeling of familiarity for what will be her home when she travels. There are a few guidelines to keep in mind as you select a portable kennel:

　　a. Be sure it is well-ventilated and sturdy (such as models made of reinforced plastic).

b. It is imperative that the kennel be large enough for your pet to move around in; measure Fido's length, height, and width to ensure that your pet can stand up and turn around in the kennel you've selected.

5. Before I leave on any trip, I throw my most comfortable slippers, time-tested sweater, and a box of chocolate chip cookies in my flight bag. These few simple objects go a long way toward making me feel more comfortable and content on trips. Similarly, your pet should have some favorite familiar possessions assembled in a bag which accompanies it whenever it travels; it'll especially appreciate its sleeping blanket, dish, water bowl, favorite food or a snack, and prized toy.

6. Hotels and motels have diverse regulations governing animals: some will not accept pets at all, others house pets in separate accommodations, and a progressive handful provide luxurious pet quarters which *you* would be happy to sleep in. Among the major hotel and motel chains which generally welcome pets are: Hilton, Marriott, Holiday Inns, Sheraton, and Ramada Inns. Once you have planned your itinerary, check with the respective hotels and motels en route to determine the reception Fido will receive. Additional details concerning housing accommodations for animals, as well as other valuable information about traveling with pets in general, can be found in the following publications:

Traveling with Your Pet ($1.00 donation would be appreciated)
American Society for the Prevention of Cruelty to Animals (ASPCA)
441 E. 92nd St.
New York, NY 10028

Touring with Touser ($1.00)
Gaines TWT
P.O. Box 1007
Kankakee, IL 60901

Traveling with Your Pet (free)
U.S. Travel Service
Department of Commerce
Washington, DC 20230

Protecting Your Pets ($3.95)
Gieseking and Clive, Inc.
Box 716
Bronxville, NY 10708

7. Virtually every state in our country requires, as a precondition for admission of pets, a Veterinarian Health Certificate and a Rabies Vaccination Certificate. It is your responsibility to check with your veterinarian and the local office of the ASPCA to be certain that your pet will be permitted to travel where you want to take him. Interstate car travel usually involves random inspections of pet kennels and documents at specified check points, while airlines routinely and systematically review health certificates for interstate air travel by pets. For travel outside the continental United States, your pet (which, in most instances, means dog) will need both Health and Rabies Vaccination Certificates. Since requirements for the admission of pets *differ* from country to country, prior to your trip you will want to call the embassy or consulate of each country to determine their respective, *current* regulations. In some cases, the embassy will require that the health certificate prepared by your vet be countersigned by an embassy official.

Even if your pet passes the necessary physical and health requirements, some countries (Great Britain, for example) will place it in an extended quarantine lasting a minimum of six months. If the country or countries you wish to travel to enforce such stringent quarantine regulations, chances are that Fido will never see the Changing of the Guard at Buckingham Palace. And it is worth mentioning here that there are a number of countries (Australia, for one) which will not admit pets from the United States under any circumstances. As part of your pretrip planning, it is imperative that you check with the various foreign offices to determine if Fido will be welcome . . . and under what conditions.

HEALTH REQUIREMENTS FOR PET TRAVEL IN THE USA

CODE DEFINITION:
*—health certificate required.
†—rabies inoculation required.
Time—rabies inoculation must be given within the time listed.
kv—killed virus vaccine.
mlv—modified live virus vaccine.
cev—chick embryo vaccine.
ntv—nerve tissue vaccine.
Puppies—are exempt from rabies vaccination requirement up to age listed.

Other:
1—show dogs exempt.
2—dogs from rabies quarantine area not admitted.
3—dogs with screwworms not admitted.
4—may be quarantined 60 days if from rabies area.
5—dogs from rabies quarantine area may enter with written permit.
6—not admitted if exposed to rabies or from an area where rabies exists.
7—cats require health certificate and rabies vaccination.
8—hunting dogs must receive rabies vaccination within 30 days of entry.
9—proof of ownership required.
10—puppies under 4 months from a quarantine area need a permit from Bureau of Animal Industry.
11—cats must be free from contagious disease.
12—cats require a health certificate.
13—dogs suspected of having rabies or being bitten by a suspected rabid animal may be quarantined 60 days.

SOURCE: Information concerning domestic and foreign regulations reprinted with the permission of the American Society for the Prevention of Cruelty to Animals.

	Health Certificate	Rabies Inocula-tion	Within This Time	Puppies	Other
Alabama	*	†	6 mo	3 mo	3, 6
Alaska	*	†	6 mo	4 mo	6
Arizona	*	†	1 yr, kv 3 yr, mlv	4 mo	2

	Health Certificate	Rabies Inoculation	Within This Time	Puppies	Other
Arkansas	*	†	1 yr	3 mo	2, 6, 7
California	*	†	30 mo, mlv	4 mo	
Colorado	*	†	1 yr	3 mo	6, 7
Connecticut	*	†	6 mo		1, 2, 6
Delaware	*	†		4 mo	1, 5, 11
District of Columbia		†	1 yr	3 mo	13
Florida	*	†	6 mo		11
Georgia	*	†	6 mo	3 mo	2, 6
Hawaii	120-day quarantine at owner's expense				
Idaho	*	†	6 mo, ntv 2 yr, cev	4 mo	2, 6, 10
Illinois	*	†	6 mo, kv 1 yr, mlv	16 wks	
Indiana	*	†	mlv or equal duration 1 yr	3 mo	7
Iowa	*	†	3 yr, mlv 1 yr, kv	6 mo	1, 12
Kansas	*	†	1 yr	3 mo	
Kentucky	*	†	1 yr, kv 2 yr, mlv	4 mo	1, 2, 6, 7
Louisiana	*	†	2 yr, cev 1 yr, ntv	2 mo	

Maine		†	mlv		
Maryland	*	†	1 yr	4 mo	2, 6
Massachu-setts	*	†	1 yr	6 mo	1
Michigan	*	†	6 mo, kv		1, 4
Minnesota	*	†	1 yr, kv 2 yr, mlv	6 mo	5, 6
Mississippi	*	†	6 mo	3 mo	2, 7
Missouri	*	†	2 yr, mlv 1 yr, kv	4 mo	
Montana	*	†	2 yr, mlv	3 mo	5
Nebraska	*	†	2 yr, mlv 1 yr, kv	4 mo	
Nevada	*	†	2 yr, ntv 1 yr, ntv	4 mo	1, 5
New Hampshire	*	†	3 yr, cev 1 yr. kv	3 mo	2, 6
New Jersey	*				1, 2, 6
New Mexico	*	†	1 yr	3 mo	7, 14
New York	*				1
North Carolina	*	†	1 yr	4 mo	1, 5
North Dakota	*	†	3 yr, mlv	3 mo	1, 2, 6, 8
Ohio		†	3 yr, cev 1 yr, other	6 mo	

	Health Certificate	Rabies Inoculation	Within This Time	Puppies	Other
Oklahoma	*	†	1 yr		2, 6
Oregon	*	†	2 yr, mlv 6 mo, kv	4 mo	5, 12
Pennsylvania					9
Rhode Island	*	†	6 mo, kv 2 yr, mlv	6 mo All dogs	2, 6
South Carolina	*	†	1 yr		2, 6, 12
South Dakota	*	†	1 yr		
Tennessee	*	†	1 yr		2, 6
Texas	*	†	6 mo		
Utah	*	†		4 mo	7
Vermont	*	†	1 yr, mlv	4 mo	2, 7
Virginia	*	†	1 yr	4 mo	2, 6, 7
Washington	*	†	2 yr, mlv 1 yr, kv	4 mo	12
West Virginia	*	†	1 yr	6 mo	1, 2, 6, 7
Wisconsin	*	†	3 yr, cev 1 yr, other	6 mo	
Wyoming	*	†	2 yr, cev 1 yr, mlv	4 mo	2, 6

HEALTH REQUIREMENTS FOR FOREIGN TRAVEL WITH PETS

The following summary suggests that countries vary considerably from each other in terms of entry requirements for dogs and cats. Inasmuch as these regulations are somewhat technical and because they are subject to change, it is always advisable to consult your veterinarian and to contact the respective embassy or consulate for any clarification you need.

Australia
Entry prohibited from United States, except Hawaii. Dogs and cats arriving from Hawaii require:
— Certificate of good health.
— Declaration from veterinarian that rabies have not existed in Hawaii for at least five years.
— Declaration of residency and import permit. Apply to Chief Quarantine Officer (Animals), Department of Primary Industries, William St., Brisbane, Australia.
— Animal must travel in a sealed container.
— Nine months' quarantine required in Brisbane.

NOTE: If arriving from countries other than the United States, check requirements with nearest Australian consulate.

Bahamas
— Obtain an import permit. Apply at least a month in advance to Ministry of Agriculture & Fisheries, P.O. Box N-3028, Nassau, Bahamas.
— Obtain a certificate of good health from a veterinarian within 24 hours of departure.
— Animals over 6 months of age require certificate of rabies inoculation (a minimum of 10 days old, maximum of 9 months).

Bermuda
— Obtain a certificate of good health from a veterinarian within 10 days before arrival. This document must indicate:
1. Breed, sex, age, and color of animal.
2. That the animal is free from external parasites and communicable diseases.
3. Has not been exposed to rabies and has not been in an area where rabies exists (in the last 6 months).
4. Has received rabies inoculations since 3 months old and that the last inoculation was administered at least 1 month and not longer than 12 months before arrival.

— Obtain an import permit from the Director of Agriculture Fisheries, Point Finger Road, Paget 6-23, Bermuda.
— Obtain a document attesting that the animal did not reside within 30 miles of any area known to be infected with foot-and-mouth disease.

NOTE: If arriving direct from New Zealand, Australia, Great Britain, or Jamaica, rabies inoculation is not required.

Brazil
— Obtain a certificate of good health from a veterinarian.
— Have this document authorized by the Brazilian Consulate before departure.

Canada
— Animals from the United States require a certificate of rabies inoculation stating that this vaccination was given within 12 months prior to departure.

NOTE: Check with consulate for regulations regarding arrival from other countries.

Chile
— Obtain a good health certificate from a public agency in the country of origin. From the same agency, obtain a certificate of rabies vaccination for dogs.
— Have the above document legalized at the Chilean consulate.

China, People's Republic of
— Obtain from a veterinarian (at the point of origin) a certificate of good health and rabies vaccination.

Denmark
— Obtain a certificate of good health and rabies inoculation which gives complete identification of animal. (Inoculation must have been given at least 4 weeks, but not more than 1 year, prior to arrival in Denmark.)

Egypt
— Obtain a certificate of good health from a government veterinarian at the point of origin (at least 2 weeks before intended arrival).

Fiji
— Dogs and cats prohibited entry into Fiji by air except those imported from New Zealand, New South Wales, Tasmania, Victoria, and South Australia. Check requirements with consulate.

France
Required documents must be issued by an authorized veterinarian at the point of origin.
1. If 12 months old or more:
— Certificate of good health obtained not more than 5 days before

transport. This document must attest that the country of origin was rabies-free in the last 36 months and that the animal has lived there since birth or during the last 6 months.

2. Over 3 months of age:
— Certificate of good health or rabies inoculation as outlined in number one.

3. Dogs must be vaccinated against distemper and hepatitis a minimum of 1 month (maximum 12 months) prior to transport (revaccination valid if given within 1 year prior to transport).

4. Cats must obtain a certificate of inoculation against typhus (minimum of 1 month, maximum 12 months prior to transport).

5. Animals younger than 3 months are denied entry.

Germany, East
— Obtain a certificate of good health from the government veterinary agency (maximum of 5 days before trip).
— Obtain a certificate of rabies vaccination. Two copies of this document are required and must be obtained at least a month, but not more than a year, prior to the trip. This must be authorized by country of origin's veterinary service.
— Animal must pass health exam at entry point.
— Obtain an import license if stay will exceed 28 days.

Germany, West
— Obtain a certificate of good health. This must be written in German (or translated into German) on the stationery of a licensed veterinarian in the country of origin. The following information must be included: animal's name, race, sex, age, color, the date of health exam, and that the animal is disease-free, and that in the last 3 months rabies has not been reported within a 13-mile radius. This certificate is valid for 10 days if importation is from Europe, 20 days if arriving from a non-European country.

NOTE: Exemption from the above regulations is granted if the animal is used professionally, by an artist, a Seeing Eye dog, a service dog (with German military, customs, or lifesaving organization) or is in transit (may not leave airport in this case).

Greece
— Obtain a certificate of rabies vaccination and good health. This document must be issued by a veterinary authority before departing country of residency and must attest that the rabies vaccination was made not more than a year (6 months for cats) and not under 6 days before arriving.
— Submit animal to health clearance upon entry.

Hong Kong
— Obtain an import permit in advance of trip from Agriculture

Fisheries Department, Canton Road Government Offices, 393 Canton Rd., 12th Floor, Kowloon, Hong Kong. When applying for this document include the animal's species, breed, age, sex, color, owner's name and address, expected arrival date in Hong Kong and how arriving (plane, train, etc.).
— Obtain a certificate of good health from the government veterinary authority of the country of origin. This is not valid if obtained more than 2 weeks prior to departure date.

NOTE: Upon arrival the animal must be quarantined at a kennel designated for this purpose. Quarantine is 6 months unless arriving from Australia, Ireland, New Zealand, or Great Britain. Animals from these countries may have quarantine waived if the following are presented: certificate attesting that the animal was living in one of the aforementioned countries for at least 6 months prior to arrival in Hong Kong, a certificate of good health obtained from an official veterinarian of the government of country of origin, a document from captain of transporting plane or ship that the animal traveled isolated from other animals.

India
— Obtain a certificate of good health and rabies inoculation from a veterinarian in the country of origin. This must be issued at least 7 days before arrival in India.
— Make arrangements to be met at airport by a veterinarian authorized by the government. He or she must issue a document certifying that the animal is in good health.

Ireland
— Obtain an import license from the Department of Agriculture, Veterinary Section, Agriculture House, Kildare St., Dublin 2.
— Air transportation permitted by air freight only.
— Quarantine is required at owner's expense. The animal will receive 2 rabies inoculations during this time.

Israel
— Obtain a certificate of good health and rabies vaccination from a veterinarian.

NOTE: An unvaccinated dog may enter but must be vaccinated within 2 weeks of arrival. Dogs from Asia and Africa are quarantined for 1 month and revaccinated during that time.

Italy
— Obtain from veterinary authority (in country of origin) a certificate of good health and rabies vaccination. This must be authorized at least 4 weeks but a maximum of 1 year (6 months for cats) before departure.
— Dogs require muzzle if being led on a chain over 1 meter in length.

Jamaica
Cats and dogs prohibited except those born and bred in Great Britain and arriving directly from there.
— Obtain an import permit. Apply to Veterinary Division of the Ministry of Agriculture, Kingston, Jamaica.
— Obtain a certificate of good health which affirms that the animal received a rabies vaccination at least 6 months before transport.

Japan
— Cats do not require any documents.
— Dogs require:
1. Certificate of good health.
2. Certificate of rabies vaccination obtained from the government veterinary authority at departure area.

NOTE: At least 14 days' quarantine is required at owner's expense unless the animal belongs to U.S. military personnel or is arriving directly from Fiji, Finland, Australia, Great Britain, Cyprus, Iceland, Hong Kong, Northern Ireland, New Zealand, Taiwan, Singapore, Sweden, Portugal, or Norway. Quarantine varies for animals arriving from these countries.

Kenya
— Obtain an import permit from Livestock Officer, Veterinary Department Post Office, Kabete, Kenya. Allow at least 1 month from submission of application for the permit to arrive.
— At point of origin obtain a veterinarian certificate of good health and rabies vaccination.

Malaysia
— Obtain a landing permit.
— Obtain a certificate of good health. Must be obtained 1 week prior to transport and must affirm that the country of origin is rabies-free and the animal was not imported there.
— Obtain an import permit from Malaysian Veterinary Department.
— Quarantine of 30 days or longer required unless arriving from Australia, New Zealand, Singapore, Great Britain, or Ireland (and if from Singapore obtain export license from government of Singapore).
— Station manager (at disembarkation) must be given complete details on animal's arrival by the originating airport. And space should be reserved for animals requiring quarantine.

Mexico
— Under 3 months of age denied entry.
— For other animals obtain a certificate of good health and rabies inoculation from a veterinarian.
— Have this document visaed by the Mexican consul (unless it is obtained from a government agency).

New Zealand
— Entry permitted only to animals from Australia, Great Britain, and Ireland.
— Animal must be sent as cargo in a strong container. Seeing Eye dogs may travel in cabin with passenger if permission is obtained from the airline.

Peru
— Obtain a veterinarian certificate of good health and rabies inoculation at point of origin.

Philippines
— Obtain (at point of origin) a veterinarian certificate of good health and rabies vaccination. This document must affirm that the animal has not been exposed to a contagious disease. Obtain an import permit in advance. Apply to Bureau of Animal Industry.
— The station manager of the transporting airline (at point of disembarkation) must notify the quarantine inspector in Manila at least 24 hours in advance of the animal's expected arrival.

Portugal
— Obtain in advance an authorization from Direccao Geral dos Servicos Pecuarios, Lisbon.
— Obtain (at point of origin) a certificate of good health from a veterinarian.
— If arriving from a country where rabies exist, obtain a certificate of rabies vaccination that states date and type of vaccination, name of the manufacturer and serial number of vaccine, the veterinarian's statement with his name, profession, signature, and stamp.
— The station manager of transporting airline (at disembarkation point) must be advised in advance of animal's arrival so that a veterinarian will be on hand to meet it.

Puerto Rico
— Obtain (at point of origin) a certificate of good health from a veterinarian. This document is valid for up to a month before arrival. For dogs, it must be stated that the animal was residing in an area free from contagious, infectious, or transmissible disease. Dogs over 8 weeks old also require a certificate of rabies vaccination (issued within 6 months before arrival).

Saudi Arabia
— Importation of dogs prohibited.
— For cats, obtain 2 copies of a veterinarian certificate of good health plus a certificate of rabies inoculation (this must state that the vaccination was given between 1 year and 1 month prior to import).

Singapore
— Obtain an import permit at least 2 weeks in advance. Apply to

Director of Primary Production, City Veterinary Centre, 40 Kampong Java Road, Singapore 9.
— Obtain a certificate of good health, issued within seven days of departure, by the Government Veterinary Authority.
— Either obtain a certificate of rabies inoculation or have the animal vaccinated upon arrival.
— Quarantine of at least 30 days imposed unless arriving from Great Britain, Australia, or New Zealand.
— Transporting airline's agent (at Singapore) should be notified at least a day in advance of arrival, so a veterinarian will be on hand.

NOTE: The above regulations pertain to importation. Transshipment requirements differ. Contact nearest consulate for details.

South Africa
— Obtain a Veterinary Import Permit from the Director of Veterinary Services, Private Bag X 138, Pretoria. Apply at least 8 weeks before planned arrival.
— Obtain a certificate of rabies inoculation. Must be issued at least 3 months, but not more than 3 years, before arrival.

Spain
— For an animal over 3 months old, obtain a certificate of good health and rabies vaccination. This is valid only if issued at least 4 weeks, but not more than 1 year, prior to shipment.
— Have this document visaed by the Spanish consulate.
— Animals are subject to examination by customs veterinarian upon arrival.

NOTE: It is advised that arrival be timed to coincide with working hours to avoid clearance delays.

Sweden
1. For animals arriving from Finland and Norway:
— Obtain a 6 week affidavit from a veterinarian before transport.
2. For arrival from other countries:
— Obtain an import permit from Lantbrukstyrelsen, 55183 Jonkopping, Stockholm.
— Also obtain (in country of origin) a certificate of good health from a veterinarian.
— Animals are subject to examination and quarantine upon arrival. Quarantine of 4 months cost about $6 (U.S. dollars) per day.

Switzerland
— Obtain a certificate (in English, German, French, or Italian) from a veterinarian indicating that the animal was inoculated against rabies at least 1 month, but not more than 12 months, prior to

arrival. The following information must appear on this certificate: owner's name and address, complete description of animal, age, statement of good health, date of rabies vaccination, kind of vaccine, name of producer and production number of vaccine, and the veterinary surgeon's signature.

Trinidad and Tobago

— Obtain a government veterinarian certificate of good health and rabies inoculation. This must state that the animal is disease-free and that the country of origin has been free from rabies for at least the last 6 months.
— An entry permit must be obtained in advance: apply to Director of Agriculture, St. Clair, Trinidad.
— Station manager of transporting airline (located at disembarkation point) must be notified at least 24 hours before animal's arrival. He will arrange government veterinary clearance.
— Quarantine of 6 months or more is imposed unless arriving directly from Anguilla, Antigua, Barbados, Ireland, Jamaica, Nevis, St. Kitts, St. Vincent, or Great Britain.
— Pets in transit are exempt from all requirements if continuing on same aircraft. If connecting with another flight within 24 hours, apply to Director of Agriculture, Trinidad, for an intransit permit.

Tunisia

— Obtain a certificate of good health from the veterinary authorities in the country of origin. This must affirm that the place of origin has been free from contagious animal diseases at least 6 weeks prior to transport. Obtain a certificate of rabies inoculation for dogs.

Turkey

— Obtain a certificate of good health and rabies inoculation.
— Have this document issued by the Chamber of Commerce or the Ministry of Foreign Affairs (in the country of origin) and legalized by the Turkish consulate.

United Kingdom

For animals in transit:

— If transit will require over 4 hours, consent must be obtained in advance from Cargo Department of the airline involved in United Kingdom. Quarantine will be imposed and owner will have to pay high fees.

For import:

— Animal must arrive as manifested cargo in a nose and paw proof container and covered by an air waybill.
— Cargo Department, at arrival station, must be advised in advance of arrival and be apprised of the license number shown on the boarding document, name of shipper and owner, type of pet, date of arrival, flight of arrival, and departure.

— Obtain a certificate of good health.

— Obtain a boarding document as proof that an import license has been issued by the Ministry of Agriculture, Fisheries and Food.

— Animals may arrive only at the following airports: Glasgow, Edinburgh, Manchester, Birmingham, London (Gatwick Airport), London (Heathrow Airport) and Leeds.

— During a 6 months' quarantine animals will receive rabies inoculations.

NOTE: Animals cannot be shipped as baggage. Failure to comply with regulations can result in fines or destruction of animal. Consult nearest consulate for more information.

United States, Virgin Islands

— Obtain a certificate of good health from a veterinarian not more than 1 month prior to transport.

— Animals must be accompanied by a document stating that a rabies inoculation was given within 12 months before transport. This certificate must affirm that no rabies have occurred during the past 6 months within a radius of 50 miles from the point of origin.

— Animals cannot leave the airport until the animal quarantine veterinarian authorizes departure.

USSR

— Obtain a certificate of good health from a veterinarian authorized by the local Board of Health. This cannot be issued more than 10 days before arrival at port of entry.

Venezeula

— Obtain from an approved U.S. government veterinarian a certificate of good health and certificate of rabies and distemper vaccinations.

— Have all documents visaed by the Venezuelan consul.

Yugoslavia

— Obtain a certificate of good health from a veterinarian. This must be legalized by the veterinary authorities at the point of origin.

SOURCE: Information concerning foreign regulations reprinted with the permission of the American Society for the Prevention of Cruelty to Animals, and Hal Gieseking *(Protecting Your Pets*, Gieseking and Clive, Inc.).

HOW SHOULD FIDO TRAVEL: BUS, TRAIN, SHIP, CAR, OR PLANE?

Bus and Train

Interstate bus lines will carry no pets with the exception of Seeing Eye dogs. Amtrak (the national railroad system) similarly makes no provisions for carrying pets. Therefore, if you want your dog or cat to travel, your options are a ship, your family car, or an airplane.

Ship

Many passenger cruise ships have special accommodations designated for pets. Some of these "floating kennels" will be substantially larger than your stateroom . . . giving new meaning to the phrase, "it's a dog's life." When booking passage, ask about the company's policy regarding the transportation of pets (i.e., cost, nature of housing, availability of "kennelmates" to exercise and care for your pet, etc.). Remember that you will be sailing to a foreign country and, here again, the responsibility is *yours* for determining health requirements for your pet at the point of disembarkation. If, for example, you and Fido land in Southampton, you won't see each other for six months because of England's quarantine rule.

Car

I recently went for a drive in scenic New England with some friends who brought along their noble, if a bit athletic, English Sheepdog. The dog, which was walking about the back seat, suddenly became distracted and leaped into the driver's lap, nearly causing a significant increase in Massachusetts' accident statistics. From that ride on, noble or not, the English Sheepdog remains on a leash or harness.

People are frequently subject to car sickness and so, apparently, are dogs. If you plan to take yours for a drive, observe a few simple rules which will add appreciably to its comfort and security and yours:

1. Do not feed it a big meal before the trip.
2. Always carry fresh water.
3. Stop regularly so that your pet can get needed exercise and have the opportunity to tend to requisite bodily functions.
4. Don't drive with the car windows wide open. (Even if your pet loves to watch its hair blowing in the wind, an

open window frequently becomes an invitation to jump outside directly into the path of oncoming traffic).

5. Do not take your pet for a drive if it has been ill; car sickness will probably not improve its disposition or its condition.
6. Remember to bring along a bag of goodies (blanket, dish, snack, toys).
7. Be sure it is on a leash and that someone in the car is holding on to the leash... or your pet.

My experience with pets traveling in cars is that they genuinely enjoy the adventure of it all except, of course, when they become bored. When that happens, a dog's bark (like your kid's yell) generally means, "Mommy, when do we get there?!"

Plane

Airlines have specific regulations and established fares for transporting pets and, since carriers tend to differ from each other as to the nature and enforcement of these regulations, you may wish to shop around a bit before deciding which airline Fido will fly. No matter which carrier you select, you may safely assume that:

1. It will require current and valid health and rabies vaccination certificates (some carriers may, in addition, request an ownership certificate). To be safe, bring all of these documents with you to the airport.
2. It will require you to bring or rent a portable kennel to transport your pet.
3. It will charge you for transporting ("shipping" is so undignified) your pet; this fare is in addition to the rental of the kennel.
4. It will allow the pet to accompany you in the passenger compartment only if it can be accommodated in a container less than eight inches high (this rule does vary, however, among carriers); if your pet cannot travel with you in the cabin or as excess baggage, you may ship it as air cargo though this is the least

desirable option because "priority" cargo could result in your pet being "bumped."

5. It will only allow one pet in each cabin of the aircraft (i.e., first-class and coach), and this is determined on a first come, first served basis.

6. It will expect you to deliver your pet to the appropriate airline receiving area at a specified time; or, if you prefer, you may contract directly with a commercial shipper specializing in pets to handle all of these arrangements (look under Pet Transport in the Yellow Pages).

7. It will want you to attach to the portable kennel any special feeding instructions or notes about your dog's unique temperament.

Though I can find no research to justify this theory, I suspect that your pet would also be grateful to be booked on a nonstop, or at least a direct, flight . . . like you, he would rather not be jostled about at airports.

Now that you have made some important decisions concerning whether you will make the trip alone or with a friend, spouse, or lover; if you will do it independently or latch onto an organized escorted tour; if you will schlepp along the kids or leave them at home; or if you will bring along your pet or check it into a kennel—you are ready to meet adventure's midwife . . . your travel agent.

4

WHOM SHOULD YOU GO TO FOR ADVICE?

Your air conditioner is on the fritz so you consult a friend who is an electrician and ask his advice about various models you are considering buying. Exhausted from manually mowing the lawn each weekend, you check out power models at several different stores in order to compare quality and prices. The rash on your elbow, acquired during your camping trip last month, won't go away and so you consult a dermatologist for information and medical advice. Before we make any major decision concerning the quality of our lives or future plans and acquisitions, we normally ask questions, make comparisons, and seek information from professionals. Except, it would seem, in the area of travel.

Friends who spend a half an hour mulling over a wine list at dinner, or take a week to select wallpaper for the bathroom, or three months shopping for a washer-dryer race into vacations that are chaotic, ill-timed, poorly planned, and overpriced. You can usually identify such unhappy victims: once home they fall to their knees, kiss the lawn, and swear on their barbecues never to leave again. Pity, because chances are that a good travel agent could have helped them to transform the ridiculous into the sublime.

HOW TO CHOOSE AND USE A TRAVEL AGENT

There are currently sixteen thousand travel agents in the United States and they probably vary from each other just as much as any other occupational group in terms of expertise, professionalism, motivation, and the ability to communicate with—and relate well to—other people. You were probably not thrilled with the first optometrist, shoemaker, butcher, or dentist you used and so you might well have to sample several travel agents in order to hit upon the correct chemistry which successfully blends your needs and their skills. But it need not be hit or miss, and it should never be at the last minute.

How to Choose a Travel Agent: Who Is for *You?*

In my opinion, the single most reliable arrow to point you in the direction of a "good" travel agent is the *recommendation of friends.* Your neighbors used their travel agent to plan a Caribbean cruise, your boss used his or her travel agent for an extended business trip to South America, your brother-in-law used his travel agent to plan a fishing trip to Mazatlán, but the extent to which all were satisfied probably was based upon the same evaluation: the travel agent was professional, helpful, informed, and interested...and the trip went off without a hitch. Then, too, your friends and business associates no doubt feel they know you, and so their recommendation of a specific travel agent reflects their instinct about what you want and who can provide the guidance you need. I happily volunteer the name of my travel agent to friends because I am impressed with his thoroughness (everything is confirmed and reconfirmed; if there's a goof-up it's not his), interest (he makes valuable, creative, *and* economical suggestions and gladly fields my probing questions), and his intuitive understanding of the ways in which I like to travel (a good travel agent knows his clients as well as he knows his countries).

People in the travel industry urge prospective travelers to *use agents who are members of ASTA* (American Society of Travel Agents). In order for agencies to be accredited by ASTA, they must have been in operation for three years and have written $500,000 in business during the year preceding initiation. ASTA therefore reflects business continuity and fiscal responsibility, and, for those professional indicators alone, you are probably in safer hands with an ASTA agency.

Here again, however, the ASTA symbol on a travel agency window does not ensure unlimited travel expertise or flawless trips. Capability within the agency may vary from agent to agent, but at least you know you're doing business with an experienced agency which is presumably in business to stay.

Check the Yellow Pages in order to determine which travel agencies are located near your home; though not essential, convenience could be a consideration. Then, too, telephone directory listings often indicate areas of specialization for agencies: cruises, charters, tours of Africa, study-abroad programs, etc., and you might appreciate having this information as you start to narrow down the field.

Call your local Better Business Bureau and ask if it has any complaints on file for the several agencies you are considering. This may seem to be an unnecessary precaution, but it is a reality of business life that some merchants are disreputable, dishonest, and distrusted; you are certainly entitled to be apprised of legitimate beefs by earlier travelers. If a charter airline has consistently canceled flights, or a tour operator has illegally downgraded hotel accommodations, or a travel agent has failed to make appropriate refunds—the Better Business Bureau might well know of these shady practices and so should you.

When you have narrowed down the field to several agencies you believe you'd like to pursue, *phone ahead and make appointments.* Travel agencies appreciate all business, but (like you when you are feeding the kids or balancing the old checkbook) they discourage unannounced interruptions. When you call for an appointment, by all means indicate the possible destinations you have in mind for your trip and request that your appointment be with an agent in the office who *knows* that area. Sorry, but I think a travel agent's value is in direct proportion to his or her familiarity with the destination—I want to talk to the agent who visited there within the last few years, don't you?

All of these preparations might seem excessive considering, after all, that this is a vacation and not a doctoral dissertation, but if you choose carefully you will find in your travel agent an invaluable ally who skillfully and successfully brings together you and where you want to go.

How to Use a Travel Agent: The Steps

Travel agents are professionals whose business it is to guide, arrange, and administer your travel plans for the purpose of making themselves a profit. Their time and their advice are valuable and they will rightfully expect that you will be respectful of both. They are not your analyst, poker pal, or hairdresser. Though they may smile benevolently at your desire to see all of Australia in two days, travel agents are not Eleanor Roosevelt with a flight schedule or Sister Kenny with a currency converter. Like your tailor and lawyer, travel agents mean business.

Homework. Prior to your meeting, discuss with your travel mates exactly what you hope to accomplish. On a pad of paper, you might indicate:

——How much time you have (must you be back on a *specific* date?).

——What kind of vacation you'd like to have (a shopping spree, a communion with nature, a quest for culture, etc.).

——How much you want to spend (think in terms of a minimum/maximum range rather than a specific dollar figure).

——When you would like to go. (Be as flexible as possible, remembering that rates are often lower off-season and that airline fares tend to be lower for extended stays overseas. Adding one day to your trip or traveling two weeks later could save you hundreds of dollars.)

——Where you have previously gone on vacation and which trips pleased you most . . . and why.

——What previous travel experiences raised questions in your mind about your "travelability." For instance: are you outraged by bad weather, impatient with slow service, irritated by convention hotels or large tour groups, or repulsed by bus travel? Confess everything to your travel agent so he or she can steer you away from a bad rerun on your next travel outing.

Commitment. When you meet with your travel agent, make an effort to determine how much time he or she is prepared to spend with you. This may seem a vague goal, but it's most essential to get a feel for how importantly the agent regards *you* and *your trip.* Presuming you are neither neurotic nor a nuisance, he or she should be generally available for your consultations and questions. Beware the agent who begins your conference with, "I'll start your trip and then my associate will handle the actual details," "I'm really swamped, but because you're a friend of Shirley's, I'll make time," or, "I usually handle much more elaborate itineraries (or first-class travel), but I'll make an exception for you." Whenever I've heard any of these harbingers of doom muttered by travel agents, my feet began running in the opposite direction.

Conditions, Clauses, and Croissants. Analyze tour brochures carefully in the presence of your travel agent. Jointly, you should be certain that you fully understand:

——Cruise details, including the ratio of days at sea to days in port, the physical layout of the ship, stateroom size and plan (especially for *your* stateroom), and dining hours on board.

——Each other's use of terms applied to hotel accommodations, such as: "superior," "deluxe," "moderate," and "first-class."

——Which charges are *fixed* (such as air fare, hotels, and airport transfers, etc.), and which are optional or *extra* such as gratuities, alcoholic beverages, additional sight-seeing, etc.).

——The cancellation clause and possible penalties if you are opting for an air charter or packaged tour.

——Which meals are included as part of the plan you are buying (don't play the sophisticate: European Plan (EP) means no meals; American Plan (AP) = all meals; Modified American Plan (MAP) = breakfast and lunch *or* dinner; Continental Plan (CP) = breakfast consisting of coffee or tea and a sweet roll.

——That you must indicate specific preferences with regard to room arrangements (king-sized beds? adjoining rooms? high floor? oceanfront?); and be sure your agent makes notations of these preferences on all hotel confirmations and vouchers.

——The value of purchasing insurance to cover trip cancellation, bad weather (honest, it's available!), lost luggage, property theft, injury, and accidents particularly if these incidents are not otherwise covered by your existing insurance policies.

Payment. There is, I suspect, quite a bit of confusion regarding payment to travel agents and the sources from which they receive their commissions. Let's lay the myth to rest—the client (you) doesn't pay anything to the travel agent for normal travel arrangements which include airline ticketing, hotel reservations, car rentals, sight-seeing tours, and airport transfers. Travel agents make their profit on trips from the commissions (ranging from 6 percent to 20 percent) they receive from wholesale tour operators, airlines, and hotels. They collect their profits from them, *not* from you.

There are, however, extenuating circumstances which would require your paying a service charge to your travel agent. If, for example, Ralph comes home from the office flushed with excitement and exclaims: "I can't take it another day; pack, Freda, we're going to Portugal!", Ralph's travel agent will need to cable or telephone Lisbon to expedite arrangements and those unusual costs will be passed on to the traveler. But the normal day-to-day business of structuring and organizing travel arrangements is done at no charge to you, the client.

In terms of your payments to the travel agent for the trip itself (i.e., hotel rooms, airline tickets, sight-seeing), keep these two guidelines in mind:

——Pay for your airline tickets when you receive them

(some agencies have a cash flow problem and will ask for your money when you make your reservations—wait till you have the tickets in hand).

——Most tour operators and hotels require a deposit on the services and/or accomodations you are contracting for; your travel agent will ask for specific amounts of money (or a lump sum deposit) in return for which he or she will give you travel vouchers specifying the amount credited in your name for each hotel, tour, etc.

Responsibility. Travel agents, like most merchants, deal with vendors they can trust—people who deliver the product promised. As you and your travel agent review brochures, discuss airline and steamship companies, and evaluate tours and itineraries be sure you ask him about his earlier experiences in referring previous clients to these same hotels, airlines, ships, and tours:

——Were your travel predecessors satisfied?

——Did they get what they paid for?

——Were there last-minute substitutions?

——What services were promised and not delivered?

——What is the company's reputation for promptness, efficiency, courtesy, and quality?

——Would clients who have taken the trip repeat it, or recommend it to others?

You must understand and appreciate that as many as two hundred *separate* service personnel and companies might be involved in providing you with what you need on a three-week tour of Europe. The travel agent contracts, as your representative, with a tour wholesaler who then "subcontracts" for facilities and services with this army of people throughout the world. The local sight-seeing bus does not arbitrarily materialize at your London hotel on the appointed morning; you are not preregistered at a quaint Bavarian inn by chance; and your kielbasy and vodka lunch doesn't just happen on a whim in Cracow—it is all part of a master plan built by a tour operator in accordance with specifications designed by your travel agent and you. With so many concerned about the welfare of so many, it is no wonder that there are snafus: delayed departures, overbooked hotels, inept guides... but you will be astonished (all right, pleased) at the responsible professionalism of the travel industry.

But what if you're not? If you fail to get what you have contracted and paid for, get to the root of the problem. First, discuss the situation with the travel agent in an effort to rescue the dollars you believe you're due. After you have waited what you regard as a sufficient period of time, perhaps you should consider a few other options:

——Write to, or telephone, your local Better Business Bureau (at least your dissatisfaction will be a matter of record).

——If you believe your travel agent is at fault, register your complaint with ASTA, Consummer Affairs Department, 711 Fifth Ave., New York, NY 10020 (212-486-0700).

——Describe your maltreatment in a letter, outlining the conditions and events of your trip, and send it to the Consumer Affairs Advocate (or Hotline) at your local television station or newspaper (this route often provides a potent catalyst for getting a problem resolved with maximum speed and visibility).

——If an airline is the culprit, write or call:

Bureau of Consumer Protection
Civil Aeronautics Board
Washington, DC 20428
(202-673-6047)

——And if all else fails, consult an attorney and consider bringing suit against the "guilty parties" in Small Claims Court.

Anticipate the best from your travel agent and trip; in most cases, you will get it.

Other Services. In addition to securing a wealth of travel information for you and handling the logistics of your trip, your travel agent—by sharing his or her considerable expertise—can smooth potentially bumpy waters in other

ways. For example, he or she is your principal source of information concerning:
——Travel documents (how to get passports, visas, and International Driver's Permits)
——Immunizations required for overseas travel
——Foreign currencies
——Climates and seasonal temperatures in your destination cities
——Clothing appropriate for where you are going and the style in which you are going there
——Customs regulations

Skilled travel agents know a great deal about many places; they cannot possibly know of every trendy boutique in Soho, every four-star restaurant in Paris, or the best place to buy jade in Hong Kong... but they may have these gems of information at their fingertips and astound both you and themselves with their knowledge and memory. More importantly, good travel agents who simply do not have the answer to your question will put you in touch with a resource (a colleague, a tourist board, an airline, a reference book) that does.

GETTING INFORMATION: LIBRARIES, TOURIST BOARDS, AND AIRLINES

There is a lovely old Spanish proverb which translates, "He who would bring home the wealth of the Indies must carry the wealth of the Indies with him." The point is that the more positive input you take with you on a trip, the more magical and meaningful will be the memories you bring back. No matter what your ultimate destination, neighboring county or Nepal, trust me that your experience will be more educational and entertaining if you read about the place and question others who have been there.

On a recent trip, an inept, uninformed guide could have ruined an excursion for me had I not read voraciously about the ruins we were examining. By reading books and brochures and from questioning well-traveled friends, I have learned what to wear, what taste treats were in store for me, what national holidays to avoid and what festivals to include, where best to change money, what not to drink, where to go on serendipitous nearby excursions, what to do for entertainment, what to expect at customs, and how to meet the locals. Should anyone you know give you the name and phone number of a person in the country you will be visiting, regard this as a potential travel bonus and take advantage of it. I learned more at dinner from two young Israelis in Haifa than I did from four days of organized sight-seeing.

Your travel agent (and perhaps your traveling friends) will, in varying degrees, be able to provide you with comprehensive, accurate, current, and practical information concerning your destinations. You have other resources as well.

The Library
You remember the library: a dimly lit place with lots of books and a lady yelling, "Shhhhh." Most libraries have a travel section where you will find the popular area travel guides and reference books by the biggies in the field: Temple Fielding, Arthur Frommer, Eugene Fodor, and Myra Waldo. Simply find the book which deals with the region of the world and specific destination you plan to visit. But while you are in the library, stretch your ingenuity a bit and consider picking up a nonreference book about the place you will soon be visiting. If, for instance, you read James Michener's *Iberia*, you'll have another window opened to the world that is Spain.

Tourist Boards
Virtually every state and some cities in our country maintain a tourist office normally located in that respective state's capital city. A letter or phone call to this office will result in a bombardment of *free*, current information regarding tourist attractions, accommodations, costs, and seasonal events in that area. The quality of these materials ranges from sketchy "you must be kidding" maps to handsome, comprehensive

travel kits which will do everything for you but pack your suitcase.

Similarly, most foreign countries (and many territories and geographic regions) maintain government tourist offices in the United States. These offices are typically located in New York City, though some governments—depending on demand—maintain branch offices in Los Angeles, San Francisco, Chicago, and Miami.

When you write to a state or foreign tourist board, it is essential that you specify your interests (family attractions, campsites, cultural events, walking tours, etc.), the time of year in which you plan to visit, and your general itinerary (a sharp tourist board representative once reviewed my itinerary and then made several excellent suggestions which I then incorporated into my trip).

Tourist boards are not travel agents; they produce and distribute information in an effort to promote tourism. If you simply write and request "all you have on Egypt" you will receive a packet which includes everything but the Nile ...which is fine if you truly plan to read and digest these materials.

This warning however: tourist boards are flooded with inquiries and some are notoriously slow in complying with requests for travel information. Write to them *well in advance* of your trip, and don't be ashamed to send them follow-up reminders if you've been ignored. I can't vouch for the individual quality of every tourist board's travel packets, but I can tell you that the free information kits these organizations generally produce can be valuable companions for any journey. With apologies to Karl Malden, "Don't leave home without them."

U.S. TOURIST BOARDS*

Alabama Bureau of Publicity and Information, State Highway Bldg., Room 403, Montgomery, AL 36130

Alaska Division of Tourism, Pouch E, Juneau, AK 99811

American Samoa Office of Tourism, Pago Pago, American Samoa, 96799
Arizona Office of Tourism, 1700 W. Washington, Room 501, Phoenix, AZ 85007
Arkansas Department of Parks & Tourism, 149 State Capitol Bldg., Little Rock, AR 72201
Baltimore Convention & Visitors Bureau, 22 Light St., Baltimore, MD 21202
Chicago Convention & Tourist Bureau, Inc., 332 S. Michigan Ave., Chicago, IL 60604
Colorado Division of Commerce & Development, 1313 Sherman St., Denver, CO 80203
Connecticut Department of Commerce, Division of Tourism, 210 Washington St., Hartford, CT 06106
Delaware Division of Economic Development, 630 State College Rd., Dover, DE 19901
District of Columbia: Washington Area Convention & Visitor Association, 1129 20th St., NW, Washington, DC 20036
Florida Division of Tourism, 107 W. Gaines St., Room 505, Tallahassee, FL 32304
Georgia Bureau of Industry & Trade, P.O. Box 1776, Atlanta GA 30301
Guam Visitors Bureau, P.O. Box 3520, Pedro's Plaza, Suite 410, Agana, GU 96910 USA
Hawaii Visitors Bureau, 2270 Kalakaua Ave., Suite 801, Honolulu, HI 95815
Idaho Division of Tourism & Industrial Development, State Capitol Bldg., Room 108, Boise, ID 83720
Illinois Office of Tourism, Department of Business & Economic Development, 222 S. College St., Springfield, IL 62706
Indiana Division of Tourism, 336 State House, Indianapolis, IN 46204
Iowa Development Commission, 250 Jewett Bldg., Des Moines, IA 50309
Kansas Department of Economic Development, 503 Kansas Ave., 6th Floor, Topeka, KS 66603
Kentucky Department of Public Information & Travel, Capital Annex Bldg., Frankfort, KY 40601
Louisiana Tourist Development Commission, P.O. Box 44291, Baton Rouge, LA 70804
Maine State Development Office, State Capitol Building, Augusta, ME 04333
Maryland Division of Tourist Development, 1748 Forest Dr., Annapolis, MD 21401
Massachusetts Department of Commerce & Development, Division of Tourism, Leverett Saltonstall Bldg., 100 Cambridge St., Boston, MA 02202
Michigan Travel Bureau, Department of Commerce, P.O. Box 30226, Lansing, MI 48909

Minnesota Department of Economic Development, 480 Cedar St., Hanover Bldg., St. Paul, MN 55101

Mississippi Agricultural & Industrial Board, 1505 Walter Sillers State Office Bldg., P.O. Box 849, Jackson, MS 39205

Missouri Division of Tourism, P.O. Box 1055, Jefferson City, MO 65101

Montana Travel Promotion Unit, Department of Highways, Helena, MT 59601

Nebraska Department of Economic Development, Travel & Tourism Division, P.O. Box 9466, State Capitol, Lincoln, NB 68509

Nevada Department of Economic Development, Capitol Complex, Carson City, NV 89710

New Hampshire Department of Resources & Economic Development, P.O. Box 856, Concord, NH 03301

New Jersey Office of Tourism & Promotion, P.O. Box 400, Trenton, NJ 08625

New Mexico Department of Development, 113 Washington Ave., Santa Fe, NM 87503

New York City Convention & Visitors Bureau, 90 E. 42nd St., New York, NY 10017

New York State Department of Commerce, 99 Washington Ave., Albany, NY 12245

North Carolina Department of Natural & Economic Resources, P.O. Box 27687, Raleigh, NC 27611

North Dakota Highway Department, Capitol Grounds, Bismarck, ND 58501

Ohio Department of Economic & Community Development, 30 E. Broad St., Columbus, OH 43215

Oklahoma Tourism & Recreation Department, Tourism Promotion Division, 500 Will Rogers Bldg., Oklahoma City, OK 73105

Oregon Department of Transportation, Travel Information Section, Transportation Bldg., Salem, OR 97310

Pennsylvania Department of Commerce, Travel Development Bureau, 423 South Office Bldg., Harrisburg, PA 17120

Philadelphia Convention & Visitors Bureau, 1525 John F. Kennedy Blvd., Philadelphia, PA 19102

Puerto Rico Commonwealth of Tourism Development, GPO Box BN, San Juan, PR 00936

Rhode Island Department of Economic Development, 1 Weybosset Hill, Providence, RI 02903

South Carolina Department of Parks, Recreation & Tourism, Suite 113, Brown Bldg., 1205 Pendleton St., Columbia, SC 29201

South Dakota Division of Tourism, Joe Foss Bldg., Room 217, Pierre, SD 57501

Southern California Visitors Bureau, 705 W. 7th St., Los Angeles, CA 90017
Tennessee Department of Tourist Development, 505 Fesslers Ln., Nashville, TN 37210
Texas State Department of Highways & Public Transportation, Travel & Information Division, P.O. Box 5064, Austin, TX 78763
Virgin Islands Government Information Center, 10 Rockefeller Plaza, New York, NY 10020
Utah Travel Council, Council Hall, Capitol Hill, Salt Lake City, UT 84114
Vermont Agency of Development & Community Affairs, 61 Elm St., Montpelier, VT 05602
Virginia State Travel Service, 6 N. 6th St., Richmond, VA 23219
Washington Department of Commerce & Economic Development, General Administration Building, Olympia, WA 98505
West Virginia Department of Commerce, Travel Development Division, 1900 Washington St. E., Charleston, WV 25305
Wisconsin Department of Business Development, Division of Tourism, 123 W. Washington Ave., Madison WI 53702
Wyoming Travel Commission, 1-25 at Etchepare Circle, Cheyenne, WY 82002

FOREIGN TOURIST BOARDS*

Afghanistan
Afghan Tourist Organization, 535 Fifth Ave., New York, NY 10017
Antigua
Antigua Information Office, 610 Fifth Avenue, NY 10020
Argentina
Argentina Tourist Information Office, 500 Fifth Ave., New York, NY 10036
Aruba
Aruba Information Center, 576 Fifth Ave., New York, NY 10036
Australia
Australian Tourist Commission, 1270 Avenue of the Americas, New York, NY 10020
Austria
Austrian Tourist Information Office, 545 Fifth Ave., New York, NY 10017
Bahama Islands
Bahama Islands Tourist Office, 30 Rockefeller Plaza, New York, NY 10020
Barbados
Barbados Tourist Board, 800 Second Ave., New York, NY 10017
Belgium
Belgian National Tourist Office, 720 Fifth Ave., New York, NY 10019

*Lists of tourist boards compiled by, and reproduced courtesy of, *The Travel Advisor*. (Now published by Travel Magazine, Inc.)

Bermuda
Bermuda Department of Tourism, 630 Fifth Ave., New York, NY 10020
Bonaire
Netherlands Antilles, Bonaire Tourist Information Office, 685 Fifth Ave.,
    New York, NY 10022
Bolivia
Bolivian Consulate General, 10 Rockefeller Plaza, New York, NY 10020
Brazil
Brazilian Consulate General, 630 Fifth Ave., New York, NY 10020
British Virgin Islands
John Scott Fones, Inc., 515 Madison Ave., New York, NY 10022
Bulgaria
Bulgarian Tourist Office, 50 E. 42nd St., New York, NY 10017
Burma
Union of Permanent Mission of Burma to the UN, 10 E. 77th St., New York,
    NY 10021
Cameroon
Embassy of Cameroon, 2349 Massachusetts Ave. N.W., Washington, DC
    20008
Canada
Canadian Government Office of Tourism, 1251 Avenue of the Americas,
    New York, NY 10020
Cayman Islands
Cayman Islands Department of Tourism, 420 Lexington Ave., New York,
    NY 10017
Ceylon (Sri Lanka)
Ceylon Tourist Board, North American Office, 609 Fifth Ave., New York,
    NY 10017
Chile
Consulate General of Chile, 866 Second Ave., New York, NY 10017
China, People's Republic of
Liaison Office, People's Republic of China, 2300 Connecticut Ave. N.W.,
    Washington, DC 20008
Colombia
Colombian Government Tourist Office, 140 E. 57th St., New York, NY
    10022
Costa Rica
Costa Rican Embassy, 211 E. 43rd St., New York, NY 10017
Curaçao
Curaçao Tourist Board, 30 Rockefeller Plaza, New York, NY 10020
Cyprus
Consulate General of Cyprus, 820 Second Ave., New York, NY 10017
Czechoslovakia
Cedok-Czechoslovak Travel Bureau, 10 E. 40th St., New York, NY 10016

Denmark
Danish National Tourist Office, 75 Rockefeller Plaza, New York, NY 10019
Dominica
Eastern Caribbean Tourist Association, 220 E. 42nd St., New York, NY
    10017
Dominican Republic
Tourist Information Office, Dominican Republic Government Tourist
    Office, 64 W. 50th St., Rockefeller Center, New York, NY 10020
Ecuador
Consulate General of Ecuador, 1270 Avenue of the Americas, New York, NY
    10020
Egypt
Egyptian Government Tourist Office, 630 Fifth Ave., New York, NY 10020
El Salvador
Consulate General of El Salvador, 211 E. 43rd St., New York, NY 10017
Ethiopia
Consulate General of Ethiopia, 866 United Nations Plaza, New York, NY
    10017
Finland
Finland National Tourist Office, 75 Rockefeller Plaza, New York, NY
    10019
France & French Community
French Government Tourist Office, 610 Fifth Ave., New York, NY 10020
Galápagos Islands
Galápagos Islands Tourist Office, 888 Seventh Ave., New York, NY 10019
Germany
German National Tourist Office, 630 Fifth Ave., New York, NY 10020
Ghana
Sontheimer & Co., 445 Park Ave., New York, NY 10022
Gibraltar
Gibraltar Tourist Office, Cathedral Square, Gibraltar
Great Britain
British Tourist Authority, 680 Fifth Ave., New York, NY 10019
Greece
Greek National Tourist Organization, 645 Fifth Ave., New York, NY 10022
Grenada
Grenada Information Office, 866 Second Ave., New York, NY 10017
Guadeloupe
French West Indies Tourist Board, French Government Tourist Office, 610
    Fifth Ave., New York, NY 10020
Guatemala
Guatemala Consulate General, 1270 Avenue of the Americas, New York, NY
    10020

Guyana
Consulate General of Guyana, 622 Third Ave., New York, NY 10017
Haiti
Republic of Haiti Government Tourist Bureau, 30 Rockefeller Plaza, New York, NY 10020
Honduras
Honduras Information Service, 501 Fifth Ave., 5th Floor, New York, NY 10017
Hong Kong
Hong Kong Tourist Association, 548 Fifth Ave., New York, NY 10036
Hungary
Danube Countries Promotion Group (Hungary), 380 Madison Ave., New York, NY 10017
Iceland
Icelandic National Tourist Office, 75 Rockefeller Plaza, New York, NY 10019
India
Government of India Tourist Office, 30 Rockefeller Plaza, New York, NY 10020
Indonesia
Consulate General of the Republic of Indonesia, 5 E. 68th St., New York, NY 10021
Iraq
Press Information Office of Iraq, 14 E. 79th St., New York, NY 10021
Ireland
Irish Tourist Board, 590 Fifth Ave., New York, NY 10036
Israel
Israel Government Tourist Office, 350 Fifth Ave., New York, NY 10001
Italy
Italian Government Travel Office—ENIT, 630 Fifth Ave., New York, NY 10020
Jamaica
Jamaica Tourist Board, 866 Second Ave., New York, NY 10017
Japan
Japan National Tourist Organization, 45 Rockefeller Plaza, New York NY 10020
Jordan
Alia—The Royal Jordanian Airline, 535 Fifth Ave., New York, NY 10017
Kenya
Kenya Tourist Office, 60 E. 56th St., New York, NY 10022
Korea
Korea National Tourism Corp., 460 Park Ave., Room 628, New York, NY 10022

Lebanon
Lebanon Tourist & Information Office, 405 Park Ave., New York, NY 10022
Liberia
Liberian Consulate General, 820 Second Ave., New York, NY 10017
Luxembourg
Luxembourg Tourist Office, One Dag Hammarskjold Plaza, New York, NY
10017
Macao
Portuguese National Tourist Office, 548 Fifth Ave., New York, NY 10036
Malaysia
Malaysian Tourist Information Center, Transamerica Pyramid Bldg., 600
Montgomery St., San Francisco, CA 94111
Malta
Malta Consulate, 249 E. 35th St., New York, NY 10016
Martinique
French West Indies Tourist Board (Martinique), French Government
Tourist Office, 610 Fifth Ave., New York, NY 10020
Mexico
Mexican National Tourist Council, 405 Park Ave., New York, NY 10020
Monaco
Monaco Government Tourist Office, 115 E. 64th St., New York, NY 10021
Morocco
Moroccan National Tourist Office, 521 Fifth Ave., New York, NY 10017
Nepal
Consulate General of Nepal, 711 Third Ave., New York, NY 10017
Netherlands
Netherlands National Tourist Office, 576 Fifth Ave., New York, NY 10036
New Caledonia
New Caledonia Tourist Information Office, 700 S. Flower St., Suite 1704,
Los Angeles, CA 90017
New Zealand
New Zealand Government Travel Commissioner, 630 Fifth Ave., New York,
NY 10020
Nicaragua
Tourist Information Office of Nicaragua, c/o Consulate General of
Nicaragua, 1270 Avenue of the Americas, New York, NY 10020
Nigeria
Consulate General of Nigeria, 575 Lexington Ave., New York, NY 10017
Norway
Norwegian National Tourist Office, 75 Rockefeller Plaza, New York, NY
10019
Pakistan
Consulate General of Pakistan, 12 E. 65th St., New York, NY 10021

Panama
Panama Government Tourist Bureau, 630 Fifth Ave., New York, NY 10020
Paraguay
Consulate General of Paraguay, 909 International House Bldg., New
    Orleans, LA 70130
Peru
Peruvian Consulate General, 10 Rockefeller Plaza, New York, NY 10020
Philippines
Philippines Tourist Information Office, 556 Fifth Avenue, New York, NY
    10036
Poland
Polish National Tourist Office, 500 Fifth Ave., New York, NY 10036
Portugal
Tourist Information Office for Portugal, 548 Fifth Ave., New York, NY
    10036
Romania
Romanian National Tourist Office, 573 Third Ave., New York, NY 10016
St. Kitts-Nevis-Anguilla
St. Kitts-Nevis-Anguilla Tourist Information Center, 39 W. 55th St., New
    York, NY 10019
St. Lucia
St. Lucia Tourist Board, 220 E. 42nd St., New York, NY 10017
St. Maarten-Saba-St. Eustatius
St. Maarten, Saba, St. Eustatius Information Office, 445 Park Ave., New
    York, NY 10022
St. Vincent and the Grenadines
Eastern Caribbean Tourist Association, 220 E. 42nd St., New York, NY
    10017
Scandinavia
Scandinavian National Tourist Offices, 75 Rockefeller Plaza, New York, NY
    10019
Senegal
Republic of Senegal Tourist Information Office, 51 E. 42nd St., New York,
    NY 10017
Singapore
Singapore Tourist Information Office, 251 Post St., San Francisco, CA
    94108
South Africa
Republic of South African Tourist Corp., Rockefeller Center, 610 Fifth
    Ave., New York, NY 10020
Spain
Spanish National Tourist Office, 665 Fifth Ave., New York, NY 10022
Sri Lanka (see Ceylon)

Surinam
Surinam Tourist Bureau, One Rockefeller Plaza, New York, NY 10020
Sweden
Swedish National Tourist Office, 75 Rockefeller Plaza, New York, NY 10019
Switzerland
Swiss National Tourist Office, 608 Fifth Ave., New York, NY 10020
Tahiti
Tahiti Tourist Office, 200 E. 42nd St., New York, NY 10017
Taiwan, Republic of China
Chinese Information Service, 159 Lexington Ave., New York, NY 10016
Tanzania
Embassy of United Republic of Tanzania, 2010 Massachusetts Ave. NW,
    Washington, DC 20036
Thailand
Tourist Organization of Thailand, 5 World Trade Center, New York, NY
    10048
Tonga
Tonga Visitors Bureau, Transportation Consultants International, 700 S.
    Flower St., Suite 1704, Los Angeles, CA 90017
Trinidad and Tobago
Trinidad and Tobago Tourist Board, 400 Madison Ave., New York, NY
    10017
Tunisia
Tunisian National Tourist Office, 630 Fifth Ave., Room 863, New York, NY
    10020
Turkey
Turkish Government Tourism & Information Office, 821 UN Plaza, New
    York, NY 10036
Turks and Caicos Islands
B.W.I. Turks and Caicos Islands Tourist Information Office, 7777 W.
    Talcott, Chicago, IL 60631
Union of Soviet Socialist Republics
Intourist Information Office, USSR Co. for Foreign Travel, 45 E. 49th St.,
    New York, NY 10017
Uruguay
District Consulate of Uruguay, Consulate General, 301 E. 47th St., New
    York, NY 10017
Venezuela
Venezuelan Government Tourist and Information Bureau, 450 Park Ave.,
    New York, NY 10022
Yugoslavia
Yugoslav National Tourist Office, 630 Fifth Ave., New York, NY 10020
Zambia
Zambia National Tourist Bureau, 150 E. 58th St., New York, NY 10022

Airlines

Since airlines, like tourist boards, are in the business of promoting travel, it will come as no surprise to you that virtually all carriers produce brochures describing the destinations to which they fly. Information available from airlines ranges from United's leaflet (free) on *Condominiums in Hawaii* to a comprehensive atlas on travel such as *Pan Am's World Guide* ($6.95). In between these two extremes of airline-produced literature, there are thousands of *free* booklets and brochures describing tour packages, suggested itineraries, restaurants, shopping, climates, clothes, tipping, customs, and currencies. To obtain any of these publications, simply call the airline that flies to the destination in which you are interested and ask for the tour desk. Explain where you want to go and what you are looking for, and the airline representative will send you whatever publications that carrier makes available to the public. If the airline you wish to contact has no local office in your hometown, call the long distance operator and ask for that airline's toll-free (usually an 800 area code) number. It's just that simple.

AIRLINES OF THE WORLD

Aerocondor Airlines, 301 S.E. 2nd St., Miami, FL 33131
Aeroflot-Soviet Airlines, 545 Fifth Ave., New York, NY 10017
Aerolineas Argentinas, 9 Rockefeller Plaza, New York, NY 10020
Aeromexico, 8400 N.W. 52nd St., Miami, FL 33166
Aeroperu, 1st Federal Bldg., Miami, FL 33131
Air California, 3636 Birch St., Newport Beach, CA 92660
Air Canada, 600 Madison Ave., New York, NY 10022
Air Afrique, 683 Fifth Ave., New York, NY 10022
Air Florida, 3900 N.W. 79th Ave., Miami, FL 33156
Air France, 1350 Avenue of the Americas, New York, NY 10019
Air India, 345 Park Ave., New York, NY 10022
Air Jamaica, 19 E. 49th St., New York, NY 10017
Air New Zealand, 510 W. 6th St., Los Angeles, CA 90014
Air Panama International, 500 Fifth Ave., New York, NY 10036
Alaska Airlines, Inc., Seattle-Tacoma International Airport, Seattle, WA 98158

Alia—The Royal Jordanian Airline, 535 Fifth Ave., New York NY 10017
Alitalia, 666 Fifth Ave., New York, NY 10019
Aloha Airlines, Inc., P.O. Box 30028, Honolulu, HI 96820
American Airlines, Inc., P.O. Box 61616, Dallas-Ft. Worth Airport, TX 75261
Ansett Airlines of Australia, 510 W. 6th St., Los Angeles, CA 90014
Ariana Afghan Airlines, 535 Fifth Ave., New York, NY 10017
Avensa Airlines, 745 Fifth Ave., New York, NY 10022
Avianca Airlines, 6 W. 49th St., New York, NY 10020
Aviateca, 999 S. Bayshore Dr., Miami, Fl 33131
Braniff International Airways, P.O. Box 35001, Dallas, TX 75235
British Airways, 245 Park Ave., New York, NY 10017
British Caledonian Airways, 415 Madison Ave., New York, NY 10017
British West Indian Airways, 610 Fifth Ave., New York, NY 10020
Capitol International Airways, P.O. Box 325, Smyrna Airport, Smyrna, TN 37167
Cathay Pacific Airways, 291 Geary St., San Francisco, CA 94102
China Airlines, 391 Sutter St., San Francisco, CA 94108
Continental Airlines, Inc., International Airport, Los Angeles, CA 90009
Czechoslovak Airlines, 545 Fifth Ave., New York, NY 10017
Delta Airlines, Inc., Atlanta Airport, Atlanta, GA 30320
East African Airways, 600 Fifth Ave., New York, NY 10020
Eastern Airlines, Inc., International Airport, Miami, FL 33148
Ecuatoriana de Aviacion, 500 Fifth Ave., New York, NY 10036
Egyptair, 720 Fifth Ave., New York, NY 10019
El Al Israel Airlines, 850 Third Ave., New York, NY 10022
Ethiopian Airlines, 200 E. 42nd St., New York, NY 10017
Finnair, 10 E. 40th St., New York, NY 10016
Frontier Airlines, Inc., 8250 Smith Rd., Denver, CO 80207
Gulf Air, 245 Park Ave., New York, NY 10017
Hawaiian Airlines, Inc., P.O. Box 30008, Honolulu, HI 96820
Hughes Airwest, International Airport, San Francisco, CA 94128
Iberia Air Lines of Spain, 97-99 Queens Blvd., Rego Park, NY 11374
Icelandic Airlines, 630 Fifth Ave., New York, NY 10020
International Air Bahama, 630 Fifth Ave., New York, NY 10020
Iran Air, 345 Park Ave., New York, NY 10022
Irish International Airlines, 564 Fifth Ave., New York, NY 10036
Japan Air Lines Co., 655 Fifth Ave., New York, NY 10022
KLM Royal Dutch Airlines, 609 Fifth Ave., New York, NY 10017
Korean Air Lines, 1813 Wilshire Blvd., Los Angeles, CA 90057
Kuwait Airways, 30 Rockefeller Plaza, New York, NY 10020
Lacsa Airlines, 300 Biscayne Blvd. Way, Miami, FL 33131
Lan-Chile International Airlines, 150 S.E. Second Ave., Miami, FL 33131
Lanica Airlines, P.O. Box 481286, Miami, FL 33148
LOT-Polish Airlines, 500 Fifth Ave., New York, NY 10036

Lufthansa German Airlines, 1640 Hempstead Turnpike, East Meadow, L.I.,
NY 11554
Malaysian Airlines System, 510 W. 6th St., Los Angeles, CA 90014
Malev Hungarian Airlines, 630 Fifth Ave., New York, NY 10020
Mexicana Airlines, 851 Burlway Rd., Burlingame, CA 94010
Middle East Airlines, 680 Fifth Ave., New York, NY 10019
National Airlines, Inc., P.O. Box 592055, AMF, Miami, FL 33159
New York Airways, Inc., P.O. Box 426, LaGuardia Airport Station,
Flushing, NY 11371
Nigeria Airways, 30 Rockefeller Plaza, New York, NY 10020
Northwest Orient Airlines, Inc., International Airport, Minneapolis, MN
55111
Ozark Airlines, Inc., Lambert Field, St. Louis, MO 63145
Olympic Airways, 888 Seventh Ave., New York, NY 10019
Pacific Southwest Airlines, 3225 North Harbor Dr., San Diego, CA 92112
Pakistan International Airlines, 545 Fifth Ave., New York, NY 10017
Pan American World Airways, Pan Am Building, 200 Park Ave., New York,
NY 10017
Philippine Air Lines, 212 Stockton St., San Francisco, CA 94108
Piedmont Airlines, Smith-Reynolds Airport, Winston-Salem, NC 27102
Prinair, International Airport, Isla Verde, PR 00913
Qantas Airways LTD., 360 Post St., San Francisco, CA 94108
Republic Airlines, Inc., 2500 Airline Dr., Minneapolis, MN 55450
Royal Air Maroc, 680 Fifth Ave., New York, NY 10019
Sabena Belgian World Airlines, 125 Community Dr., Great Neck, NY 11201
San Francisco Helicopter Airlines, Inc., P.O. Box 2525, Oakland, CA 94614
Saudi Arabian Airlines, 747 Third Ave., New York, NY 10017
Scandinavian Airlines System, 138-02 Queens Blvd., Jamaica, NY 11435
Singapore Airlines, 510 W. 6th St., Los Angeles, CA 90014
South African Airways, 605 Fifth Ave., New York, NY 10017
Southwest Airlines, Inc., 1820 Regal Row, Dallas, TX 75235
Spantax, 500 Fifth Ave., New York, NY 10036
Swissair, 608 Fifth Ave., New York, NY 10020
Taca International Airlines, New Orleans International Airport, Kenner, LA
70062
Tan Airlines, P.O. Box 222, Miami International Airport, Miami, FL 33148
TAP-Portuguese Airlines, 1140 Avenue of the Americas, New York, NY
10036
Tarom Romanian Airlines, 200 E. 38th St., New York, NY 10016
Texas International Airlines, Inc., P.O. Box 12788, Houston, TX 77017
Thai Airways International, 251 Kearny St., San Francisco, CA 94108
Trans America Airlines, 2504 Airport Station, Oakland International
Airport, Oakland, CA 94614
Trans World Airlines, Inc., 605 Third Ave., New York, NY 10016

United Airlines, P.O. Box 66100, Chicago, IL 60666
U.S. Air, National Airport, Washington, DC 20001
UTA French Airlines, 9841 Airport Blvd., Los Angeles, CA 90045
Varig-Brazilian Airlines, 485 Lexington Ave., New York, NY 10017
Viasa-Venezuelan International Airways, 18 E. 48th St., New York, NY
    10017
Western Airlines, Inc., P.O. Box 92005, Airport Station, Los Angeles, CA
    90009
Wien Air Alaska, Inc., 4100 International Airport, Anchorage, AK 99502
Yugoslav Airlines-Jat, 630 Fifth Ave., New York, NY 10020
Zambia Airways, 150 E. 58th St., New York, NY 10022

How You Can Help Yourself

Incredible as it may seem, you're moving steadily closer to getting your trip off the ground. You have researched the literature, collaborated with your partner in adventure (your travel agent), and together you have drafted an itinerary which will take you where you want to go, at a price you can afford, at a time you want to be there. Having planned all of the logistics with precision not observed since the Berlin Airlift, you must be prepared to be flexible and spontaneous from the moment you set foot outside your home. It is possible that delays might occur at any point: an air traffic controllers' strike, a flooded mountain road, or two 747s landing at the same moment at almost any airport in the world. Some delays are avoidable, others aren't, but both could occur on your trip. You can either cope or develop colitis.

It's advisable, then, to leave a little pad in your planning for time and money. Though you have conscientiously drawn up what you consider to be a realistic budget for your trip, you should always add on a slush fund to deal with emergencies and other unexpectables that might happen. Keep a couple of extra bucks earmarked for any last-minute decision to take an optional excursion to Mykonos, or to splurge on a spectacular creole dinner in New Orleans, or to pay a doctor's bill after a particularly revengeful Mexican visit from Montezuma. You know how much you can afford to spend on a vacation, but you also know that counting every penny can make the whole experience a lot less pleasurable.

Anticipating a trip can be filled with almost as much excitement as the trip itself. As the departure draws closer, days seem mysteriously to shorten so that you feel you're about to open in a play for which you haven't yet rehearsed. Relax . . . it will all get done, but you must allot a fair amount of time in which to do it. Make a list of what needs to be accomplished, by whom, and when.

PREDEPARTURE CHORES

Chore	To Be Done by	Deadline for Departure: (December 1)
Get new passport	Sally	October 1
Finalize itinerary with travel agent (get confirmations thus far)	John and Sally	October 15
Get necessary immunizations	John and Sally	November 1–15
Buy luggage	John and Sally	November 10
Pick up airline tickets, vouchers, and copies of itinerary from travel agent	Sally	November 20
Put dog in kennel	John	November 30

This might seem frighteningly businesslike for a vacation, but it will spare you the last-minute migraines, anxiety, and frantic racing around to get it all accomplished when you just have two days left before lift-off. Keep calm, get your act together, and address yourself to the nuts and bolts of how you want to go there.

5

HOW SHOULD YOU GET THERE: BY AIR OR BY SEA?

Except for cruises to Alaska and Hawaii, travel within the United States is typically via car, bus, train, or plane. And, where air travel is concerned, we are apparently finding those skies very friendly indeed since an astonishing two hundred million of us flew in 1978. The advent of wide-body jet aircraft, deregulation of airlines (in terms of routes and fares), and a treasure chest of discount air fares have combined to get most Americans airborne. Still, a significant one-third of our population has never flown...thereby denying themselves a unique and economical adventure in travel.

AEROPHOBIA: FEAR OF FLYING

When I was in college, I flew to Las Vegas with Sandy from Chicago. Sandy's approach to flying was as joyous as an index card. At the airport, she was tense, nervous, and distraught; these symptoms were only occasionally relieved by her monologue which focused on how her loved ones could manage without her. On board, she clutched the seat, armrest, tray table, and me. I used to think Sandy was crazy; now I realize she was aerophobic. Many people fail to fly because they have a fear of flying, while others fly in a state of terror and panic. Many individuals can be helped to overcome this potent phobia through desensitization courses offered by a number of clinical psychologists and some airlines (Pan Am, for one) as well. After Sandy told me what she hated about flying ("the takeoff, the landing, and what happens once you're up there"),

I referred her to an airline-sponsored course for aerophobics. Here she became familiar with aerodynamics (how planes fly), what safety measures are involved, and which feelings surface for her when she's up there. She got to taxi around the airport in a plane and ultimately participated in the graduation exercise which consisted of a short hop on a flight from Los Angeles to Las Vegas. Recently, she and her husband got to see Paris.

Once you have overcome any inherent anxiety about flying, all you need to determine is when you want to get there and how much you wish to spend.

GETTING THE LEAST EXPENSIVE AIR FARE ON THE BEST FLIGHT WITH THE RIGHT SEAT

In order to understand the current maze of available air fares, you would need to have a Ph.D. in accounting, a digital computer, the services of a specialist in finite mathematics, and a great deal of patience. The tidal wave of deregulation left behind it a stream of "peanut fares," "chicken feed fares," "freedom fares," "supersaver fares," "standby fares," and "sky trains." At last count, there were twenty possible fares between Atlanta and London, and when I recently asked an airline reservations clerk for the various options between Los Angeles and New York, she answered, "You must be kidding." Since fares are changing even as I write these words, better to work with guidelines rather than figures.

1. *How can I get the least expensive air fare?*
——As a general rule, you will get a lower fare if you are able to travel on weekdays (Monday through Thursday) and at night (typically, after 9:00 P.M.)
——"Supersaver" air fares, available for travel within the United States (excluding Hawaii), permit savings of 30 percent to 50 percent provided you make your reservation and purchase your ticket seven days prior to departure and stay away a minimum of seven days.
——For travel overseas, ask your travel agent about excursion

fares (which require that you stay away specified lengths such as seven to sixty or twenty-two to forty-five days—generally speaking, the longer your trip, the more money you will save in air fare) and "group inclusive tours" or "GITs" (these vacation packages, created by tour operators, combine air and land arrangements and can help you realize genuine savings on your trip depending upon the size of the group).

——It is often cheaper to fly to some destinations off-season; before making travel plans, always check with your travel agent or an airline to determine when peak season ends—by postponing your departure for a few weeks, you could save several hundred dollars.

    2. *How can I get the best flight?*

——Avoid weekend travel (airports and airplanes are veritable disaster areas especially on Friday and Sunday).

——Fly off-peak hours (airport and airplane rush hours roughly coincide with those on the ground; if you avoid flying during these times, you will do much to increase the chances of your departing and arriving on time).

——Select night flights (if your body can stand a night flight, you will be rewarded with a less congested airport *and* airplane).

——Always choose a nonstop or, at least, a direct flight (the less frequently you need to take off and land, the greater the likelihood you will arrive at your destination on time).

——For lengthy domestic and all international flights, ask your travel agent which airline has the lowest load factor or seat occupancy percentage on a given route (presuming in-flight service is equivalent, you will welcome an airplane that is half full, thereby allowing you to stretch out on a long flight).

——Select a flight which gets you into the most convenient airport at your destination city (do you want to land at Dulles Airport in Virginia, Baltimore/Washington International Airport in Maryland, or National Airport in Washington D.C.?—all three serve our nation's capital).

——Experiment with different airlines ... to determine which

airline is best for you, you'll need to sample flights on a variety of carriers (here, be guided by the recommendations of your travel agent and flying friends—they can give you valuable advice about which airlines provide the best service on specific routes).

——Choose, if you have the option, to fly on wide-bodied jets which incorporate the latest innovations in technology and design to make your flight as safe, smooth, and comfortable as possible.

3. *Should I consider flying first-class?*

——If you can afford it, sure: the difference in air fare between first-class and economy on coast-to-coast domestic flights is currently just 20 percent; on international flights first-class fare might be as much as twice the economy fare. Still, on a fifteen-hour nonstop to Hong Kong, it may be well worth it.

——First-class passengers enjoy a number of amenities not shared by their fellow passengers in the economy cabin, to wit: more seat space, greater legroom, free booze on board, free use of stereo headsets ($2.50 international for economy passengers), better quality meals (I'll opt anytime for caviar, pâté, and filet mignon over that dreadful weary chicken), and more personalized attention by in-flight personnel; in addition, you might also receive a better selection of reading materials, slippers, eyeshades, and toiletries.

4. *What do I need to know in order to select the right seat?*

——First, of course, decide if you wish to be in the smoking or no smoking sections of the cabin; if you select no smoking, ask that your seat be at least five rows behind the last row of the smoking section (the billowing smoke clouds travel . . . at least protect yourself with a buffer zone).

——As you consult the adjacent diagram of a 747 wide-body jet, consider whether or not you are likely to feel claustrophobic sitting in the center bank of seats (DEFG); if so, request seating on the two-seat or three-seat sides of the aircraft.

——If you want a quiet flight, avoid seats in busy, noisy areas such as the lavatories and service centers (in-flight kitchens).

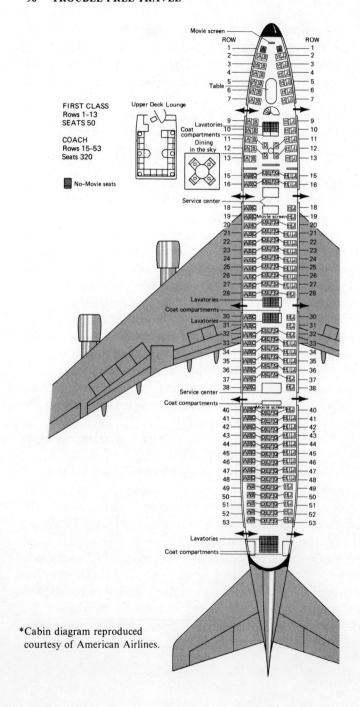

FIRST CLASS
Rows 1–13
SEATS 50

COACH
Rows 15–53
Seats 320

▪ No–Movie seats

*Cabin diagram reproduced
courtesy of American Airlines.

——If, more than anything, you crave legroom, ask for a seat immediately behind the exits (represented in the diagram by arrows).

——If your flight features a movie and if you wish to watch it, ask for a seat that permits you to do so (avoid the row immediately behind the movie screen).

——Convey your specific needs or requests to your travel agent or the airline *when you make your reservation* (don't wait until your arrival at the airport to make your seat selection), and be sure to indicate, at the same time, any dietary requirements that will necessitate your having a special meal on board.

The current availability of some incredible bargains in discount air fares can help you realize real economies on your next trip. In addition to saving you a pile of bucks and being perhaps the safest means of transportation, air travel is also the most expedient way in which to get there. Flying is faster, cheaper, and safer, and for me—"Mr. High and Mighty"—the thrill of flying remains one of the major adventures of travel.

SELECTING THE RIGHT CRUISE

I've been on cruises to South America, Mexico, and the Greek Islands and—based on my sybaritic experiences on each of those voyages—I still can't figure out why they mutinied on the *Bounty*. The word "cruise" sounds exactly like what it is: slow, easy, and tranquilizing. The word cruise can provide a hint as to your seaworthiness, since selecting this particular kind of vacation presumes that you are as interested in *how* you get there as you are in *where* you are going.

Remember those wonderful movie musicals filmed on ocean liners and bursting with beautifully tanned and gowned people who consumed enormous quantities of food while simultaneously dancing and falling in love? Romance on the high seas, or at least the promise of it, lures many passengers to cruise ships. As a matter of fact, one of television's most popular series is set on a ship and is called *The Love Boat*. The tempting setting at sea is certainly right, but there can obviously be no assurance that you will ship out, shack up, and settle down.

The cruise business, much like the airline industry, has been bracing itself in recent years to handle a mass market of millions of travelers. In 1979, more than a million passengers embarked on cruises, and the ships sailing the very popular Caribbean, trans-Panama, Alaska, and Mediterranean routes report that business is better than ever. As a matter of fact, far more people are choosing ships for cruises than for transatlantic crossings; as a result, most major passenger ships are now in the cruise business. Since increased quantity often affects quality, some steamship lines have sacrificed service standards in order to accommodate the highest number of passengers at the lowest possible per passenger rate. In practical terms, this means that the number of crew members on board to serve passengers has changed from the halcyon years' 1:1 to the current crew/passenger ratio of 1:2 or 3:5. No matter, your wine will still be poured, your cigarette lit, and your cabin cleaned.

Your travel agent can help make you aware of the remarkable diversity of seagoing adventures available to you. While the trend is unquestionably toward shorter, less expensive, and less formal cruises, you can sail for as little as three days from Miami to Nassau at a cost of $145, or for as long as three months around the world for a mere $145,000.

   1. As a vacation, what makes a cruise unique?
——In the first place, you will know in advance approximately what the entire voyage will cost. Your fare includes all services, accommodations, transportation, food, and entertainment (extras *not* included: shore excursions, alcoholic beverages, tips, and departure/port taxes).
——The entire adventure has been designed to relieve you of any responsibility (and, hopefully, of most inhibitions): the "driving" is left to the captain, the itinerary is left to the steamship company, cooking is left to the chef, and entertainment is left to the social director.

——A cruise strips all urgency from travel. If you wanted to get there fast, you would have flown.

——Because the ship is your hotel for the length of the voyage, you need to unpack only once, and you may bring aboard virtually an unlimited amount of clothing since often the baggage allowance is 200 pounds per passenger.

——Normally, the cruise company will arrange and make available to you a complete program of shore excursions so you get to go sight-seeing whenever you're not at sea; ship-to-shore transfers and ship-to-airport transfers are usually arranged as well.

  2. *In selecting a cruise, are there any pitfalls I should be particularly alert to?*

——Beware of bait and switch tactics in which you are lured to, or promised, a cabin at a given rate and are then switched to one that is more expensive—that is illegal and unethical, so raise hell with the steamship company and your travel agent.

——Understand that ads for cruises normally spotlight the price for *minimum* cabins; as a practical matter, these low-priced cabins constitute about 5 percent of the ship's capacity, so you will rarely be booking a cruise at the minimum rate.

——Several less vigilant ships have had dramatic problems with their safety, health, and sanitation maintenance; if you have any reservations concerning your prospective ship, question your travel agent about its record in these areas or contact: Chief Sanitation Officer, U.S. Public Health Service, 1015 N. American Way, Room 17, Miami, FL 33132, and ask for a "Vessel Sanitation Report."

——The single traveler (or individual traveling alone) is clobbered by steamship companies in that very few single cabins are available; as a result, people traveling alone must pay a hefty surcharge (from 50 percent to 100 percent) for the privilege of having a cabin for themselves, *or* they may ask to share a cabin with another independent cruise mate.

——Ships are slow, so cruises take time *and* they are expensive:

on a typical passenger cruise ship, figure that your per-day costs will be in the neighborhood of $75 to $150 per person. Given what you are getting, it's probably worth it.

3. *What should I look for in a cruise?*

——In reviewing the cruise company's brochure with your travel agent, study the itinerary carefully: a ship which calls at five ports in seven days will not afford you much of a *cruise* experience since you will be doing little more than sleeping on board.

——Study the hours the ship spends in each port: it is reasonable to assume that you need at least six hours ashore in order to make a dent in your sight-seeing/shopping agenda; cruise ships normally spend a minimum of six hours in less important ports, while devoting twelve hours or more to popular ports like San Juan, Istanbul, Mykonos, and Santo Domingo.

——Ask your travel agent and other knowledgeable "seafarers" about the ship's accommodations, activities, and reputation for atmosphere *and service*.

——Inquire about air-sea packages in which the cruise company will either fly you free to your port of embarkation or at least offer a discount on your air fare if you choose above a minimum-priced cabin.

——Decide *whom* you want to sail with: the longer the cruise, the older the passengers . . . and it is likely to be more expensive and a bit more formal as well; summer cruises seem to attract younger passengers.

——Ask about the typical male/female, single/married ratio on this particular cruise: as a rule, cruises attract more women than men, more marrieds than singles, and more couples than families.

——Ask if there are any cruises which focus on one of your special interests, such as opera, bridge, art, the stock market, Broadway shows, gourmet cooking, etc.

——Find out how many passengers and how many in crew the ship carries (this ratio will provide a hint as to the company's emphasis on personalized service); while you're at it, ask how many people can be accommodated in the ship's main salon: will there be a nightly scramble for the available seats in order to watch the show or movie?

——If you are traveling by yourself, ask about the line's policy regarding single occupancy of cabins. What is the single occupancy surcharge? Will they book you a half share (and find you a cabin mate) or a guaranteed share (committing the cruise company to finding you a cabin mate or allowing you to sail alone in a double occupancy cabin at the single rate)?

4. How far in advance should I book passage?

——Once you have selected your cruise, ship, and cabin, *book as far in advance as possible*; it is not unusual for cruise space to be reserved a year in advance—three months in advance would be an absolute minimum.

——If the cruise you want is booked, by all means have your name wait-listed; there are always cancellations prior to sailing.

——Understand all cancellation penalties before paying for your cruise.

——When booking, choose a travel agent who specializes in cruises (check your Yellow Pages for likely candidates), as he or she is most apt to benefit from continuous feedback from previous cruise customers.

——Since cruise lines are extremely anxious for their ships to sail full, there is a flurry of last-minute bookings from which you can benefit: call the reservations manager directly and see if you can book late in exchange for guaranteed upgrading of your cabin (i.e., you pay for C Deck and get B Deck; other deals are possible).

5. What kind of activities may I expect on board?

——A cruise is designed to be relaxing and fun, and the activities on board reflect both of those goals; still, the option is entirely yours as to whether or not you wish to attend or participate in the: Captain's Champagne Party, Singles Night, Masquerade Party, Piano Concert, Caribbean Night (on ships that ply that route), Casino Night, Talent Night (do you *really* need to hear a fourteen-year-old girl sing "My Way"?), Crew

Show, Continental Revue, as well as such shipboard staples as bridge, canasta, gin rummy, horse races, swimming, shuffleboard, tennis, trapshooting, bingo, table tennis, dance classes, exercise classes, jogging, and buffets... whew!

——A principal activity on board any ship is eating: there are normally two sittings for meals and you may indicate your preference either when you book passage with the cruise company or immediately after you embark (see the chief dining room steward); as a generalization, you may expect that older people and passengers with children will favor the first sitting while younger passengers (anxious to linger over cocktails or to take a nap before dining) will opt for the second sitting.

	First Sitting	Second Sitting
Breakfast	7:30 A.M.	9:00 A.M.
Lunch	Noon	1:30 P.M.
Dinner	6:30 P.M.	8:00 P.M.

——God forbid you should get hungry, the ship will also destroy your diet by offering you: early riser's coffee and sweet rolls, "elevenses" (or mid-morning) snacks, afternoon tea with cakes and cookies, and a spectacular midnight buffet... when you disembark, your gross tonnage could equal the ship's.

6. *What kind of clothes should I bring?*

——Just because ships permit passengers a virtually unlimited baggage allowance, don't go overboard: review the cruise brochure, consider the length of the trip, climate en route, and schedule of social activities that might require special clothing; generally, you will want really to "dress up" (tux or suit and tie for men; gown or cocktail dress for women) for the Captain's Welcome Party and Farewell Party; other than that, your cruise wardrobe should reflect a blend of "informal dress" (sports jacket and slacks with tie for men; dress, cocktail dress, or pantsuit for women) and "casual dress" (sports shirt and slacks or leisure suit for men; sundress, skirt and blouse for women).

——Since cruises have gradually become less formal, it is not at all surprising to find passengers wearing shorts and blue jeans during the day both on board and ashore.

7. *What about tipping aboard ship?*

——With the exception of Holland America Line which has instituted a no-tipping policy (gratuities are included in your fare), you will have to deal with greasing of palms in several strategic locations around the ship.

——Assuming you have received satisfactory service, the standard tip for cabin stewards and dining room waiters is $1.50 to $2.00 each per day, per passenger; *exceptional* service should be reflected in a more generous tip.

——Bar stewards and wine stewards should be tipped 10-15 percent of the bill when each service is rendered.

——If you are taking a short cruise, say less than two weeks, you may tip at the end of the voyage; on longer cruises, the ship's staff would expect and be grateful to be tipped at the end of each week.

——As you ponder how generous you wish to be with your gratuities, remember that the longer (therefore more expensive) the cruise the bigger the tip, and, philosophically, you may wish to consider that European crews traditionally get higher wages while Caribbean crews rely rather heavily on tips to boost their earnings.

8. *How will I be able to pay for extras during the cruise?*

——You should plan to use traveler's checks and cash since very few cruise lines will accept personal checks.

——Ask, *before you sail*, which credit cards the cruise line honors; do not assume that all credit cards will be accepted.

9. *Will I get seasick?*

——Probably not, since a recent medical survey revealed that less than 10 percent of all seagoing passengers become seasick; still, if you're one of the 10 percent, it's not a pleasant prospect.

——Prior to sailing, ask your doctor to suggest an antidote for motion sickness and don't hesitate to take it as soon as the ship gets under way and until you get your sea legs.

——Smart sailors restrict their intake of *all* liquids; a modest amount of liquor seems to do no harm.

——There will be a magnetic urge to overeat—don't.

——Get lots of fresh air ... the kind at sea is an invigorating brand all its own.

——If you should get sick at sea, don't become alarmed since any ship carrying more than sixteen passengers is required by law to have a doctor on board; normally, ships' doctors will not charge you for any minor illness that develops during the voyage; however, they are much more likely to bill you for any treatment based upon a preexisting condition.

——As a general policy, most cruise lines will not accept passengers over sixty-five years of age unless they present a certificate of good health from their family physician.

10. *Where do I get additional information concerning the various passenger steamship companies and their schedules of cruises?*

——Your travel agent should have a harvest of cruise information; if not, simply write to the respective companies in which you are interested (see list that follows).

PASSENGER STEAMSHIP AND CRUISE SHIP LINES

American Cruise Lines, Inc., Steamship Landing, Haddam, CT 06438
Bahama Cruise Lines, Inc., P.O. Box 4460, Miami, FL 33101
Carnival Cruise Lines, Inc., 820 Biscayne Blvd., Miami, FL 33132
Carras Cruises, 75 Rockefeller Plaza, New York, NY 10019
Chandris, Inc., 666 Fifth Ave., New York, NY 10019
Commodore Cruise Line, Ltd., 1015 North America Way, Miami, FL 33132
Costa Line, Inc., 245 Park Ave., New York, NY 10017
Cunard Line, Ltd., 555 Fifth Ave., New York, NY 10017
Delta Lines, Inc., One World Trade Center, New York, NY 10048
Delta Queen Steamboat Co., 511 Main St., Cincinnati, OH 45202
Eastern Steamship Lines, Inc., 1317 Biscayne Blvd., Miami, FL 33101
Epirotiki Lines, Inc., 608 Fifth Ave., New York, NY 10020
Flagship Cruises, 522 Fifth Ave., New York, NY 10036
Holland America Cruises, 2 Pennsylvania Plaza, New York, NY 10001
Home Lines, One World Trade Center, New York, NY 10048
Italian Line World Cruises, 17 Battery Place, New York, NY 10004
K Lines Hellenic Cruises, 521 Fifth Ave., New York, NY 10017
Lauro Line Cruises, Inc., One Biscayne Tower, Miami, FL 33131
Lindblad Travel, Inc., 133 E. 55th St., New York, NY 10022
March Shipping Passenger Services, One World Trade Center, New York, NY 10048
Monarch Cruise Lines, 1428 Brickell Ave., Miami, FL 33131
Norwegian American Line, 29 Broadway, New York, NY 10006

Norwegian Caribbean Lines, 100 Biscayne Blvd., Miami, FL 33132
Orient Overseas Line, 9060 Wilshire Blvd., Beverly Hills, CA 90211
Pacquet Cruises, Inc., 1370 Avenue of the Americas, New York, NY 10019
Pacific Far East Line, One Embarcadero Center, San Francisco, CA 94111
Princess Cruises, 2020 Avenue of the Stars, Century City, CA 90067
Royal Caribbean Cruise Line, Inc., 903 South America Way, Miami, FL
    33132
Royal Princess Line, 924 Biscayne Blvd., Miami, FL 33132
Royal Viking Line, One Embarcadero Center, San Francisco, CA 94111
Sitmar Cruises, 10100 Santa Monica Blvd., Century City, CA 90067
Sun Line Cruises, 1 Rockefeller Plaza, New York, NY 10020
Windjammer Cruises, P.O. Box 120, Miami Beach, FL 33139

Selecting the Right Cabin

Cruise brochures can be downright hypnotic filled, as they are, with vistas of sandy beaches, quaint waterfronts, smiling locals, and yawning buffet tables. But a major function of these brochures is to provide you with important information concerning the ship's itinerary and its interior design plan. However sensational the shopping, no matter how spectacular the weather, and despite midnight buffets that Henry VIII would envy—your cruise could be miserable if you have selected the wrong cabin.

The brochure is your introduction to the ship—a prospectus for the place that will serve as your home for three days or three months. Once you've read it, arrange to review it with your travel agent in an effort to decide where—aboard this floating city—you want to sleep each night. Normally, you will find a cutaway model of the ship from which you can learn where each deck is in relation to the others. This photograph tells you at a glance how high or low you are on the ship depending upon which deck you select.

1. True sailors regard the middle decks of the ship as the most desirable location since cabins in this area are least subject to the ship's motion. Another incentive for selecting a middle deck is that cabins in this location will normally place you much closer to the areas of the ship to which you will want easy access (i.e., dining rooms, swimming pools, nightclubs, etc.).

CUTAWAY MODEL OF SHIP*

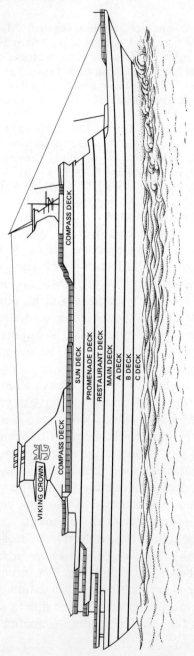

*All diagrams of the M/S *Sun Viking* reproduced courtesy of Royal Caribbean Cruise Line.

2. Though traditionally more expensive, the higher decks on a ship are *not necessarily better*. For one thing, air conditioning has typically resulted in sealed portholes so you don't necessarily get a breath of fresh air even if you want it. Then, too, the top decks are most likely to have two other bothersome distractions: suspended lifeboats (which obscure your view), and peeping deck strollers (who invade your privacy). For the record, cruise veterans seldom spring for the expense of luxury cabins. Considering the time spent in your cabin, the simpler and cheaper accommodations will probably prove to be adequate.

3. On the adjacent cutaway diagram, cabins on the Main Deck would probably be less resistant to the ship's motion.

The deck plan of the ship logically enough shows you which of the ship's elements (cabins, dining rooms, gift shops, bars, elevators, etc.) are located on each deck *and where*.

1. If possible, avoid a cabin on the Restaurant Deck since there is a predictable amount of noise and traffic on this deck throughout the day and into the night. (The ship used in our diagram wisely designed its Restaurant Deck to exclude cabins).

2. You will be less likely to encounter noise if you avoid cabins on main corridors, near bars and shops, and across from elevators.

3. Some die hard sailors I know insist that the quietest and smoothest ride on the ship can best be obtained in cabins amidships, that is, those cabins located toward the middle of the ship between the bow (front) and stern (rear). If you believe these cruise veterans, you would probably select one of the center block of cabins in the diagram.

The final essential information typically contained in a cruise brochure are diagrams of the representative accommodations. Cabins are compactly designed and every inch of available space is utilized. Study these diagrams carefully and ask yourself (and your travel agent) some important questions which will assist you in narrowing down your choices.

DECK PLAN
OF SHIP

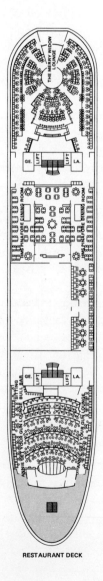

RESTAURANT DECK

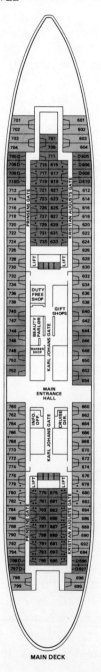

MAIN DECK

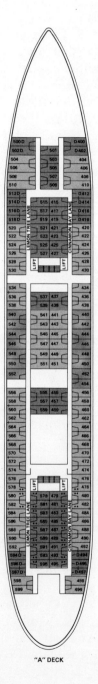

"A" DECK

DIAGRAMS OF SHIP'S CABINS

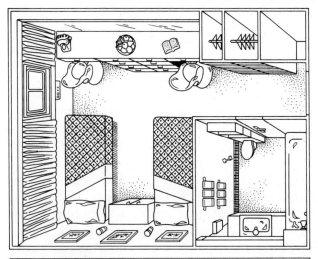

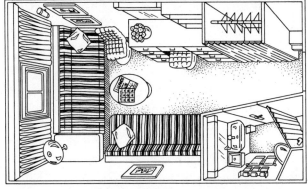

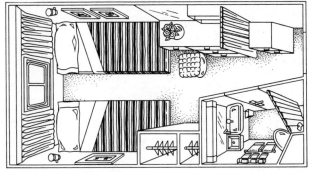

1. Do I want an outside or inside cabin (ocean view vs. no ocean view)?
2. Do I want berths or beds?
3. Do I want a shower, a tub, or both?
4. How much drawer space is provided?
5. Is there enough closet space?
6. How much do I want to spend? The higher up, larger, outside cabins will always be the most expensive on the ship.

STANDARD OUTSIDE/INSIDE STATEROOM

Our Standard Stateroom is a sitting room by day. Bedroom by night. Two lower beds easily convert into comfortable sofas and vice versa. There is also a private shower and facilities and 110 volt outlets for small appliances. The room is furnished with a large dressing table and there's a wardrobe as well. You'll also find added comforts like individual room temperature control, telephone, three-channel radio, tap ice water, wall-to-wall carpeting, and (in the outside stateroom illustrated) a view from your window that changes daily.

LARGER OUTSIDE STATEROOM

Our Larger Stateroom is furnished with two lower beds (that convert to comfortable sofas by day), a side chair, dressing table with settee and a cocktail table. Besides ample drawer space there is a full-length wardrobe. The room also has a private shower and facilities. Plus added conveniences of home such as 110 volt outlets for small appliances like hair dryers or electric shavers. A three-channel radio. A telephone. Tap ice water. Individual room temperature control. (So that you can adjust your room to your comfort.). Wall-to-wall carpeting. And a window with an ocean view.

PROMENADE DECK—DELUXE STATEROOM

Our Deluxe Staterooms are located mid-ships on Promenade. Each suite has plush wall-to-wall carpeting throughout and its own unique color decor. It is furnished with side chairs. A large dressing table with plenty of drawer space. Two lower beds side by side. And a large wardrobe for hanging long gowns and suits. It also has a complete private bath and tub and shower. And you can keep your stateroom at the temperature you desire by simply adjusting a thermostat. In addition there is tap ice water, telephone, refrigerator, three-channel radio and 110 volt outlets for small convenience appliances. In short, it's one of our stateliest staterooms.

All of this cruise stuff was much less complicated in the good old days, for then, before the opening of the Suez Canal, distinguished oceangoing clientele sailing from England to India were simply assigned the shadiest cabins on the portside going out and the starboard side coming home. Instead of cabin numbers, passenger tickets read, 'Portside Out; Starboard side Home," thereby specifying accommodations and providing us with at least one theory for the origin of the word "posh."

SOMETHING ABOUT FREIGHTERS

Though perhaps not as "posh" as cruise ships, freighters have a unique appeal, since passage on board promises visits to exotic ports, camaraderie with crusty crews, fascinating firsthand glimpses of the intricate cargo operation, and time. Most of all ... time. Some freighters carry a handful of passengers while Delta Lines' sleek cargo liners, which circumnavigate South America, carry as many as a hundred. In either case, the freighter experience is not every sailor's keg of rum. In evaluating your candidacy for this particular brand of oceangoing adventure, consider the following characteristics of most freighter voyages:

1. Time matters less on a freighter than it does on a cruise ship; though there is a scheduled itinerary for port arrivals and departures, less emphasis is placed on getting there on time.

2. The priority cargo is *cargo*; passengers are happily accommodated, but there is no question that what's in the hold matters more than what's in the cabins.

3. The ship's itinerary might well change after you have booked passage and, for that matter, after you have sailed; such adjustments are typically in response to variable cargo conditions and could cause you to miss some scheduled ports while adding a few new ones.

4. The number of passengers normally won't exceed sixteen (if there are more, a doctor must be provided on board), so you will be dependent upon a handful of passengers, the crew, and yourself for amusement.

5. Because a freighter is about the business of transporting freight, there is less emphasis and space given to the comfort of its passengers. Though passenger cabins might be as large (or larger) than those on cruise ships, you should not expect fancy public rooms, swimming pools, or the countless other amenities found on cruise ships. Passenger accommodations on freighters are generally air-conditioned . . . *ask*!

6. Passengers typically have their meals with the crew and, since the chef is cooking for perhaps sixty people and not six hundred, you might be astonished at the quality of the delectable stuff that comes out of a freighter's galley. Incidentally, the opportunity to eat with the crew could provide you with as many vivid memories of the trip as your camera does.

7. Freighters which carry passengers do not necessarily offer a comprehensive program of shore excursions. You may be on your own when the ship docks, but chances are that if you're on a freighter—that's the way you want it anyway.

8. "Casual dress" is as dressy as you need to bring for any voyage on a freighter. Leave the tuxedo and gowns at home and select, instead, the most informal and comfortable clothes you own. If you insist upon carrying every item of clothing in your wardrobe, at least you will be heartened to learn that freighter companies are exceedingly generous with baggage allowances.

9. Accommodations on a freighter, which can range from semi-Spartan to near-deluxe, are predictably cheaper than those on a cruise ship. If you shop around diligently, you may

well find yourself spending as little as $35 per person, per day, and rarely more than $80.

10. Because a freighter usually carries only between eight and sixteen passengers, space on board is at a premium. If you decide to go the freighter route, make every effort to reserve space from six months to a year in advance of the sailing.

A voyage on a freighter can be the answer to your travel dreams provided your time is ample, your schedule is flexible, your style is casual, and your disposition is self-sufficient. In return for these considerations, you could be rewarded with Yokohama, Singapore, Valparaiso, Haifa, Rotterdam, Funchal, and Pago Pago. Before you race to pack your seabags (which you should do carefully because you probably won't find your favorite shampoo, lotions, and medicines on board), you might wish to obtain valuable freighter information from among several sources:

TravLtips Freighter Travel Association
40-21 Bell Blvd.,
Bayside, NY 11361

Ford's Freighter Travel Guide
P.O. Box 505
Woodland Hills, CA 91365

Pearl's Freighter Tips (Pearl Hoffman)
175 Great Neck Rd., Suite #306-A
Great Neck, NY 11021

Ask your travel agent about the various steamship lines with regard to accommodations, freighter itineraries, and reputations for service. You may book passage with your travel agent or, in most instances, directly with the steamship companies themselves.

CARGO/PASSENGER STEAMSHIP COMPANIES

Alcoa Steamship Co., 2 Pennsylvania Plaza, New York, NY 10001
American Export Lines, 17 Battery Place, New York, NY 10004

American President Lines, 601 California, San Francisco, CA 94108
Delta Lines, One World Trade Center, New York, NY 10048
Farrell Lines, 1 Whitehall St., New York, NY 10004
Gulf Container Lines, Sanlin Bldg., New Orleans, LA 70130
Gulf-Puerto Rico Lines, P.O. Box 8400, Gentilly Station, New Orleans, LA 70182
Holland America Lines, 2 Pennsylvania Plaza, New York, NY 10001
Matson Navigation Co., 215 Market St., San Francisco, CA 94105
Moore-McCormack Lines, 2 Broadway, New York, NY 10004
Orient Overseas Lines, 510 Montgomery Ave., San Francisco, CA 94111
Pacific Far East Lines, One Embarcadero Center, San Francisco, CA 94111
Polish Ocean Lines, One World Trade Center, New York, NY 10048
States Steamship Co., 320 California, San Francisco, CA 94104
United States Lines, 1 Broadway, New York, NY 10004

The Roman philosopher Seneca once said, "Voyage, travel, and change of place impart vigor." And Seneca had never flown a 747SP nonstop from San Francisco to Hong Kong, nor had he sailed on a luxury liner through the Panama Canal or the Strait of Magellan. Seneca may have had the Roman Forum, but he never gazed upon a cruise ship's midnight buffet. These adventures await *you* now that you've decided exactly how you plan to get there. But before you fasten your seat belt or throw kisses to envious friends on the pier, there are a few more things you need to do in order to get ready.

6

WHAT DO YOU NEED TO DO TO GET READY?

To get ready for any trip outside the United States, you will have to attend to a number of required travel documents (passport, visa(s), and international driver's permit), immunizations, and household maintenance and security in your absence. Somehow, the lawn must be mowed! All of these preparations can be accomplished with a minimum of hassles if you get them under way well in advance of your trip. Ignore, I beg you, those friends who brag, "I got my passport in forty-eight hours," "You don't need a smallpox shot for where you're going," and, "Your driver's license is all you need to rent a car over there." Remember that these same friends once urged you to build a home on an earthquake fault in California and to buy an Edsel.

The emphasis here is on foreign trips since interstate travel within the United States is blissfully free of bureaucratic red tape except, of course, for special state rules regarding pets. Your travel agent should provide you with the information you need regarding required travel documents (how to apply, where, when, cost involved, etc.), so consult him or her first.

THE PAPER CHASE

Passports
A passport is a document issued by the U.S. State Department which entitles you, as a citizen, to leave and reenter the United States.

1. Where do I apply for my passport?
—At the Passport Agency of the U.S. State Department, or clerk of the Federal Court, or at certain designated post offices.

2. What do I need to apply?
—*Proof of citizenship:* this may consist of either a certified birth certificate *or* a census certificate *or* a baptismal certificate *or* a letter from the registrar in your state of birth.

—*Identification document:* this document can be your driver's license since it *must* contain your photograph or physical description and signature; if you have no such document, bring a witness (who knows you) and has such identification—he or she can then "testify" in your behalf.

—*Photographs:* two (2) recent full-face photographs are required; these photos should measure 2 inches by 2 inches, may be color or black-and-white, and should be signed in the left-hand margin and on the reverse side of the photo in the center.

3. How much does a first passport cost, and how long is it good for?
—The first passport will cost $14 and is valid for five (5) years from the date issued.

4. How do I renew my passport once it has expired?
—Simply present your old expired passport, plus $10, and two recent passport-size photos at any of the agencies or offices designated to issue passports.

—The Passport Agency no longer uses the term "renewal"; it prefers to regard each passport as a new one valid for five years from the date issued.

5. Can I get a new passport by mail?
—Sure, *provided* your last one was issued:
  a) within the last eight years; and
  b) when you were over eighteen years old.
—When ordering by mail, don't forget to send your old passport, two recent photos, your check or money order for $10, and the completed application.

6. Who can be included in my passport?

—Because it is now considered impractical and inconvenient, spouses may no longer be included on a passport; however, all minor children (under thirteen years of age) may be included in their parent's passport.

7. *How long will it take me to get my passport once I have submitted the completed application?*

—This will frequently depend on the time of year when you apply; at the minimum, *allow four weeks* for passport processing and a few extra weeks if you are applying during the summer tourist crush.

8. *Are there any foreign countries to which a U.S. citizen may travel* without *a passport?*

—Yes: Mexico and Canada simply require proof of citizenship. Many Americans use their passports for this purpose, but you could use a voter registration card or birth certificate as well.

9. *Any tips to expedite the processing of my passport application?*

—Assemble all the required documents and photographs in accordance with the regulations (sorry, your 5 by 7 photograph in uniform, however dashing, is *not* acceptable—nor is the one of you being kissed by Fido).

—Indicate your itinerary on your passport application since the Passport Agency will then expedite (give priority to) applications indicating travel to countries that require visas.

Securing a passport sounds much more complicated than it actually is; in practice, most of the twenty-six million Americans who travel outside our country each year do so carrying passports obtained without a hitch or delay. Since a passport is required for most travel outside the United States, you are well advised not to pay for your trip until you have your passport in hand. Wouldn't it be a sad and expensive mistake to pay for a trip that's canceled because you didn't receive your passport prior to departure? Allow ample time for unexpected delays or heavy traffic at the Passport Agency, and *don't* count on being bailed out by a passport magically processed in forty-eight hours.

Once you have secured your passport, treat it like the valuable document it is. There is a vigorous black market in passports throughout the world, with those from America sometimes fetching up to several thousand dollars each. Many people from other countries would like the freedom to exit and enter America which is guaranteed to you by your U.S. Passport. As you travel abroad, carry your passport with you at all times, surrendering it only when registering at hotels, if requested. Should you lose your passport while traveling outside the United States, report the loss (or theft) at once to the local U.S. consulate or embassy. Your world will not come to an end, but the loss of a passport could cause complications and delays which might have been avoided had you been more careful.

Additional information concerning passports is available in a concise, readable brochure called, logically enough, *You and Your Passport*. To get a copy, telephone your local Passport Agency office or write to:

> Passport Agency
> U.S. Department of State
> Washington, DC 20524

Visas

A visa is an official travel authorization that permits you to enter, travel through, and exit the specific country which has issued this document to you. Your U.S. Passport gets you into and out of only the United States; visas get you into and out of the respective countries which have issued them. Which countries require visas of whom is based upon diplomatic relations, agreements, and a system of reciprocity with which you don't have to bother your already bulging head. Just know that you must confer with your travel agent as soon as your itinerary is fixed to determine visa requirements for each destination along the way.

1. How can I find out which countries on my itinerary require visas?
—Begin with your travel agent. If he or she doesn't know, telephone (or write to) the consulates or embassies maintained in the United States by the countries you plan to visit.

2. May I assume that countries with which the United States has friendly relations will waive any visa requirements?
—No, you can't: the countries that require visas of U.S. citizens run the gamut from Australia and Japan to Russia.

3. Do many countries require visas of U.S. citizens?
—Yes: currently about a hundred nations in the world make this requirement of American travelers, so your chances of needing a visa are quite high.

4. How do I get a visa?
—Initially, you should call the consulate or embassy of the respective country (or countries) and determine their specific regulations governing visas; also request a visa application.
—Generally, to secure a visa, you will need to send your valid U.S. Passport, two passport-size photos, the visa application and fee (if any) to the embassy or consulate involved.

5. How much does a visa cost?
—Some are free; others might cost as much as $75, depending upon the country involved, length of your stay, and purpose of your visit.

6. How long is a visa valid?
—Again, this varies with the country in question and your purpose (business, education, pleasure) in visiting it.
—Visas may be valid for as little as several days or for as long as four years.

7. How much time should I allow for a visa to be processed?
—Many embassies and consulates will process your visa while you wait or at least provide you with same day service; others will require three to four weeks (*and sometimes more*) in order to process your application.

8. How do I locate the nearest office of a foreign embassy or consulate?

—Most foreign nations maintain embassies or consulates in New York City (the telephone listing normally would be under the name of the country or territory); some countries have consulates and/or missions in other American cities such as Chicago, Miami, Los Angeles, and San Francisco—logically, you should begin by contacting the nearest office.

   9. *Any tips for expediting my visa application(s)?*
—As soon as you have finalized your itinerary and have secured your U.S. Passport, determine which countries you plan to visit require visas and get your application(s) in the works.

—Since you must present or send your U.S. Passport *with each visa application*, it is essential that you allow enough time for the processing of your application with *each* of the respective countries you plan to visit (for the record: my visa for Yugoslavia was processed in fifteen minutes while I waited; my visa for Costa Rica took two hours while I waited; my visa for Zambia was prepared in seven hours and I returned to pick it up; and my visa for Poland—mailed to the embassy in New York—took three weeks to process).

—In some cities in the United States, there are visa services which—for a nominal fee *in addition to* the consular visa charges—will help you prepare the visa application and see that it is expeditiously dispatched (usually by hand delivery) to the respective embassies or consulates involved; these services, as offered by such companies as Intercontinental Visa at the World Trade Center in Los Angeles, are particularly appreciated by travelers who plan to visit many countries requiring visas but do not have the time or inclination to secure them themselves.

—Be advised that some consular offices will not accept personal checks when visa applications are presented in person; cover yourself with the necessary cash or traveler's checks just to be safe.

International Driver's Permit
Driving in many foreign countries presupposes that you have served a successful apprenticeship with Mario Andretti.

Though you have fought rush-hour traffic in midtown Manhattan or the bumper-to-bumper madness on the Santa Monica Freeway, no prior experience will adequately prepare you for the adventure of sharing a foreign country road with oncoming bulls, goats, horses, wagons, soccer players, and a village wedding. Remember that in many countries in Asia, Central America, and Africa the road is an extension of the living room, and so your car can be considered the intruder and not the local people.

Still, driving abroad opens up many vistas of opportunities and experiences which a tour bus simply can't guarantee. Determined to drive "over there," you need simply to equip yourself with an ample supply of tranquilizers and an International Driver's Permit.

1. Which countries require the International Driver's Permit (IDP)?
—Currently, there are about a hundred countries in the world that require an IDP.
—There is a separate IDP required in order to drive in Latin-American countries.
—An IDP is *not* required in order to drive in either Mexico or Canada (it can't hurt to have one so you might get an IDP nonetheless).

2. Where do I apply for an International Driver's Permit?
—At the local office of your state automobile club; when applying by mail, write (or call) and request an application for an IDP.

3. How do I apply?
—You may apply in person or by sending your application by mail.
—Your petition for an IDP consists of the application itself, your valid U.S. driver's license, two (2) passport-size photos, and a check or money order for $3 payable to your automobile club.

4. Any tips for expediting the processing of the IDP?
—By all means handle this process in person rather than through the mails; first, the entire procedure takes just a few minutes in the office and would require four to five days via the

postal service, and second, the application requires that you submit your driver's license and, if you mail your license, you will have to do without this important document for at least several days.

Once you get to your destination and hire a rental car, be certain to learn quickly about local driving regulations, customs, and etiquette. Take your crash course on rules and not on the road.

IMMUNIZATIONS: AN OUNCE OF PREVENTION

S. J. Perelman once said, "I don't know much about medicine, but I know what I like." Like Perelman, I have my preferences too: I respond to any prescribed treatment which includes convalescence in Polynesia and a daily half-gallon of butter pecan ice cream. Unfortunately, I still haven't found the right disease for which this treatment is the cure.

Doctors and scientists have made strides in conquering diseases, but it is a reality of life that the traveler will still be subjected to tenacious illnesses that continue to appear and flourish all over the world. Luckily, there are preventive (or prophylactic) steps which the traveler can take to avoid—or at least reduce—illness overseas. Enter immunizations.

Prospective travelers' own doctors are the appropriate source of information regarding immunizations which are required or recommended for a trip. First, they have access to current information concerning the status of diseases and epidemics in countries their patients plan to visit, and second, the doctors have before them the comprehensive medical histories which will help them decide which precautionary immunizations are indicated. Sometimes our bodies react strangely to shots, and doctors, aware as they are of their patients' unique medical history, should be the ultimate authority as to what shots are needed and which ones their patients are able to take.

The World Health Organization issues a universally used booklet, *International Certificates of Vaccination*, which you can get from your local Public Health Service, County Health

Office, doctor (if he or she stocks a supply), or travel agent. In this booklet, your doctor will enter the date of each vaccination, its manufacture and batch number, and his or her own professional status and address. There is a space next to the doctor's signature for an approved stamp of an official vaccination center. Carry the booklet in a safe place (perhaps with your passport) since this document can be critical to your good health and freedom of movement among countries.

   1. How do I find out which immunizations are required for overseas travel?
—Give your family doctor a list of the countries you will be visiting and ask for a list of required *and* recommended shots.
—If your doctor does not have this information, call your local Public Health Service, County Health Service, or your travel agent.
—If all else fails and you are unable to secure accurate, *current* information concerning immunizations for specific destinations, write to:

> Public Health Service
> U.S. Department of Health, Education, and Welfare
> Atlanta, Ga. 30333
> *Attn:* Health Information for International Travelers

or call:

> Center for Disease Control
> (404-329-3671) Atlanta, Georgia

   2. What shots can be required *in accordance with international regulations?*
—Only three vaccinations can be *required* by the World Health Organization, depending upon current disease conditions in the area to which the traveler is going: smallpox (valid for three years after primary vaccination or on date of revaccination), cholera (initial course is two injections a week apart; valid for six months), and yellow fever (given at certified centers, this immunization is valid for ten years).

   3. Must I have all the required shots in order to leave the United States?

—Absolutely not: you need only have the shots required by the country or countries you are planning to visit.

—The United States does not require any immunization, *at this time*, of a U.S. citizen leaving or reentering the country unless, of course, you are returning home from an "infected area."

    4. What shots might be recommended *for overseas travel?*

—Depending upon your destination and your own health (as determined by your doctor), you might be encouraged to be immunized against: tetanus/diptheria (this is a combination given in one shot and repeated one month later; tetanus boosters are required every ten years); polio (Salk vaccine is given by injection; Sabin vaccine is given orally); and typhoid (initial series consists of two shots each given four weeks apart).

    5. Are there parts of the world for which even additional protection might be warranted?

—Yes, but your doctor should make a decision as to whether or not you are a candidate for other inoculations.

—For some journeys, particularly to countries where sanitation is inadequate and water is likely to be polluted, you might be advised to be additionally vaccinated against typhus, plague, influenza, tuberculosis, and hepatitis.

    6. Will I have any reaction to the shots?

—It depends on your body chemistry and the vaccine with which you're being inoculated; some people experience redness, some swelling, and heat at the site of the vaccination— remember you have been given a dose of the live virus so don't panic when your body reacts with the blahs.

    7. Does the immunization guarantee that I will not contract the disease?

—No, but it gives you strong insurance against the prospect of developing the strain against which you've been inoculated, and, depending upon the vaccine, the immunization will at least dilute the severity of the illness and leave you with a much milder case.

8. When should I get my shots?
—After you and your doctor have determined which shots you need, make up a schedule so that you can *space your inoculations over a period of time*; do not leave all of your shots to the last minute: your body will never forgive you for this unspeakable (and painful) injustice.

—Complete your necessary immunizations at least a week prior to your trip; that way, any discomfort or reaction will be well behind you when you board the plane for the long flight overseas.

9. When should I check immunization requirements for the countries I plan to visit?
—Check several months before your trip and again closer to departure since a sudden outbreak of a disease (or even an epidemic) will result in a change in that country's immunization requirements governing tourists, and that change affects *you.*

10. What happens if I am about to enter a country for which I don't have the required immunizations?
—Your host country has a number of options: it can (a) vaccinate you on the spot, (b) put you in quarantine, or (c) refuse you entry and immediately reboard you on the next available flight out.

11. Suppose my doctor feels that a specific vaccination might be detrimental to my health; does that mean I can't travel?
—Not necessarily: have your doctor write a letter explaining your condition (technically, "contraindication to vaccination") to the chief medical officer of the country (or countries) you plan to visit; have this letter validated by that respective country's embassy or consulate prior to your departure from the United States.

The question that then remains is if vaccinations are so safe and so sure, why are we so scared? Because, like S. J. Perelman, we may not know much about medicine, but we know what we like.

TRAVEL INSURANCE

Ever since I discovered that my previous insurance policy only protected me against muggings by werewolfs in countries whose names begin with the letter *G*, I have become considerably more cautious about the kind of coverage I want and need. Many of us foolishly depart on trips with insurance coverage that under- or overprotects us, when professional guidance by our insurance broker or travel agent would help us secure the coverage we need.

Is travel insurance necessary at all? Probably, only because the number of things that can go wrong on a trip are considerable: we race exhausted bodies through foreign countries and allow excitement to lower our defenses, we become less careful with valuables and personal property, and we use countless conveyances and visit many public places. For a reasonably modest amount of money, your travel agent or insurance broker can help you secure the coverage which will give you necessary protection *and* peace of mind.

1. Is it possible that I am already covered for property loss and damage under my regular homeowner's (or apartment owner's) policy?

—It's possible, but don't assume that you have such protection away from the premises unless your insurance broker points out this clause to you in your policy.

—If you don't have such coverage already, consider adding a personal articles floater to your homeowner's policy; this option will protect your valuable possessions both at home and during your travels.

2. Can I buy a single policy which will provide me with the protection I need for a specific trip?

—Sure, you should ask your insurance broker (or travel agent) about a package of short-term travel insurance which will protect you and your family for the duration of the trip against accidents, damage, or loss to baggage and personal effects, and cancellation of a charter flight (if applicable).

—Shop around, though, since premiums quoted for the same basic coverage may vary considerably.

3. Once I purchase a policy that covers loss or damage to personal property and luggage, can I rest easy?
—Yes, but only if you have carefully read the policy and understand its deductible clause and any existing exclusions (such as money, airline tickets, gold, etc.).

4. Can I purchase insurance which will protect me if my trip is canceled or interrupted?
—Yes, insurance brokers and travel agents can sell you a policy which protects your advance charter payment if you must cancel the trip because of personal illness or a death in your immediate family (specific conditions and exceptions vary).
—The trip interruption element in these policies usually provides you with compensation for economy fare home if you must interrupt your trip for any of the acceptable reasons.
—"Advance booking charter" (ABC) operators, who provide air transportation only, are required to give you the option of buying insurance policies protecting you against trip cancellation. Your travel agent or the charter operator will have details.

5. Do I really need to buy flight insurance?
—This depends upon your very personal responsibilities of financial protection for members of your family; then, too, you should take into consideration the adequacy of your existing life insurance coverage before buying additional in-flight protection.
—Flight insurance, against accidental death on a specific flight, may be obtained at insurance booths or from insurance vending machines at the airport.

Insurance provides emotional as well as material protection, especially when you are feeling hypervulnerable when travels take you away from home. If you have coverage and need it—it's a godsend; if you have it and never use it—it's still a relief.

HOUSEHOLD CHORES

Three months ago, my next-door neighbors left on a two-month tour of Africa and for some time I watched strange activities taking place in and around their apartment. I'm not nosy, I'm certainly not spying, and I suspect no foul play—but I do confess to a certain degree of suspicion when I see garbage cans filled to the brim and placed in the hallway, or when I hear *A Chorus Line* blaring from an apartment that is allegedly empty, and when I see lights on a terrace that promise a party I know cannot be taking place. Magic? Mystery? Not exactly: it seems my security-prone friends rigged their apartment with electrical timers to turn on terrace lights, to activate the record player (okay, but at least make arrangements to change the record), and to have a willing friend pop by once a week to fill their refuse cans with garbage. All of these precautions had one purpose: to prove to the world-at-large that my neighbors' apartment was consistently occupied so as to discourage burglars during their two-month absence. It worked; they were not robbed, but I was. So much for poetic justice.

In the frenzied weeks before any trip, we become consumed with getting inoculations and passports, buying new clothes and sorting through old ones, packing and repacking luggage, and distributing trip itineraries to families and friends. Sometimes, in our excitement to get to where we are going, we forget to make the necessary preparations at the place we are leaving behind—home. It's important that you give some thought to maintaining household chores and security in your absence, whether you're going away for a long weekend or for three months. Without transforming yourself into a psychotic checklist maker, you might want to list a few items that need attention while you're away. For instance:

1. If you plan to be away for more than several days, stop deliveries of milk and newspapers (if you want the back issues of newspapers, have them delivered to your neighbor until you return).

2. Have the post office hold your mail until you return or, if your vacation is brief, simply instruct the postman to leave your mail with your neighbor.

3. Securely lock and bolt all doors and windows in the house.

4. If your trip is of a sufficiently long duration to warrant it, arrange to have the lawn mowed in your absence.

5. Turn off all electrical appliances, gas jets, and water faucets in the house.

6. If you will be gone for at least a month, ask if your telephone company has a vacation service whereby you are charged at half the usual rate (or lower) during your absence since your phone is technically not in use. Also, some electric companies will turn off your current upon request and charge only a minimal fee.

7. Leave a copy of your trip itinerary (including phone numbers, if available) with your neighbor so that you may be reached in case of an emergency.

8. Whenever possible, it's desirable to find a trustworthy house sitter to tend to your pets, plants, and home while you're away; this failing, at least leave your house key with your neighbor who can make periodic inspections.

9. Inexpensive, automatic timers are available for many electrical appliances; following the example of my neighbors, you might wish to attach timers to one or two lamps in the house, and to a record player as well (light and noise will normally discourage intruders from investigating your house any further).

10. If you make it a practice to keep valuables (jewelry, bonds, cash, etc.) in your home, you are courting disaster, particularly when your home is unattended; before you leave on your trip, stash all of these goodies in a bank safe-deposit box.

11. If you don't trust friends with your prized plants (I don't, ever since a friend of mine watered the plastic fern in my bathroom for two weeks), there are timerlike, wick-action gadgets which will measure the moisture in the soil and water your plants on cue.

12. Put your pet in the kennel several days before your departure so you can check on its adjustment (feeding, sleeping, disposition, etc.) before you leave town.

13. Consider any business or personal financial obliga-

tions which will need to be handled while you are away; if necessary, mail postdated checks or ask a business associate or neighbor to mail preaddressed payment envelopes on the prescribed dates.

14. Defrost the refrigerator.

15. Do not consciously leave any odious chore to await you on your return; images of cluttered garages that need to be cleaned and storm windows that need to be washed tend to make the trip with you.

16. Finally, do not discuss the details of your trip (departure date, length of stay, etc.) in the presence of strangers—in doing so, you may inadvertently be extending an invitation to have your home burglarized.

Now that you have attended to the security and sanctity of your home, there's another temple equally demanding of some care and attention: your body. You need not be a physical fitness expert to appreciate the rigors to which your body is subjected on a trip. How well it serves you will depend on what preparations you take before the trip and what precautions you take during the trip. As if you didn't know, your aching ankles and pulsating pancreas have feelings too.

7

HOW CAN YOU STAY HEALTHY?

I am the type of traveler who delights in tasting a new, unexpectedly scorching curry which causes a three-alarm fire in my mouth. I am the adventurous type first to volunteer for a trek through a tropical rain forest or a swim in an unknown, but oh-so-inviting lagoon. And you can count on me to make a toast as I taste the local ouzo, viniak, or sangria. These quirks of personality suggested to me long ago that I should travel with a paramedic unit or a portable pharmacy. I usually opt for the latter.

I believe, as Emerson did, that "the first wealth is health," and I take every precaution prior to the trip to keep my body's account solvent. The lesson is simple: travel can be only as enjoyable as your physical, mental, and emotional health permit. If your ulcer is acting up, fair Verona will be just another town where you can't find Gelusil; and if your long-absent migraines choose Dubrovnik for a reunion, you will see more of your hotel room than you will of the Adriatic. A trip to India that took months to plan and cost thousands of dollars to take can be ruined by a recurring chronic back problem; a decidedly relaxing and potentially romantic Mediterranean cruise can be clobbered by a sensitive wisdom tooth that screams each time you open your mouth; and a winter skiing holiday (in the works since last summer) can be destroyed by overexposure to the wind and sun.

Most travel-related health problems can be anticipated and prepared for even before you leave home. Other more serious, chronic, or unexpected illnesses might require medical attention once you are under way. In any case, you must strike a balance between being consumed with precautions that rob your trip of its fun and spontaneity, and that "let the chips fall where they may" attitude which is not only foolish but dangerous as well. It will come as no surprise to you that the advice of your doctor, coupled with your own common sense, will be very valuable travel allies indeed.

GETTING READY TO GO: VISITS TO THE DOCTOR AND DENTIST

1. Several months prior to any major trip, you should be given a complete physical by your doctor.

—Discuss your trip with your doctor: are the destinations realistic and advisable given your unique medical history?

—Are there any special precautions he or she would advise in your case (to deal, for example, with high altitudes, oppressive heat, vigorous physical activity, or a strange diet)?

—Ask him or her to determine required *and* recommended inoculations and to set up your schedule for immunizations; remember to space the shots.

—Ask your doctor to write prescriptions for any drugs you regularly use; request these drugs in sufficient quantity to last you for your entire trip since many medications are not universally available.

—Are there, in addition, any medications your doctor would prescribe for common problems (constipation, diarrhea, colds, minor infections, etc.) which you might experience in your travels?

—Increasingly, some physicians are preparing a brief personal medical history form which they encourage their patients to carry with them in their travels around the world; this practice is more necessary in the cases of patients with serious or chronic disorders (heart ailments, kidney dysfunction, hypertension, etc.) that could be problematic during a trip—a company called Probe Medi-Guard (19 W. 44th St., New York, NY 10036) will even microfilm your complete health history and attach it to a small laminated card that can be read with a collapsible viewer.

—If you must take any preventive medicine (an antimalaria drug, for instance) be certain you understand both the required dosage *and* the period of time during which you must continue to take the drug in order to have valid protection against the disease.

—If you are currently on a restricted diet, review with your doctor what nutritional procedures you should follow, what substitutes you might be allowed, and what essential dietary ingredients you should take with you on your trip.

—If you normally take a significant quantity of habit-forming drugs (tranquilizers, narcotics, sedatives), request your doctor to write a brief note outlining your need for such medication (this note might eliminate potential problems with customs officials at home and abroad).

—Travel, even the relaxing kind, takes something of a toll on our bodies. Ask your doctor what, if anything, you might do to get in shape for the trip.

2. Have a complete examination by your dentist at least six weeks prior to your trip.

—Allow ample time for the examination and for any necessary dental work indicated.

—By all means urge your dentist to tend to *potential* problems of the "this filling is a bit loose" variety; it is much better to anticipate and correct dental problems at home than to waste your time in a strange dentist's chair overseas.

WHAT TRAVEL DOES TO YOUR BODY

Most of us have had the experience of walking off an airplane after an endless overseas flight feeling as if we had just kissed a bus doing eighty. What we are feeling is a combination of physical exhaustion (due to a flurry of pretrip activities and the flight itself), inactivity (from the confinement imposed by the airplane), nervous anticipation, and—if we are crossing time zones—a disruption in our body's biological clock. Jet lag, alas, has made the trip with us.

Think about your trip and the effect it has had and will

have on your body. For several weeks prior to departure, and despite careful planning, you raced around doing chores which seriously cut down on needed nutrition and rest (famous last words: "I'll catch up on sleep during my vacation"). You are about to take your body to strange countries where it will be subjected to varying abrupt changes in climate, and filled with different, unusual, and maybe even exotic foods. You will then force it to climb countless steps, take marathon walks, sit endlessly on tour buses, sleep on unfamiliar (often uncomfortable) beds, and get up earlier and go to sleep later than it probably has ever done since the two of you have been together. In return for this barrage by alien stimuli, you expect your body to be supple, alert, rested, energetic, and absolutely free of pain and problems. If you're going to be that demanding of your body, at least give it some help along the way.

1. What can I do to feel better during, and after, the flight?

—Though you will be tempted by seemingly continuous meal service on long-distance flights, eat moderately.

—Alcohol does strange things to us at 37,000 feet; drink carefully and exercise even greater restraint than you would on the ground. Combat dehydration by drinking water.

—Wear comfortable clothes that allow your body to breathe; tight-fitting clothes can be torment on a long flight.

—Throw a pair of slippers or comfortable shoes in your flight bag, and slip into them for the duration of the flight.

—Aircraft cabins tend to be over-air-conditioned, so carry along a sweater that can be worn when icicles start forming on your tray table.

—Since poor blood circulation can be a problem on long flights, you should move about the cabin as often as possible; exercise your legs by walking several times from one end of the cabin to the other.

—Several airlines have actually developed programs of simple exercises designed to keep the body fit in flight; for copies of these programs—which essentially consist of stretching and isometric exercises—telephone the local office of Lufthansa German Airlines and ask for a copy of *Fitness in the Chair*, or buy a copy of Scandinavian Airlines' *Exercises in the Chair* (Bantam, $3.95).

2. What is jet lag and how can I prevent it?

—Jet lag is your body's reaction to a disruption in its normal biological clock. The changes that travel imposes on your body's usual system of eating, sleeping, and waking often result in a general feeling of malaise (headache and fatigue are the most common symptoms).

—The discomfort produced by subjecting your body to extreme variations in its normal body functions is "diurnal and circadian dysynchronization"; this means, in essence, that you know where you are but your body doesn't.

—You can avoid, or certainly reduce, jet lag by getting ample rest *prior to the flight* and by allowing at least a full day for rejuvenation once you have landed on the other side of the country or ocean; as a general rule, the more time zones you cross, the more time your body will need to bounce back. (I need one full day to recuperate from travel U.S./Europe, and two days for travel to Africa or the Far East.)

—Whenever possible, it is advisable to break up your trip into legs or portions so that you can recuperate a bit after each moderately long flight rather than trying to revive yourself after a single, endless one.

—Unless you combine the best of Superman and Wonder Woman, I would strongly advise you *not* to plan any sight-seeing or business activities after a transoceanic or transcontinental flight; you'll function better and appreciate more after a good night's rest.

—Though travelers continue to debate the merits of morning versus evening arrivals in foreign cities, I personally opt for the latter: the hotel room will be ready to receive you, and your body (exhausted from the journey) will be content to have a short stroll, a good dinner, and a rejuvenating night's sleep.

YOUR OWN MEDICAL KIT

Although it is unnecessary to travel as if you were a mobile pharmacy, there are some indispensable items you will probably wish to take along. Here again, follow your doctor's recommendations before assembling your supplies.

1. What items must *be included?*
—An ample supply of any medications which you are required to take, together with prescriptions for drugs (using their generic rather than brand names) which your doctor feels you might need on the trip.
—An extra pair of your prescription eyeglasses.
2. What items might *be included?*
—Assorted bandages
—Band-Aids
—Gauze pads
—Q-tips
—Adhesive tape
—Cotton
—Safety pins
—Scissors
—A thermometer
—Tweezers
—An antidote for motion sickness (such as Dramamine)
—An antidiarrheal agent (such as Lomotil)
—Antiallergy medication
—An antidote for constipation (such as Milk of Magnesia)
—Antifungal skin ointment
—Water purification tablets (if appropriate)
—An antihistamine nasal spray (especially helpful during the flight)
—Antibiotics (as recommended by your doctor)
—Antacid tablets
—Aspirin
—Cough medicine (or throat lozenges)
—Eyewash or drops

—Vitamins and minerals
—Sleeping pills (if prescribed by your doctor)
—Soap (preferably surgical)
—Insect repellent (particularly if your trip involves travel to the tropics)
—A simple first-aid booklet (better yet, get a copy of *The Year-Round Travelers' Health Guide* by Drs. Patrick J. Doyle and James E. Banta; Acropolis Books, $4.95 in paperback—this guide tells you all you need to know about first aid and staying fit when traveling).

To determine which of the above items you should take, consult your doctor, particularly concerning your possible use of antihistamines, antibiotics, and sleeping pills, each of which can be obtained only by prescription. If you ultimately carry *all* of these medical supplies with you, you will resemble Madame Curie's laboratory, but why should you risk not finding what you need—elsewhere in the world—when you need it?

3. How come no one has thought of a traveler's first-aid kit?
—Someone has . . . it's called Medi Case and consists of aspirin, allergy tablets, cold and cough tablets, antinausea pills, antacid tablets, laxative pills, a thermometer, Band-Aids and gauze pads, vials for your own medication, and an information booklet on first aid. This tidy, compact leather case (the size of a book) sells for $8.50 at stores that cater to travelers.

Is all of this *really* necessary? To this question I can simply reply that there have been trips when I would have sold my soul for a decongestant nasal spray to help me breathe again, and there were times when I would gladly have given away new Italian loafers for a skin cream that stopped my itching. After a few early trips for which I was ill-prepared, I have begun to carry almost all of the recommended medical supplies with me and, at one time or another, I've used every one. And I must confess that I enjoy my instant popularity as soon as fellow travelers get their first glimpse of my portable pharmacy. Just having me (it?) around must be a relief.

STAYING HEALTHY ABROAD: DO'S AND DON'TS

Whether you call what you have "Montezuma's revenge," "Delhi belly," "turistas," or "giardiasis," no one enjoys an upset stomach. Alas, there is no fail-safe system to guarantee you will be spared from diarrhea, nausea, cramps—but there are certainly lots of precautions you can take to avoid becoming a statistic. If you are on a defiantly crazy "I can eat everything, nothing ever bothers me" rampage, chances are there will be moans from your room around two in the morning. Somehow, there has to be a happy midpoint between stuffing yourself with every exotic dish in sight and limiting yourself to tea and toast. A little bit of common sense applied to what you eat and drink, and where, will dramatically improve your chances of staying healthy.

Food

Do *not:*

—Overdo your intake of fruits since this could cause diarrhea.
—Eat meat unless it is *well done* (red or rare meat is an invitation to tapeworm).
—Eat salads, mayonnaise, cream fillings, custards, or buffet dishes prepared far in advance (these kinds of foods, especially if poorly refrigerated, are subject to spoilage).
—Deceive yourself into thinking that highly seasoned or spicy foods are "safe" (often the heavy seasoning masks contamination).
—Be smug about sanitation standards where food preparation is concerned: some of the world's worst stomachaches have come out of some of the world's fanciest resorts.

Do:

—Eat vegetables if they are well cooked.
—Eat fruits *if* they have been washed in safe water and *if* you are able to peel them yourself (a fruit with punctured skin is probably entertaining a foreign body you don't want to know).
—Be careful where you eat seafood (like crabs, oysters, and

shrimp, etc.) since such delectable morsels might be coming to your plate directly from polluted waters ... hello hepatitis!

—Exercise restraint when experimenting with unfamiliar or exotic dishes. Taste selectively so you don't put your stomach on overload.

—Stick with toast, tea, and hot soup if you're beginning to feel queasy.

Beverages

Do *not:*

—Drink tap water (I don't care what guarantees the locals give you, play it safe).

—Accept ice cubes or shaved ice in your drinks (ice is made from the water you're trying to avoid, remember?!).

—Drink from any container unless it is clean (dirty container= dirty water).

—Use tap water for brushing your teeth (in Samoa, I used root beer—my caps have been clicking ever since).

—Deceive yourself into assuming that alcohol sterilizes the water (it's an attractive notion, but booze does nothing whatever to decontaminate water).

—Order carafes of wine (only because the wine may have been diluted by the same water you want to avoid).

—Sing in the shower (okay, okay, admittedly this is a bit extreme, but you might keep in mind that it takes only one swallow of those bacteria to make you sick).

—Drink fresh milk (even in countries with the highest standards of hygiene, pasteurization tends to mean different things to different people).

Do:

—Drink established brands of bottled water and, to be absolutely safe, ask that the bottle be brought to your table with the seal unbroken (the dilution dilemma again).

—Drink ordinary tap water only *if* you are able to boil it for about ten minutes, or *if* you have water-purification tablets

(such as Halazone or Globaline) which will render the water safer to drink.
—Drink coffee or tea if the water used has been properly boiled.
—Drink dry or canned evaporated milk.
—Drink bottled beer and wine, both of which are usually safe (ah, some good news at last).
—Carry an unbreakable flask in which to hold the safe beverage of your choice during long trips or tours, and also carry a collapsible cup so that you can avoid having to drink from communal bottles or flasks if that kind of unsanitary sharing makes you uneasy.

You'll be okay if you use your head to protect your stomach. Consider where you are and the standards of hygiene and sanitation in that respective country, and who you are and the diet to which your body is normally accustomed. It's perfectly all right to experiment with new foods and untried drinks; as a matter of fact, that adventure is a part of the joy of travel . . . just moderate your enthusiasm with good judgment.

HOW TO FIND A DOCTOR OVERSEAS

If you're like most travelers, you will have a trip filled with perfectly good health and return home with nothing more painful than bills and overexposed film. But some people begin journeys in excellent health only to encounter trouble along the way. Sadly, there are even those would-be tourists so intimidated by the notion of getting sick in a foreign place that they forgo the trip altogether. Pity, because medicine is not a science limited in practice to the United States, and there is every likelihood that you will be able to find a capable doctor wherever in the world you need one.

There are, of course, exceptions. Several years ago, a fellow journalist and myself visited the destination of our dreams: Egypt. He and I rode camels at sunset and felt fine, we cruised in feluccas on the Nile and were radiant, we toasted the pharaohs with wine and rejoiced, my friend ate a hamburger in

Cairo and nearly died. At four in the morning, I heard moaning and groaning from the bathroom which was subsequently followed by noises of a much more distinctive variety. Between gasps, I heard him yell (like some ancient curse), "The hamburger, the hamburger!!" I called the desk clerk who in turn connected me with a nurse who spoke "better English than the doctor standing adjacent." The nurse would be my interpreter. "My friend," I began, "has severe stomach cramps, a slight fever, a terrible headache, and he is throwing up over most of Cairo." The nurse then translated all of these symptoms to the doctor. Presumably, he diagnosed the case for her because she then returned to the phone. "Sir," she began, "I told the doctor everything you said and he wants you to tell your friend not to worry—the first pregnancy is often difficult."

You can have better luck if you prepare for such an emergency, taking any one of the following steps:

1. Ask your family physician if, by chance, he or she can give you names of any colleagues in the various countries you might be visiting. Even if your doctor doesn't personally know physicians overseas, he or she can check with colleagues or a faculty member at a nearby medical complex who might be able to provide the recommendations you seek; it's a long shot, but at least ask.

2. Consider membership in either of the following organizations, both of which maintain a current international listing of English-speaking member physicians who meet their criteria for training and education throughout the world:

> Intermedic, Inc.
> 777 Third Ave.
> New York, NY 10017
> (212-486-8974)

NOTE: The single membership fee is $6 for one year or $10 for a family membership entitling the member(s) to a worldwide directory of English-speaking physicians all of whom have agreed to work for uniform, standardized fees.

International Association for Medical Assistance
to Travelers (IAMAT)
350 Fifth Ave., Suite 5620
New York, NY 10001
(212-279-6465)

NOTE: The IAMAT listing of 3000 English-speaking
physicians in 120 countries is available free of charge; since
IAMAT is a nonprofit organization, contributions are
appreciated.

3. If you are an American Express credit-card member,
you might consider purchasing a copy of its recent publication,
U.S. Certified Doctors Abroad ($3)—this booklet lists 3500
English-speaking doctors around the world and fully enumer-
ates individual certification, educational background, and
training. In addition, American Express members will receive
(at no additional charge) a Med Chart in which members can
record their current medical history, medications, and other
critical data that could be of value in an emergency.

4. If you find yourself in an emergency situation and do
not know where to turn, go directly to the local medical school
hospital or university-affiliated hospital. The staff and
facilities at such complexes will probably provide the best
available treatment and service in the area.

5. Carry necessary medical insurance documents with
you on any trip outside the United States; in some cases, your
company's major medical plan or those available from Blue
Cross and Blue Shield make provisions for reimbursing
members for hospitalization once receipted bills have been
submitted.

Check your insurance protection for overseas medical
services and hospitalization *before* you go, and buy additional
or more comprehensive coverage if you feel it is warranted.

Congratulations! You've taken all the precautions, made
all the preparations, and are feeling just fine. Then you spot
your empty suitcase on the bed and realize it's time, at last, to
pack.

8
WHAT SHOULD YOU TAKE WITH YOU?

I recently took my mother to Los Angeles International Airport for her flight to Las Vegas. For this particular getaway, Mom had assembled three suitcases, one valet bag, one jewelry case, one carry-on tote bag, and a wig box . . . and she was only going away for the weekend. The national company of *The King and I* travels lighter.

Packing, like a visit to the dentist, is approached with some trepidation: we know that no matter how careful we have been, something awful is going to happen. As a protection against the inevitable, we stuff yawning suitcases beyond their limits, carry enough garments to clothe the Rockettes, and throw in—for good measure—items we have never worn in our lives but are certain we will wear on this trip. To make matters worse, we take clothes that occupied an entire walk-in closet and attempt to squeeze them into an undernourished two-suiter last used in 1964. There has got to be a better way, and there is.

For one thing, travel today is different: discount air fares and inexpensive package tours, coupled with the recent waves of liberation (including, but not limited to, women's and gay) have unleashed upon the world's market a whole new breed of footloose, fun-seeking, and faintly funky travelers. And I'm glad. Today's travelers often seem to be in pursuit of shorter, cheaper, and less formal getaways . . . objectives which have been transformed by the travel industry into wilderness vacations, "cruises to nowhere," and "party vacations for singles." In a not-so-subtle way, these vacations and vacationers have brought with them a whole new set of standards regarding what we do *and how we dress* on trips. Guys are giving up tuxedos and dark blue suits for unstructured, loose-fitting linen jackets; gals are forsaking elegant gowns and cocktail dresses for dramatic silk shirts and slacks; and everybody, everywhere, is wearing jeans. Nightclubs are out, discos are in, and "trendy tasteful" seems to be going further than "fussy formal."

Naturally, the current tide of fashions might not appeal to all of us, especially if we have a predilection for leisure suits, pantsuits, and beaded cocktail dresses. Still, it's wise to remember that the world's tourist centers seem to be accepting (even enjoying) the new, relaxed dress codes and, as a consequence, you can pack less and make your travel wardrobe go just as far. I wouldn't wear jeans to Maxim's, sneakers to La Scala, or my Boy Scout shirt to Claridge's, but, short of that, almost anything goes.

As you develop a contemporary fashion "set" for the journey, consider what you will carry to accommodate the clothes you ultimately will take.

LUGGAGE: WHAT KIND AND HOW MUCH?

1. How much luggage am I allowed to take?
—The luggage allowance for all flights within the United States is two checked pieces not exceeding 62 inches for the first bag and 55 inches for the second; note that bags are now *measured* (not weighed) by adding together the figures for length, width, and height; in addition to the two larger bags, you may check or carry on a tote or flight bag (whose total measurements cannot exceed 45 inches).
—Most, *but not all*, international carriers similarly have adopted a system of measuring luggage: first-class overseas passengers may check two bags which must not exceed 62 inches each; economy passengers are permitted to check two bags whose *total* measurements do not exceed 106 inches (you'll probably be safe as long as you carry regular-sized, *not* oversized, luggage).

—A number of international carriers still *weigh* luggage—it is imperative, therefore, that you and your travel agent review your itinerary to determine if you have flights on these particular carriers. If you do, you will need to adhere to weight as well as measurement regulations (66 pounds for first-class passengers; 44 pounds for economy).

—The added costs involved for carrying oversized or overweight luggage, particularly on overseas flights, can be stiff; know the luggage allowance and adhere to it.

—Luggage allowances vary among railroad, interstate bus, and steamship companies; as a rule, however, you may expect that a ship will carry more of your luggage *free* than any other kind of carrier (typically: 200 pounds).

2. *What kind of luggage should I buy?*

—If you are selecting a new set of luggage be absolutely certain, before buying, that you can make use of *every piece* included in the set however attractive the package price (will you, for instance, ever use a garment bag?).

—Hardside luggage is generally most durable, but the softside variety has the distinct advantage of usually being lighter (my hardside luggage has lasted twelve years and it is heavy—even empty it registers a 3.5 on the Richter scale).

—If you are determined to buy softside luggage, at least select a nylon (strongest of the man-made fibers) or a hearty canvas fabric which will last far longer than cotton.

—Inspect the zippers on the bags carefully to determine if they are durable, strongly reinforced, and double stitched (faulty zippers can cause lots of travel problems; inspect them well).

—Select a suitcase with a single handle which is securely hinged, fastened, or sewn to the frame of the bag (if you have double handles, you and porters will still grab just one, placing damaging stress on the other).

—Favor luggage which has a combination lock (such locks provide considerably more security from pilfering and theft than the uniform suitcase keys that can open *every bag* made by that respective manufacturer). If you select a suitcase without a combination lock, buy a lock and put it on the bag for added protection . . . and consider using the first three digits

of your street address for an easily remembered combination number.
—Read the label carefully: are you buying leather or vinyl? They may look alike, but they don't necessarily wear alike.
—Because of the trauma they are likely to experience at the hands of airport porters and conveyer belts, suitcases in *darker* colors seem to survive better than those which are lighter.
—Choose luggage that is, most of all, well-crafted: are the seams secure? are the threads tied off? is the lock durable? is the zipper well-supported? A well-manufactured, attractive set of luggage can cost as much as a new television set; make your selection based on durability (will it last?), manageability (can you carry it yourself if you have to?) and attractiveness (are you proud to say, "That one's mine"?).

    3. Do I need a piece of carry-on luggage?
—Absolutely; this piece of luggage (in the form of a tote, flight, or overnight bag) is invaluable in that it allows you to carry on essential items which you may need during the flight or immediately upon arrival at your destination (especially, God help us, if your checked luggage is lost).

    4. How can I prevent my luggage from being lost or stolen?
—Affix, to the outside of each suitcase, an identification tag that includes your name and phone number (most seasoned travelers will *not* indicate their home addresses since shady types who prowl around airports copy this information and use it to burgle vacant homes).
—Inside your suitcase, place an identification tag which includes your name, address, and telephone number; you might also wish to list the phone number for your office, or travel agent, or tour operator in order to facilitate reaching you if your bag has been located.
—If you have recently purchased your luggage, keep the sales slip with you as you travel (this will expedite any claim report if your bag has been lost or damaged).
—Lock your bags before airport check-in.
—Use a marking of some kind (adhesive tape, sticker, a piece

of cloth) to distinguish your suitcase from the countless others it may resemble. I always mark my luggage ever since a lady in Costa Rica accidentally ran off with my suitcase, leaving me with hers and an abundance of see-through lingerie and other assorted titillations.

—Remove all previous baggage claim checks from your suitcases before airport check-in. If you don't, you could compound the probability that your bag will be misrouted.

  5. What do I do if my suitcase is damaged?

—Take your damaged bag to the airline's baggage service office (usually located near the baggage claim area) and fill out a Property Irregularity Report outlining the nature of your claim and the extent of the damage.

—Have an airline representative inspect the damage *on the spot.*

—Ask the airline to arrange to have your bag repaired *or* have it suggest luggage repair shops in the area which they consider reliable; if you choose to have the suitcase repaired on your own, secure an estimate of the repair and get approval from the airline before giving the luggage shop the go-ahead (this step could eliminate later problems due to outrageous overcharges and possible refusal by the airline to reimburse you for repairs).

  6. Can I buy luggage insurance?

—Such coverage is possibly available as a rider to your homeowner's insurance policy (as a personal articles floater), or it can be purchased from your insurance agent to protect you on a specific trip (watch out, however, for typical exclusions such as money, jewelry, and furs, etc.).

—If your luggage and its contents exceed in value the airline's normal liability ($750 on domestic flights; $9.07 per pound international), you may wish to purchase excess value insurance from the carrier prior to your departure (this protection may be available for as little as $1 per additional $100 in coverage).

  Now that you've selected your luggage and have every reasonable expectation that whither you go it will go, address yourself to the problem of what you will put inside it.

PACKING: WHAT TO PACK AND HOW TO PACK IT

When we pack, most of us have had the experience of putting a sweater in our suitcase, then taking it out, then putting it back in, etc., until it falls apart in our hands from the wear and tear. We vacillate between packing items which are "absolutely necessary" for our trip, those which would "be nice to have along," and those which we "wouldn't be caught dead in." Somehow, all three categories of clothes are crammed into a little box originally designed to hold two suits.

Though packing experts might advise otherwise, I have never traveled with more than one suit, discovering, in the process, that I rarely wore that one when my trusted navy blue blazer would do. Turtlenecks cover a multitude of chins (and situations) and, in the bargain, they are quickly restored by a quick soak in the hotel sink. Women with whom I've traveled have sworn off wrinkle-prone chiffon, opting, instead, for more classic "travel suits" (in easier fabrics) that stretch one's wardrobe by encouraging countless opportunities to mix and match.

Some trips are more formal than others; so are some travelers. Still, I'd rather have my cordovan loafers and comfortable sneakers than my distinguished-looking vested suit and, though I'd gladly give you the formal, starched shirt off my back—I will *never* surrender my bathing suit, Windbreaker, shorts, and jeans.

1. What determines the kinds of clothes I should take?
—Most of all, this obviously depends upon the nature of the trip you're taking: though both adventures are on water, river rafting on the Colorado is different from a Mediterranean cruise on the QE II.
—The purpose of your trip: if your itinerary involves lots of social activities, you'll need more formal (or dressier) clothes since it may be difficult to make your sight-seeing and shopping wardrobes double.
—The mode of transportation: you'll have to dress more often and more elegantly aboard a ship than you would, for instance, on a bus, train, or in the privacy of your own car.

—The class of accommodations: some luxury hotels and fine restaurants require men to wear ties and jackets for dinner and they may prohibit women from wearing slacks or pantsuits (high standards in food and service often dictate high standards in dress . . . and I, for one, will put on a tie for a good pâté anytime).

—The length of your trip: I find it easier to pack for a three-week trip than for a weekend, but most of us believe that the longer the trip, the greater the number of clothes we'll need to take along (*rethink this theory* before loading yourself down).

—Climates along the way: weather, or at least the extent to which anyone has ever been able to predict it, is a major consideration in determining when we will visit which places and what clothes we will take with us. As you scan some of the following average temperatures around the world, consider how the contents of your suitcase would change to accommodate each:

SOME CLIMATES AROUND THE WORLD

City	Avg. Temp.—February	Avg. Temp.—August
Miami	76	89
New York	41	85
Chicago	34	83
Honolulu	80	90
Los Angeles	64	83
Athens, Greece	55	90
London, England	44	71
Rome, Italy	54	87
Stockholm, Sweden	27	60
Vienna, Austria	37	72
Lima, Peru	74	62
Rio de Janeiro, Brazil	80	70
Hong Kong	59	83
Tokyo, Japan	39	79

—The local customs: before you take off, ask your travel agent about, or do your own research on, any special dress codes with which you might be confronted during your trip; for instance, in many Middle Eastern countries shorts and bikinis (for either sex) are strictly taboo—while in French Polynesia bikinis are a way of life; in the Vatican and at many other sacred sites, women are expected to cover their heads, shoulders, and arms, while at shrines in the Orient visitors are required to take off their shoes. It's a courtesy to know before you go.

2. *Suggest a sample, essential wardrobe for a two- to three-week trip**:

WARDROBE FOR WOMEN
    1 suit (either skirt and jacket or pantsuit for travel)
    1 coat (for day *and* evening)
    1 two- or three-piece knit outfit
    2 daytime outfits
    2 interchangeable tops
    1 long skirt (for evenings; optional)
    1 pair of jeans (or shorts)
    3 pairs of shoes (including one pair of *comfortable* walking shoes or tennis shoes)
    2 sweaters in basic colors (or one sweater and a lightweight Windbreaker for daytime wear)
    2 scarves (one of which is a headscarf)
    1 foldaway umbrella (or pocket raincoat)
    4 to 5 pairs of panty hose
    3 sets of quick-drying underwear
    1 pair of pajamas (or a nightgown)
    2 handbags
    1 travel robe

* These wardrobe checklists follow the guidance offered in TWA's excellent brochure *Climate and Clothes,* and should be supplemented by the traveler's individual needs.

Handkerchiefs
1 pair of slippers (that can double as beach sandals)
1 flat bag (for evening)
Cosmetics as needed (contained in a zippered and
  rubberized cosmetics bag)
Electrical aids (hair dryer, rollers, etc.)
For summer or beach trip: swimsuits, tennis shorts, swim
  cap, sneakers, suntan lotion, etc.
For winter trip: boots, gloves, heavy sweaters, and
  woolen hat

WARDROBE FOR MEN
1 suit (a dark color works better for evening wear)
1 all-weather coat (preferably a raincoat with a lining)
1 sports coat (a blazer works in a variety of situations)
2 pairs of slacks
1 Windbreaker
1 pair of jeans
2 belts
5 shirts (drip-dry is often recommended, though mine
  usually drip in one country and don't dry until the next)
2 pairs of shoes (one pair should be *comfortable* walking
  shoes or sneakers)
4 sets of undershirts and shorts
3 ties
5 pairs of socks
1 sweater (either cardigan or pullover in a basic color)
Handkerchiefs
1 pair of pajamas (drip-dry)
1 travel robe
1 pair of slippers (that can double as beach sandals)
Shaving kit (electrical aids as needed)
Cuff links, tie clasp, and collar stays (if worn)
For summer trip: swim trunks, shorts, beach hat,
  sneakers, suntan lotion
For winter trip: gloves, hat, scarf, and heavy sweaters

3. What should I keep in mind as I get ready to pack?
—Carefully go through your own wardrobe before making new and expensive purchases of items you may not need or may never wear.
—Take only those clothes (and especially shoes) which you have worn and tested for comfort; do *not* experiment with new purchases on the trip.
—Try to select items that can perform double duty—such as thongs that can serve as bedroom slippers and beach sandals, and robes that can be worn both in your bedroom and at the pool.
—Stick to one basic color (at the most, two) and find items in your wardrobe that work well with it; this policy will drastically reduce the need to pack special shoes, belts, and accessories for each outfit and color (even if you do, you'll still forget *something*).
—Take a good, all-purpose raincoat that can serve you day and night for casual sight-seeing and more formal on-the-towning; a raincoat outfitted with its own lining, plus a medium-weight sweater, will get you through even the most unseasonable dips in temperature.
—Pack for the climate you are going to and not for the one you are leaving. Don't fill half of a suitcase accompanying you to sunny Bermuda with a winter coat you need only at the airport in freezing New York (your raincoat should work at both destinations).
—Avoid overpacking since this practice not only puts a serious strain on the suitcase, it prevents you from carrying any purchases you've made along the way.
—Don't be nervous about the prospect of having to wear the same clothes several (or more) times on the trip: the people whom you'll meet in your travels don't know how frequently you've worn the brown dress or blue blazer—for them your clothes are new.
—Transfer all bottled goods (colognes, perfumes, shampoo, etc.) to plastic bottles before packing.
—Put masking tape over the tops of aerosol cans in order to

avoid the mess that in-flight "explosions" can cause in your suitcase (a shaving can once spilled its contents on the lining of my suitcase, bequeathing me a decidedly abstract mural).
—Put all shoes in shoe mitts or old socks (to avoid soiling your clothes and the suitcase itself).
—Do not take along valuable, irreplaceable jewelry. Why worry about potential loss or theft? Besides, you can show off at home.
—Select items from your wardrobe that easily complement each other so that you can expand what you have to work with by mixing and matching.
—Remove any space-consuming items which perform no function (shirt cardboards and collar guards, for instance).
—Throw in several plastic bags that can serve as containers for soiled laundry and as safe, insulated packets for wet bathing suits (face it, they will never dry before checkout time).
—Replace your bulky, space-consuming wig stand with a balloon which, when inflated and secured to a table with masking tape, will do exactly the same job.
—Take only those clothes that wear well (prints usually travel better than solids, for instance).
—Take clothes which can withstand the ultimate test: the rigors of hotel laundry and dry-cleaning services. Standards vary dramatically, so you should avoid packing any items that require supersensitive care and handling. Remember that your clothes are accompanying you on the trip and not vice versa.
—Place everything you have decided to pack on a bed, and then cut back by at least one-third; I promise you'll still have far more than you need.

4. Okay, I'm ready. How do I pack?
—There are as many theories on packing as there are lines for gas; luckily, one suitcase manufacturer has developed practical instructions not only for men and women, but for owners of hardside and softside luggage as well—get out your suitcase and your clothes and see how easily one of these plans works for you.

PACKING FOR MEN: HARDSIDE LUGGAGE*

Follow this system for carefree packing: Pack firmly to avoid shifting but don't overpack. Heavy things are placed on bottom near hinges, on one side of divider, so they won't shift down and rumple other things.

1. *Shoes.* Use shoe mitts of fabric, since plastic may mark leather. For one pair—place soles along hinge.

2. *Toiletries Kit, Alarm Clock, Flashlight.* Place these heavy items near hinge between shoes, or next to them. Carry shaving cream, especially aerosol, in a plastic bag in your carry-on luggage.

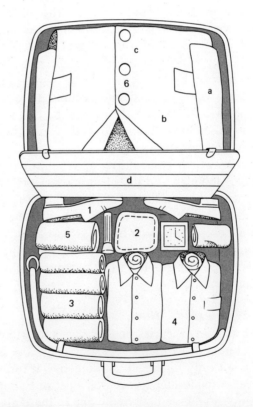

* All drawings and text on packing courtesy of the Samsonite Corporation, Denver, Colorado.

3. *Underwear—Socks.* Fold shirt and shorts in thirds, lengthwise. Place shorts, and a pair of socks, on shirt and roll up. Voilà, a set.

4. *Shirts.* You can't wear that cardboard from the laundry so why carry it? Fold buttoned shirt lengthwise to back of shirt, carefully pulling arms down straight. In shorter sizes, you may have to fold back only once; for longer shirts, a short fold at the bottom, then near the waist. Place a roll of socks in the collar of each shirt, to keep its shape.

5. *Pajamas, Robes, Sweaters.* Pajama top and robe are folded to the back in thirds. Place pajama bottoms on these, lengthwise, and roll up. Sweaters should be folded to back, same way, then placed on top of underwear, socks, and pajamas to cushion shoes.

6. If you have a men's two- or three-suiter, follow these hints. First raise the packing bar.

a. *Trousers.* Zip the fly, fold lengthwise on creases. Place back (or seat of pants) toward hinges, on hanger side of case, with the beltline touching side of case, legs hanging out over other side. Fold another pair with the back (or seat) side to hinges, in the opposite direction.

b. *Jackets.* Button as you would when you wear them. Place hanger hook through tab on jacket neck, remove keys and hard items so they won't cause lumps. Place jackets facedown, collar next to hinge. Pull sleeves to back of jacket and straighten down carefully. That way, your shoulders will fill out any creases at the back when you wear the jacket. Bring the bar back down.

c. *Final Folding.* Now, fold trouser legs hanging over case sides back over jacket, one pair at a time. Carefully fold one jacket sleeve at a time, then fold jacket bottom, back over bar and into case. (Don't flip them together, or sleeves will crease.) After folding, there will be a depression in the center of the case, suitable for a sweater or a knit shirt.

d. *Tie Bar.* This handy convenience on the case divider in two- and three-suiters will hold ties, scarves, handkerchiefs in perfect order.

PACKING FOR MEN: HARDSIDE CARRY-ON AND SOFTSIDE LUGGAGE

The technique used to pack a softside case is similar to that used in hardside, but the organization is just a little different.

1. Shoes, shirts, underwear, sleepwear, toiletries kit: Pack in bottom in rows. Keep heavy items opposite handle of suitcase. Suits are packed in second layer, on folding fixtures.

2. Remove hanging fixture. Fold trousers over the center bar. Drape the coat on the hanger.

3. For a small case, leave the coat unbuttoned and overlap the lapels until the coat fits within the width of the case. For a larger case, button the coat as you would when you wear it and lay in it the case, on the folding fixture, facedown. Coattails hang out over the front.

4. Fold each sleeve lengthwise around the sides of the coat as shown.

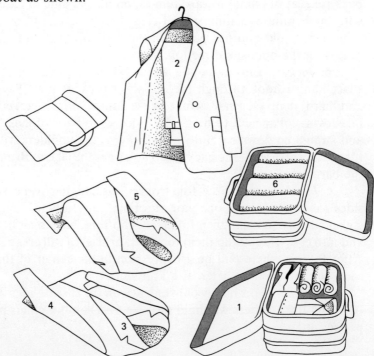

5. If the folding fixture bends, raise the lower part toward the shoulders of the coat (as illustrated). Otherwise, lay the pants in the case on top of the coats with the waistbands at opposite sides of the case. Fold the coattails over the pants, and then the pants legs over the coats.

6. Packing in larger case is completed. For the smaller case, place folding fixture in case and wrap coattail under fixture. Fasten tie tapes.

PACKING FOR WOMEN: WOMEN'S HARDSIDE LUGGAGE

Follow this system for carefree packing:

1. *Shoes.* Place shoes heel to toe, in fabric shoe mitts, along hinge of case, so they won't shift and crush things. Packing one pair, put shoes on opposite sides; two pairs, put one pair on each side (see diagram). Tuck soft things in shoes to conserve space.

2. *Purse.* Cushion on flat scarves, toward hinges. Take hard things out (they'll mark it) and fill with stockings, etc. to keep shape. Other heavies such as electric curlers should also be placed near hinges.

3. *Lingerie.* Fold slips, panties, and girdles lengthwise to back in thirds, following body lines. Place in sets, roll up smoothly, pack in sections.

4. *Bras and Bathing Suits.* This trick works especially well for padded cups, to avoid crushing. Fold the bra or suit in half, turn one cup inside out and place smoothly in the other. Then stuff the space with stockings or panties, or roll up securely.

5. *Nightgowns and Robes.* Fold lengthwise in thirds, following body lines. Roll securely from top, in sets. Place in lingerie section of suitcase.

6. *Cosmetics.* Carry small amounts (you *know* one bottle can last months at home) in plastic containers. Much makeup comes that way; if not, buy containers in notions department. Packing in tote is best, or secured in side pouch of suitcase. Pressed powders, unspillables can go in a separate case, near hinge, with other heavy irregular-shaped items.

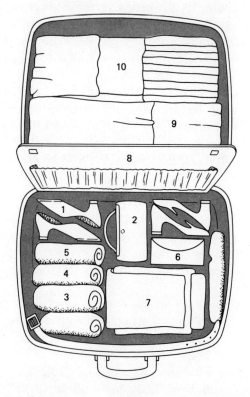

7. *Pants, Sweaters, Sport Clothes.* Fold pants flat-out, lengthwise, carefully on natural creases. Place first pair, waistband to side of case, back (or seat) of pants toward hinge, and let hang out of case. Then, place a sweater folded in thirds lengthwise, facedown on pants, letting half the sweater hang out at right angles to the pants. Fold pants back over sweater, once, then fold rest of sweater back on top, before folding last part of pants legs back. This procedure will provide a natural cushion and help resist wrinkles.

8. *Gloves, Scarves, Stockings.* Place in the pocket of the divider; extra jewelry goes here, too, and synthetic wigs, folded inside out. For human hair wigs, you need a wig box with head form. Chain belts go in the pocket; leather ones stretch around side of case.

9. *Folding Dresses/Skirts.* Start with the most fragile. Fold lengthwise on bed, front down, in thirds on natural curves. All zippers and buttons fastened, sleeves folded down back. Place in suitcase, collar touching edge, and let end hang out. Place other dresses folded same way, in opposite directions, one on another, ends hanging out. Suit jackets should be placed on their skirts, folded in thirds toward back.

10. *Final Folding.* Now you have all the garments, facing opposite directions. Start folding them carefully back over one another, layer after layer, smoothing wrinkles. Your fragile dress, on the bottom, will fold back last—with the biggest fabric "cushion" of all for its folds.

11. *Removing and Replacing Garments.* The packing system outlined allows you to take out and put back individual garments without disturbing the others. When you have packed according to the system, each dress, skirt, and jacket will be interfolded with the others.

    a. To take one out, grasp it at the fold, on the suitcase edge, and pull gently.

    b. If necessary, slide other arm in under it to keep other things in place.

    c. To replace a single item, fold lengthwise along body lines. For dresses, place facedown on the divider, with end hanging off.

    d. Slide one arm under all the other clothes in the case, and lift them gently.

    e. Slide garment from divider into case, face still down.

    f. Drop other clothes back on top, and fold ends back into case.

PACKING FOR WOMEN: WOMEN'S SOFTSIDE LUGGAGE

The technique used to pack a softside case is similar to that used for hardside, but the organization is just a little different. *Before You Start:* Put shoes in shoe mitts or some other porous

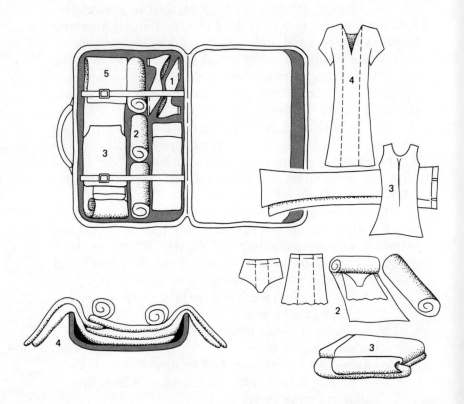

material. Fasten all zippers and buttons and remove all hard belts. Be sure any spillables are in plastic containers. Pack your case in two layers. Pack the first layer the way you'd pack the bottom of your hardside case, the top layer as you would pack the lid.

1. Pack shoes and other heavy items opposite the handle. Be sure to keep the weight in your case evenly distributed from side to side. It's easier to carry . . . better for your luggage.

2. Roll lingerie, sleepwear, and swimwear and place it in a section in the center of your case.

3. Fold sportswear, using one garment to cushion the folds in the other . . . and place it in sections, near the handle.

4. Fold dresses to the back in thirds, lengthwise along the bust and leg lines. Lay these in facedown on top of the first layer. Alternate the directions of the collars from right to left. Leave the skirts hanging over the sides.

5. Fold skirts back over each other. Fasten tie tapes.

5. What items should be packed in my carry-on bag?

The following articles should be packed in your carry-on bag and *not* in the luggage you check. As you read through this list, it will be apparent that the need to replace any of these articles will present you with a chore that ranges from the mildly inconvenient to the frankly impossible. If you carry these items with you (in a tote, flight, or handbag), you will reduce your anxiety about damage, loss, or theft:

—Passport.

—Visa(s), and two or three passport-size photographs should you wish to apply for a visa during your trip.

—Airline tickets.

—Travel documents (trip itinerary, hotel and car rental confirmations, sight-seeing vouchers, etc.).

—Traveler's checks, credit cards, cash, and any other negotiable instruments (including letters of credit).

—International Driver's Permit (*and* valid U.S. driver's license should you need to apply for a foreign license during your trip).

—Pocket money: some travelers carry small amounts of foreign currencies to expedite their arrival in foreign airports and hotels.

—Keys (carry with you your luggage, house, and automobile keys . . . not smart to pack luggage keys in locked suitcase).

—Jewelry (it would be better if you left the good stuff at home, but if you and your gold can't be parted—at least carry your expensive or irreplaceable jewelry with you).

—Medicine (carry with you any prescription medications, especially those you might need during the flight).

—Camera and a reasonable portion of your film supply (you never know what you'll see on arrival).

—Aerosols (aerosol cans should be taped at the top and preferably carried in a tote; cabin pressurization does strange things to these containers and you will have added protection against "explosive" accidents if you put the cans in your carry-on and not in your suitcase).

—Travel slippers (however comfortable the shoes that you've selected for the flight, slippers may feel better; if you've forgotten to carry yours in your tote, ask the flight attendant if she has an extra pair on board and look desperate—the slippers are normally given only to first-class passengers).

—Language book of key phrases (it could help you on arrival).

—Currency converter.

—"Critical cosmetics" and "trusted toiletries" that you may want or need in flight (items such as a toothbrush and toothpaste, mouth spray, soap and washcloth, and cologne or after-shave will conspire to make you feel almost human after an endless, sleepless flight).

—Ball-point pen and writing pad (a long flight provides you with an excellent opportunity to catch up on correspondence, thank-you notes, and perhaps even to make a few preliminary entries in your travel diary).

Though it may mark me for life as a pessimist, I confess I always add in my carry-on those few items of "survival" clothing that will see me through if my checked luggage is lost. A fresh shirt, some socks, and a few changes of underwear (cleverly stashed in the bottom of my flight bag) have—on at least two occasions—provided me with my only link to civilization. If you're lucky (and typical) you will never need to dip into these emergency rations; however, if you land in Lisbon and your suitcase somehow goes on to Lusaka, you'll be astounded at how important one set of clean underwear can be.

MONEY MATTERS

Not long ago, I found myself standing in line outside the Grand Opera House in Warsaw. Determined to see the Polish production of *Madame Butterfly*, I waited behind other excited tourists, including a large group from Chicago. One of the Americans turned to me and asked if I knew how much tickets sold for. "Fifty zlotys," I said. "How much," he asked, "is that in real money?"

"Real money" is a genuine concern to all travelers because we never seem quite sure of what we should take and how much. Remember that you have a number of choices, and even in the case of dire emergencies when you desperately need additional funds, you are probably just a cable away from getting them. To help you decide what to take, a few words about your currency options:

Traveler's Checks (or "travelers cheques")
These are clearly the safest way to carry funds overseas.

—Buy checks in small ($10 to $20) as well as in large ($50 to $100) denominations so that you can cash them in as needed without accumulating large sums of foreign currencies which you will only have to reconvert when you leave the country.

—Traveler's checks are sold by banks usually at a fee of $1 per $100, but your savings and loan association might provide them free of any service charge to customers with accounts there.

—In most foreign countries you will get the best exchange rate for your traveler's checks at banks; if you are exchanging only a small sum or are rushed for time, your hotel is your next best bet (restaurants and shops less so).

—Do *not* carry the receipt for the checks (indicating denominations and check numbers) with the checks themselves; keep your receipt in a separate place for easy reference if the checks are lost or stolen.

—Traveler's checks have no expiration date so they are always valid; if you don't spend them on this trip, you can save them for the next one.

—This form of currency also has the distinct advantage of being virtually instantly retrievable in case of loss or theft; simply report the incident to the local office of the company involved and they will issue replacement checks (your receipt for the missing checks will certainly help to expedite this process).

—Many stores offer discounts to shoppers ranging from 5 percent to 20 percent if payment is made with traveler's checks; ask about the store's policy in this regard before deciding on the form of payment.

Credit Cards
—It is unlikely that you will need more than one or two internationally accepted credit cards for travel anywhere in the world; only carry cards you need.
—Select the card(s) which you believe will afford you maximum usability on your trip: ask your credit card company for a list of hotels, restaurants, and shops which accept its card in the countries that you'll be visiting; most travelers feel they get more comprehensive charge coverage by carrying *two* internationally accepted cards.
—Several major credit card companies also provide limited check-cashing service for cardholders (American Express, for instance, permits cardholders to cash checks, up to $1000, once within any 21-day period overseas).
—If you run out of traveler's checks, you may be able to use your credit card to purchase an additional quantity of checks while you're overseas (this option is obviously available only if your credit card company sells traveler's checks).
—Charges made on your credit card outside the United States are converted based on the rate of exchange in effect on the day your foreign charge is posted in the company's American office. This means that the amount of your charge is based on the value of the dollar on the day the charge is posted, and *not* on the day the charge was made (depending upon how the dollar is fluctuating; therefore, you could lose or gain a few bucks by using your credit card).

Cash
—Generally speaking, you should avoid carrying large sums of cash with you; cash is an invitation to theft, and you have little hope of retrieving this kind of currency if it is lost or stolen.
—You might consider carrying twenty $1 bills in your passport

case or wallet; this cash can be useful for tips when you lack local currency, as well as for unexpected last-minute expenses as you leave, and then reenter, the United States.

Letter of Credit
—This document, often carried in lieu of cash or traveler's checks, enables you to draw funds from a bank overseas.
—Any arrangement with your local bank for a letter of credit should be made well in advance of your trip.

Personal Checks
—My own experience overseas has been that personal checks are the least reliable and acceptable instruments of currency; if you have trouble cashing a check at your local supermarket, can you imagine what will happen when you try to use one to pay a hotel bill in Bali?
—If you expect to use personal checks to pay for prearranged services and accommodations (hotels, rental cars, sightseeing), at least have your travel agent notify all of the respective parties well in advance; even with this warning, you and your personal checks may have problems.
—With appropriate identification, personal checks are usually accepted by credit card companies as payment for traveler's checks and by airlines which may cash personal checks, for their cardholders, if written for modest amounts (typically, under $50).

Foreign Currencies
—Prior to your departure, you may wish to purchase small amounts ($10 to $50) of foreign currencies to be used upon your arrival (it is especially convenient for airport tipping, taxis to town, and hotel check-in, etc.).
—Variously referred to as "pocket money" or "trip tips," these packets can be purchased at your local bank (to be safe, place your order in advance) or through Deak-Perera, an international foreign currency company with many local offices.

Finally, it is relevant to note here that U.S. Customs

Service requires you to file a report (Form 4790) if you are transporting more than $5000 in monetary instruments into, or out of, the United States. For the record, monetary instruments include U.S. or foreign currency, traveler's checks, money orders, and negotiable instruments. If you *are* carrying such quantities of currency, I'd like to know too—you sound like the kind of person I could get used to traveling with.

ELECTRICAL APPLIANCES: THEM AND YOU AGAINST THE WORLD

On my very first trip to Europe, I naively plugged my 110-volt (AC) hair dryer into a Parisian hotel's 220-volt outlet. Technically speaking, I was causing my hair dryer's motor to function twice as fast as it was designed to. In rapid order, I burned out the dryer's motor and caused a blackout in the hotel. Luckily, the French like candlelight.

Converters
It's a simple fact of the traveler's life that, in the United States, we operate on 110-volt alternating (AC) while most of the world runs on 220 AC. In order to convert the foreign current (220 volts) into the domestic current (110 volts), you will need to purchase a *converter* which, miracle of miracles, cuts in half the number of volts flowing to your appliance.

1. Will one converter work for all my electrical appliances?

—No. Because appliances are built differently, it's electrically impossible for a single converter to do all the jobs.
—You'll need *two* converters: one handles all appliances up to 1600 watts (hair dryers, curling irons, razors, etc.) while the other works with all electronic equipment up to 50 watts (cassette players, radios, photoflash guns, etc.).

2. I remember bulky converters that weigh more than the appliance itself; is that what I need to buy?

—No. Modern converters are lightweight and weigh just a few ounces each.

    3. Do I need to carry a converter even if I wish to use only my electric shaver overseas?

—Probably not, since many hotels in foreign cities have 110-volt outlets clearly marked For Electric Shavers Only; still, to be absolutely safe, you might take the converter along.

    4. Is there any situation in which the converter will not work?

—Yes. Converters are not designed to work with direct current (DC) which is found in some countries, and on some ships and planes as well.

    5. Aren't there some appliances designed to operate on 110 volts and 220 volts?

—Yes. These are dual-voltage products which, with a flip of the switch, allow your appliance to operate on either 110 volts or 220 volts (AC) *without a converter*: some models of hair dryers, shavers, travel irons, and coffee makers are equipped for dual voltage.

Adapters

Now that you feel terribly smug and well-informed as an apprentice electrician, it will come as some shock to you that—converter or no—your appliance is still not ready for its foreign connection. In the United States, we're used to a plug with two flat parallel blades; most foreign wall outlets require two long, thin round pins, while other sockets have three holes or two angled ones. What do you do with your electrical appliance in such situations? You adapt. It's really quite simple, actually, since a set of four adapter plugs will connect you and your appliance to virtually any outlet in the world.

    1. If I have adapters, can I forget about converters?

—No, silly, adapters *do not convert voltage*, they simply enable you to plug into the differing kinds of wall outlets you'll encounter throughout the world.

    2. Will one adapter plug be sufficient for most trips overseas?

—No. A Continental Adapter (two long, thin round pins) will work for you in Europe, Africa, Asia, and the Middle East; a British Adapter #1 (two short, round thick pins) will function in England and Central Europe; a British Adapter #2 (three square flat blades) will work for appliances in England, Africa, Hong Kong, and Israel; and a U.S.-type Adapter (two flat blades) will be fine in the Caribbean and South America.

   3. If I spring for all four adapters, will I then have universal coverage for my appliances?
—Almost, except for Australia and New Zealand which have unique plugs with flat blades set at an angle; you'll have to get a special adapter for these two countries down under.

   Before buying converters and adapters, seriously consider whether or not you could live without your hair dryer, cassette player, travel iron, or electric shaver while you're away. If you must have these appliances with you, then you must also have converters and adapters.

   1. How much will these items cost?
—*Converters* are about $12.95-$15.95 each. Remember, however, you may need *two* separate converters to deal with appliances operating on different wattages.
—*Adapters* are available for about $6.95 in a four-plug set (which will get you into most outlets).
—*Converter-adapter sets* cost approximately $29.95 and consist of the two necessary converters plus four adapter plugs all packaged in a lightweight, compact travel case the size of a paperback book.

   2. Where are converters and adapters sold?
—At most hardware, electronics, department, and luggage stores.

   3. How can I find out more about "current information" in countries around the world?

—The following list provides a guide to foreign voltages; if you require additional information, write directly to the experts in the field: Franzus Company, 352 Park Ave. S., New York, NY 10010.

CURRENTS AROUND THE WORLD

Aden 220V
Afghanistan 220V
Algeria. 110/220V
Angola. 220V
Anguilla 220V
*Antigua 110/220V
†Argentina. 220V
Aruba 110V
†Australia. 220V
Austria 220V
Azores 110/220V
Bahamas 110/220V
Bahrain 220V
Bangladesh 220V
Barbados. 110/220V
Belgium. 110/220V
Bermuda 110/220V
Bhutan. 220V
Bolivia. 110/220V
Bonaire 110/220V
*Botswana 220V
†Brazil. 110/220V
British Honduras 110/220V
British Virgin Islands . . . 110/220V
Bulgaria. 110/220V
Burma 220V
Burundi. 220V
Cambodia 110/220V
Cameroon. 110/220V
Canada 110V
Canal Zone 110/220V
Canary Islands 110/220V
Cayman Islands 110V
Central African Republic . . . 220V
Ceylon (see Sri Lanka) . . . .
Chad 220V
*Channel Islands (British). . . . 220V
†Chile 220V
China. 220V
Colombia 110V
Costa Rica. 110/220V

Cuba 110V
Curaçao. 110V
*Cyprus. 220V
Czechoslovakia 110/220V
Dahomey 220V
Denmark. 220V
Dominica 220V
Dominican Republic . . . 110/220V
Ecuador. 110/220V
Egypt. 110/220V
El Salvador 110V
Ethiopia 110/220V
Fiji. 220V
Finland 220V
France 110/220V
French Guiana 110/220V
Gabon 220V
Gambia 220V
†Germany 110/220V
Ghana 220V
Gibraltar 220V
*Great Britain. 220V
†Greece 110/220V
Greenland 220V
*Grenada 220V
Grenadines 220V
*Guadeloupe 110/220V
Guatemala 110/220V
Guinea. 220V
Guyana 110/220V
Haiti 110/220V
Honduras 110/220V
*Hong Kong. 220V
Hungary 220V
Iceland. 220V
†India 220V
Indonesia 110/220V
Iran 220V
Iraq 220V
*Ireland. 220V
Isle of Man 220V

CURRENTS AROUND THE WORLD— *Continued*

Israel	220V	Niger	220V
Italy	110/220V	*Nigeria	220V
Ivory Coast	220V	*Northern Ireland	220V
*Jamaica	110/220V	Norway	220V
Japan	110V	Okinawa	110V
Jordan	220V	Oman	220V
*Kenya	220V	Pakistan	220V
Korea	110V	Panama	110V
Kuwait	220V	Papua New Guinea	220V
Laos	110/220V	†Paraguay	220V
Lebanon	110/220V	Peru	220V
Lesotho	220V	Philippines	110/220V
Liberia	110/220V	Poland	220V
Libya	110/220V	Portugal	110/220V
Liechtenstein	220V	Puerto Rico	110V
Luxembourg	110/220V	Qatar	220V
Macao	110/220V	*Rhodesia	220V
†Madeira	220V	Romania	110/220V
Majorca	110V	Rwanda	220V
Malagasy Republic	220V	Saba	110/220V
*Malawi	220V	Samoa	110/220V
*Malaysia	220V	St. Barthélemy	220V
Mali	110/220V	St. Eustatius	110/220V
Malta	220V	*St. Kitts	220V
Martinique	110/220V	*St. Lucia	220V
Mauritania	220V	St. Maarten	110/220V
Mexico	110/220V	St. Vincent	220V
Monaco	110/220V	Saudi Arabia	110/220V
Montserrat	220V	*Scotland	220V
Morocco	110/220V	Senegal	110V
Mozambique	220V	Seychelles	220V
Nepal	220V	Sierra Leone	220V
Netherlands	110/220V	*Singapore	110/220V
Netherlands Antilles	110/220V	Somalia	110/220V
*Nevis	220V	*South Africa	220V
New Caledonia	220V	Spain	110/220V
New Hebrides	220V	Sri Lanka (Ceylon)	220V
New Zealand	220V	Sudan	220V
Nicaragua	110V	Surinam	110/220V

Swaziland	220V	Uganda	220V
†Sweden	110/220V	United Arab Emirates	220V
Switzerland	110/220V	Upper Volta	220V
Syria	110/220V	Uruguay	220V
Tahiti	110V	USA	110V
Taiwan	110/220V	USSR	110/220V
Tanzania	220V	U.S. Virgin Islands	110V
Tobago	110/220V	Venezuela	110V
Togo	110/220V	Vietnam	110/220V
Tonga	220V	*Wales	220V
Trinidad	110/220V	Yemen	220V
Tunisia	110/220V	Yugoslavia	220V
Turkey	110/220V	Zaire	220V
Turks & Caicos Islands	110V	Zambia	220V

* Denotes countries in which plugs with three square pins are used (in whole or part).
†Countries using DC in certain areas.

TRAVEL AIDS: GADGETS AND GIFTS

Having been the grateful recipient of my fair share of bon voyage gifts, I think I've become a reasonably good judge of what was useful and what wasn't. Romantic extravagances are certainly appreciated, but the beautiful bottles of bubbly champagne are cumbersome to carry, enormous boxes of chocolates are designed to melt in your hands during airport check-in, and flowers seem to be an embarrassment with which only former Miss Americas can cope.

Friends frequently ask if there is any travel item I need ("Yes—money") or if I can make some suggestions for practical bon voyage gifts for others. Frankly, it's unlikely that you or any other traveler will have the need or space for most of the items contained in the following list. Nonetheless, I believe you'll find some helpful and even imaginative suggestions here designed to dehassle your own trips and to increase the travel pleasures of others. (NOTE: all prices are approximate.)

1. *Converter/Adapter Set.* Designed to convert voltage of electrical appliances and adapt plugs to all foreign outlets, this kit is an essential ally of the frequent traveler ($29.95).

2. *Electronic World Time Alarm Clock.* Alarm clocks come in numerous styles, but this model is battery-operated and helps to orient you by indicating time zones around the world; every traveler needs an alarm clock (I am still waiting for a hotel wake-up call I left in 1974) ($32.50).

3. *"Voyager's Valet."* This is a fancy, euphonious name for an all-purpose kit which consists of soap packets, sewing kit, jiffy moisturized towels, deodorant pads, spot removers, and shoeshine polish; it contains lots of helpful, frequently forgotten items in one kit ($6.00).

4. *Laundry Kit.* Consists of six individual packets of soap suds for small laundry loads done in the hotel room ($2.00).

5. *Stretch Clothesline and Pins.* Once you have done laundry in your hotel room, you will appreciate the need for some kind of clothesline on which to hang it (don't depend on finding shower curtain bars or towel racks en route) ($4.00).

6. *Inflatable Hangers.* We've all experienced the horror of opening hotel room closets only to discover there are no hangers on which to put our travel-weary clothes; get a package of two rubber, inflatable hangers for protection ($4.00).

7. *Toilet Seat Covers.* Travelers who are especially sensitive in matters sanitary will want to purchase a packet of toilet seat covers to use on the trip ($2.00).

8. *Instant Coffee Packets.* If you are trembling at the prospect of having to drink alien coffee with the color of mud and the consistency of oil, relax—you can buy six single-serving packets of instant coffee ($2.00).

9. *Money Belts.* These "portable safe deposit boxes" are useful for the traveler who wishes to carry cash and other valuables on his or her person; available in leather ($12.50), cloth ($7.00), or as a bra money cache for women ($4.00).

10. *Passport Case.* Though many varieties are available,

the traveler will particularly welcome a case which has separate compartments for passport, foreign currency, credit cards, and sales receipts all protected by a clasp which secures the contents ($12.50 to $30.00).

11. *Currency Converter.* To help decipher foreign currencies and determine what your dollar will buy, take along one of the various kinds of currency converters ($1.95 to $3.95).

12. *Travel Diary.* I have derived great pleasure from rereading diaries I've kept of earlier trips and I know that such a gift is equally appreciated by other travelers anxious to remember "that quaint hotel in Lausanne," or "the fabulous place for seafood in Cabo San Lucas"; a travel diary also provides a handy place for listing phone numbers, addresses, expenses, and purchases ($6.00 to $10.00).

13. *Foreign Road Maps.* Any plans to drive overseas make it essential to carry the appropriate foreign road maps; these maps also are a practical gift for the traveler on an extended bus tour abroad... it's nice to know where you're going ($2.50).

14. *Language Phrase Book.* To help you get through customs formalities, ordering in a restaurant, securing directions for sight-seeing, or any of the other amenities and necessities of travel—a language phrase book provides key expressions, greetings, and travel-related questions used in countries throughout the world (the Berlitz version covers fourteen countries) ($2.95).

15. *European Menu Reader.* Though not critical to your survival overseas, this handy little booklet can help you (in a dozen or more languages) to ask for a glass of water, some sugar, or a knife; to distinguish between Bordelaise and Hollandaise, and a Burgundy or a Bordeaux; and to avoid the embarrassment of selecting an item on the menu which turns out to be "not responsible for items lost or stolen" ($2.95).

16. *Swiss Army Knife.* This is an especially valuable item for the outdoorsman, camper, hiker, and traveler-who-wants-to-be-prepared. The knife has separate blades for paring fruit and cutting bread, and a corkscrew, scissors, nail file, and screwdriver—as a matter of fact, it does everything but sing "Swanee" ($19.50).

17. *First-Aid Kit.* Here again there are several variations on the same theme but the previously described Medi Case contains essential first-aid ingredients ($8.50).

18. *Compass.* For the hiker, biker, backpacker, and camper, a compass could be an invaluable travel tool ($4.75).

19. *Unbreakable Flask.* If you're the thirsty type and like to have your own beverage supply with you, buy a flask that can be used for those parched moments en route ($2.25).

20. *Collapsible Drinking Cup.* If you are going on a group tour or will be visiting rural areas where drinking from communal bottles, glasses, or jugs is de rigueur—you may wish to carry a drinking cup of your own ($1.25).

21. *Drizzle Boots.* Women whose travels will take them to places where it is likely to rain (and that means anywhere) may feel better protected by carrying a pair of drizzle boots to slip over their shoes ($6.00).

22. *Pocket Raincoat.* This is an ingenious creation providing the traveler with a folded raincoat (the size of a purse) for unexpected showers; the compact version for women and men can be carried in a handbag or jacket pocket ($2.00).

23. *Travel Umbrella.* This popular, indispensable travel item normally consists of a half-size truncated or collapsible umbrella that folds up into itself (good luck refolding it after the initial "collapse"). Try to find a lightweight model sold in its own carrying case ($11.95 to $25.00).

I can't truthfully say that all of these wondrous articles have accompanied me on every trip, but I am amazed at how many I have added as need and convenience have dictated. If something in this inventory rings a bell—either in terms of your own travel needs or as a gift for a friend—you can probably locate the article at luggage, electrical appliance, or department stores (be sure to check the notions counter). You will have predictably better success if you investigate two specialty shops which are veritable treasure houses for the traveler (well, at least they're lots of fun):

Intercontinental Visa Service
Los Angeles World Trade Center
350 South Figueroa St., Room #187
Los Angeles, CA 90071
(213-625-7175)

The Complete Traveler
199 Madison Ave.
New York, NY 10016
(212-679-4339)

You now have all you need to take with you: luggage, clothes, electrical appliances, money, and travel aids.... Isn't it about time someone said, "Bon voyage"?

9

WHAT SHOULD YOU BRING BACK?

In addition to the fact that my closet looks as though it were organized by a threshing machine, it's unusual because it contains a Mexican sombrero, an Irish stocking cap, a Moroccan djellaba, and an Indian war bonnet (for the time being, we'll overlook the Portuguese tiles, Turkish samovar, and Roman funerary urn). All of these items were carefully chosen on various trips, fastidiously packed for the journey home, and then never worn (or used) once they got there. What is there about travel that prompts staid bankers to buy flowered shirts, undernourished bikinis, and itching lederhosen; what happens away from home to coax sensible housewives into grabbing leaden ponchos, see-through caftans, and cathedral-size woodcarvings? A person who comparison-shops at three supermarkets before choosing a chicken will spontaneously buy "precious gems" of undetermined quality and pay an excessive price. Travelers who have never bargained for anything in their lives will get palpitations, hypertension, and turn blue as they barter hysterically for a $3 ashtray. I know I have.

SHOPPING: WHY AND HOW

Though the motivation for shopping may have deeper psychological roots, I believe most of us simply enjoy the playlike experience of finding, selecting, and obtaining (at the "best possible price") something we would enjoy owning or giving. There is a feeling of contented achievement, sometimes even exhilaration, in getting what we think we want at a price we think we can afford. And besides, "we're on a vacation, aren't we?" Often lost in this process of wanting and getting is the practical question of using. I wanted a Moroccan robelike djellaba (it's the Omar Sharif in me), found one I liked, secured it at an excellent price (which at one-third the asking price was probably what it was actually worth), and stuck it in my closet at home where it remains a halfway house for moths.

Many of us shop overseas because the items we buy help us to relive and share the trip and, in a way, to extend the experience much like photographs do. Friends admire a tray bought in Jerusalem and we are at once sparked to a monologue of Israeli reminiscences. Each time you walk on your prized rug, you recall the merchant in Lisbon who invited you to have tea with him and his family. Shopping can provide an extraordinary opportunity to meet the locals and to experience a most personal contact, so don't approach each boutique, kiosk, and souk with the notion that you are a sucker about to be taken.

Shopping overseas is rather different from shopping at home; for one thing, you probably won't find items on a trip that you absolutely *must have*. A jade pin is lovely, but it's not a much-needed winter coat; the temple drawing is decorative, but you won't be serving it for dinner tonight. Therefore, shopping on trips can have an air of extravagant, even flamboyant, play about it: there is probably little you will purchase that you actually need. This carefree lack of necessity, within reason, can be fun and fulfilling too.

Then there are the crazy shoppers. I once traveled in Greece with a woman who collected brass pots. She stopped at almost every shop in the Plaka, examined pots as if she were performing an autopsy, and bought enough of them to equip all the kitchens in Brooklyn. Suspicious of shipping procedures, she decided to carry all of her purchases with her; she was the one you heard going through customs long before you saw her. Visions of this psychotic, pot-laden shopper still stay with me: she looked like a caravan and sounded like reindeer.

If you are traveling with others it makes good sense to

talk, in advance of your trip, about the priority shopping will be given. Allow for the shopping fiend to indulge his or her whims just as you must indulge yours; but if you continuously compromise your own interests, I promise you will inevitably feel deprived, imposed upon, frustrated, and angry.

You enter the first shop, your eyes are popping from the panorama of goodies, your pulse is quickening with the excitement of person-to-person contact with "the real people," and your wallet is tingling with anticipation at the adventure in bargaining that awaits. What should you be aware of as you shop? Here are some suggestions to make you smarter during your spree:

1. Try to purchase merchandise manufactured, grown, or produced in the country where you are buying it.

—You'll probably get a better deal and, besides, no one wants a shirt from Paris whose label reads "Made in Hong Kong."

2. If you are buying items of apparel for yourself, try the garment on first; if you are buying for others, take along their correct sizes and then refer to the following list of approximate comparative sizes:

COMPARATIVE CLOTHING SIZES
MEN'S CLOTHING

Suits

USA	34	36	38	40	42	44
UK	34	36	38	40	42	44
European	44	46	48	50	52	54

Shirts

USA	14½	15	15½	16	16½	17	17½
UK	14½	15	15½	16	16½	17	17½
European	37	38	39	40	41	42	43

Shoes

USA	7	8	9	10	11	12
UK	6½	7½	8½	9½	10½	11½
European	39	41	43	44	45	46

Hats

USA	6⅞	7	7½	7¼	7⅜	7½	7⅝	7¾
UK	6¾	6⅞	7	7⅛	7¼	7⅜	7½	7⅝
European	55	56	57	58	59	60	61	62

COMPARATIVE CLOTHING SIZES

WOMEN'S CLOTHING

Dresses

USA	6	8	10	12	14	16	18	20
UK	6	8	10	12	14	16	18	20
European	34	36	38	40	42	44	46	48

Junior dress sizes

USA	7	9	11	13	15	17
UK	7	9	11	13	15	17
European	34	36	38	40	42	44

Cardigans, sweaters, blouses

USA	30	32	34	36	38	40	42	44
UK	30	32	34	36	38	40	42	44
European	38	40	42	44	46	48	50	52

Shoes

USA	5	5½	6	6½	7	7½	8	8½	9	9½
UK	3½	4	4½	5	5½	6	6½	7	7½	8
European	35	35	36	37	38	38	39	39	40	41

Women's stockings

USA	8	8½	9	9½	10	10½	11
European	0	1	2	3	4	5	6

Women's gloves
Same as in USA

COMPARATIVE CLOTHING SIZES

CHILDREN'S CLOTHING

Dresses and coats

USA	3	4	5	6	6X
UK	18	20	22	24	26
European	98	104	110	116	122

Shoes

USA	8	9	10	11	12	13	1	2	3	4½	5½	6½
UK	7	8	9	10	11	12	13	1	2	3	4	5½
European	24	25	27	28	29	30	32	33	34	36	37	38½

3. Do not buy articles of wearing apparel as gifts unless you are reasonably certain as to the size and preferences (in style and color) of the prospective recipient.

—You can't return to Shannon to exchange a sweater that's too big or is the wrong color.

4. Try to select one meaningful gift for each person on your gift list rather than carting home a suitcase full of cheap, fragile souvenirs that have no meaning for anyone.

—If you are going to take the trouble to remember someone, let the gift you choose reflect your selectivity and care whenever you shop.

5. Bargain until you are breathless and your caps fall out—*unless* you are at a store that clearly adheres to a fixed-price policy.

—When bargaining, it's a safe rule of thumb to offer half the asking price...and then adjust your offer according to the merchant's reaction and your desire for the object in question.

6. Determine which items are best crafted and are most representative of the country in which you are making the purchase; often, these articles are the most treasured gifts—there are exceptions, of course: few of your friends will want a camel's harness from Khartoum.

7. If you are making more than one purchase in a given shop, see if you can get a better (i.e., discount) price on your total transaction.

8. Before you decide how you want to pay for your purchases, ask what discount the merchant offers for payment made with traveler's checks, or credit cards, or cash, respectively.

—For example, merchants throughout the world offer discounts possibly ranging from 10 percent to 20 percent on purchases paid for with traveler's checks or cash.

9. Whenever possible, have the shopkeeper wrap your purchase so you can carry it with you.

—If you choose instead to ship your packages home, you might be astounded at how handling, insurance, and postage charges will transform a "bargain" into an extravagance.

—In addition, it's worth mentioning that merchants are not universally honest; some will take your money and promise to mail your package.... I have a friend who is still waiting for the flokati rug he purchased in 1964.

10. The use of a credit card in payment of purchases affords you some protection if the article is never received.

—You should notify the credit card company of your failure to receive the goods in question and it probably will ask its local representative to contact the merchant and investigate the matter; obviously, you would not pay your credit card charge until you receive the purchase or resolve the problem.

11. If you must mail items home and they do not qualify as "unsolicited gifts—value under $25" (see later discussion on U.S. Customs in this chapter), by all means send them via prepaid parcel post.

12. Though some local merchants may plead their honesty in convincing you that it is legal to send alcohol, cigarettes, meat, and fresh fruits through the mail, it is *not* legal and *they* are not honest.

—If you have any doubts regarding items admissible to the United States under customs regulations, check with customs authorities (and not with local merchants).

13. However alluring the bait and attractive the proposition, do not change money in, or buy merchandise on, the black market.

—The temptation to deal on the black market could be enormous, and so are the penalties if you get caught.

14. It's an unwritten rule of travel that the closer a shop is to tourists' row, the more expensive its merchandise is likely to be.

—The most expensive and overpriced shops are typically found in hotels frequented by tourists.

15. Buy an item you like when and where you see it, *unless* you have reasonable assurance from someone who is in a position to know that a better price or quality can be obtained elsewhere.

—Beware the "there are better rugs in the next village"

syndrome. Who knows if the shops will still be open and if they will truly have what you want once you get there?

16. When making a purchase in a foreign country, always ask the merchant to write down the exchange rate he or she is giving you, as well as the arithmetic for the sale.
—Language may present an obstacle, but numbers are universally understood.

17. It does not take a Ph.D. in transportation to know that fragile goods travel badly.
—However desperately you wish to make a specific purchase, be assured that you can safely carry it, or ship it, home.

18. If you anticipate making quite a few purchases, you might consider taking along a sturdy cloth or net shopping bag to make your "gift marketing" easier.

19. If you are planning, or get caught up in, a true shopping binge, at least know the dutiable rates for items you purchase, thereby avoiding a truly expensive shock as you go through customs (rates of duty for most items of potential interest to travelers are presented later in this chapter).
—Some items, embroidered clothing for example, are subject to as much as 42½ percent duty—this consideration might alter your decision about making the purchase.

20. Finally, understand that while an item purchased at a duty-free or free port shop is not dutiable in the country where it is purchased, the same item may be subject to duty when you make your U.S. Customs declaration.
—Even old hands at travel seem confused by the meaning of duty-free. You may save money on your purchase in the duty-free port where it is acquired, and then get clobbered with the duty imposed on it when you reenter the United States.

Shopping overseas should be fun, and yet it requires some measure of seriousness and expertise. Whether you are paying for the purchases with lira, francs, marks, or rupees—*it's your money*; have fun, but spend it wisely. And please, don't cart home any more brass urns that convert into lamps, or wooden beads that become room dividers, or tribal masks that decay over the fireplace.... I'll give you mine.

U.S. CUSTOMS REGULATIONS

Few things in life make me nervous. Going through customs makes me nervous, and I'm not quite sure why. Perhaps it's because I usually find myself in line behind an elegant matron who opens her suitcase and reveals two salamis, a blossoming fruit plant, three pornographic books, and a pistol. This kind of returning traveler tends, I think, to predispose the customs inspector to be suspicious of the rest of the line—if not for the rest of his life.

Like the great majority of travelers processed through U.S. Customs (there were 270 million of us in 1979), I have never had a problem with my customs declaration; the explanation for this excellent track record is simple: I am honest. In case you didn't know, penalties for underestimating the value of acquired articles or for failing to declare them altogether are quite steep and should, in themselves, discourage dishonesty on the part of returning travelers.

Too frequently, I think, we approach customs inspectors as if "they are out to get us." Trust me, they are not. They are, however, "out to get" the professional smuggler intent upon filtering billions of dollars of illicit drugs into the United States each year. Similarly, in their efforts to enforce some four hundred regulations in behalf of four governmental agencies, the inspectors are on the lookout for travelers who willingly or unwittingly bring animals, insects, or bacteria back into this country and cause disasters they could not have imagined possible. In 1971, for instance, one returning traveler concealed a parrakeet in her handbag and smuggled the bird through customs. That traveler could hardly have known that the parrakeet was carrying Newcastle's Disease which, before being eradicated by governmental intervention, would kill eleven million chickens and cause a loss to the poultry industry of $20 million. One sick parrakeet did that... and there are countless other horror stories which underline the need for careful port-of-entry inspections to protect our national health.

The system of duties imposed on articles acquired abroad

was designed to protect American industry and American-made products, as well as to regulate our spending overseas. The system of duties is neither arbitrary nor especially complicated, and some recent legislation (enacted in late 1978) should help to simplify and expedite the entire procedure—and we're all for that.

1. As a returning U.S. citizen, what is my duty-free exemption?

—Each traveler, including children, has a $300 duty-free exemption (this means you may now bring back $300 worth of articles acquired abroad without paying any duty); in addition, you may bring back duty-free 200 cigarettes and a quart of alcohol (but regulations governing duty-free exemptions for alcohol *differ* from state to state; note also that children are not entitled to the duty-free exemption for alcoholic beverages).

—If you are returning from one of the U.S. Territories (U.S. Virgin Islands, American Samoa, and Guam) you are entitled to a $600 duty-free exemption, or exactly double what you'd be able to bring back duty-free from anywhere else in the world.

2. What do I have to do to qualify for these exemptions?

—(a) You must have been outside the United States for at least 48 hours (except in the cases of Mexico and the U.S. Virgin Islands for which this requirement does not apply), and (b) you must not have used your duty-free exemption within the last 30 days.

3. What happens if I go over my $300 duty-free exemption?

—Once you have exceeded your duty-free allowance, the next $600 in articles acquired is dutiable at a flat 10 percent rate (suppose you bought or received $900 worth of merchandise during your trip, then your total duty would be $60—or 10 percent of the $600 over your duty-free $300 allowance).

—And if you go on a wild spending spree and exceed the $600 taxed at a flat 10 percent, any additional dutiable articles are then taxed at the duty rate established by U.S. Customs for the articles involved.

—The customs inspector who examines your declaration and

luggage will make the ultimate determination concerning all dutiable items you may be carrying. The following condensed list of representative tourist items and duty rates might be useful to you as a guide:

U.S. CUSTOMS: RATES OF DUTY

ANTIQUES produced prior to 100 years before the date of entry—Free.
 (Have proof of antiquity obtained from seller.)
AUTOMOBILES, passenger—3%
BAGS, hand, leather—8½% to 10%
BEADS
 Imitation precious and semiprecious stones—7% to 13%
 Ivory—10%
BINOCULARS
 Prism—20%
 Opera and field glasses—8½%
BOOKS
 Foreign author or foreign language—Free
CAMERAS
 Motion picture, over $50 each—6%
 Still, over $10 each—7½%
 Cases, leather—8½% to 10%
 Lenses—12½%
CANDY
 Sweetened chocolate bars—5%
 Other—7%
CHESS SETS—10%
CHINA
 Bone—17½%
 Nonbone, other than tableware—22½%
CHINA TABLEWARE, nonbone, available in 77-piece sets
 Valued not over $10 per set—10¢ doz. + 48%
 Valued over $10 but not over $24 per set—10¢ doz.+ 55%
 Valued over $24 but not over $56 per set—10¢ doz. + 36%
 Valued over $56 per set—5¢ doz.+ 18%
CIGARETTE LIGHTERS
 Pocket, valued at over 42¢ each—22½%
 Table—12%
CLOCKS
 Valued over $5 but not over $10 each—75¢ + 16% + 6¼¢ for each jewel
 Valued over $10 each—$1.12 ea. + 16% + 6¼¢ for each jewel

U.S. CUSTOMS: RATES OF DUTY—*Continued*

CORK, manufactures of—18%
DOLLS AND PARTS—17½%
DRAWINGS (works of art)
    Original—Free
    Copies, done entirely by hand—Free
EARTHENWARE TABLEWARE, available in 77-piece sets
    Valued not over $3.30 per set—5¢ doz. + 14%
    Valued over $3.30 but not over $22 per set—10¢ doz. + 21%
    Valued over $22 per set—5¢ doz. + 10½%
FIGURINES, china—12½% to 22½%
FILM, imported, not qualifying for free entry is dutiable as follows:
    Exposed motion-picture film in any form on which pictures or sound
    and pictures have been recorded, developed or not developed,
    is dutiable at 48/100ths of a cent per linear foot.
    Other exposed or exposed and developed film would be classifiable as
    photographs, dutiable at 4% of their value.
FLOWERS, artificial, plastic—21%
FRUIT, prepared—35% or under
FUR
    Wearing apparel—8½% to 18½%
    Other manufactures of—8½% to 18½%
FURNITURE
    Wood, chairs—8½%
    Wood, other than chairs—5%
GLASS TABLEWARE valued not over $1 each—20% to 50%
GLOVES
    Not lace or net, plain vegetable fibers, woven—25%
    Wool, over $4 per doz.—37½¢ lb. + 18½%
    Fur—10%
    Horsehide or cowhide—15%
GOLF BALLS—6%
HANDKERCHIEFS
    Cotton, hand embroidered—4¢ ea. + 40%
    Cotton, plain—25%
    Other vegetable fiber, plain—9%
IRON, travel type, electric—5½%
IVORY, manufactures of—6%
JADE
    Cut, but not set and suitable for use in the manufacture of
        jewelry—2½%
    Other articles of jade—21%

JEWELRY, precious metal or stone
  Silver chief value, valued not over $18 per doz.—27½%
  Other— 12%
LEATHER
  Pocketbooks, bags—8½% to 10%
  Other manufactures of—4% to 14%
MAH-JONGG SETS—10%
MOTORCYCLES—5%
MUSHROOMS, DRIED—3.2¢ lb. + 10%
MUSICAL INSTRUMENTS
  Music boxes, wood—8%
  Woodwind, except bagpipes—7½%
  Bagpipes—Free
PAINTINGS (works of art)
  Original—Free
  Copies, done entirely by hand—Free
PAPER, manufactures of—8½%
PEARLS
  Loose or temporarily strung and without clasp:
    Genuine—Free
    Cultured—2½%
    Imitation—20%
  Temporarily or permanently strung (with clasp attached or
    separate)—12% to 27½%
PERFUME—8¢ lb. + 7½%
POSTAGE STAMPS—Free
PRINTED MATTER—2% to 7%
RADIOS
  Transistors—10⅖%
  Other—6%
RATTAN
  Furniture—16%
  Other manufactures of—12½%
RECORDS, phonograph—5%
RUBBER, natural, manufactures of—6%
SHAVER, electric—6½%
SHELL, manufactures of—8½%
SHOES, leather—2½% to 20%
STEREO EQUIPMENT
  Depending on components—5% to 12⅖%
STONES, CUT BUT NOT SET
  Diamonds not over one-half carat—4%
  Diamonds over one-half carat—5%

U.S. CUSTOMS: RATES OF DUTY—*Continued*

Others—Free to 5%
SWEATERS, of wool, over $5 per pound—37½¢ lb. + 20%
TABLEWARE AND FLATWARE
    Knives, forks, flatware
        Silver—4¢ each + 8½%
        Stainless steel—1¢ to 2¢ each + 12½% to 45%
    Spoons, tableware
        Silver—12½%
        Stainless steel—17% to 40%
TAPE RECORDERS—5½% to 7½%
TOILET PREPARATIONS
    Not containing alcohol—7½%
    Containing alcohol—8¢ lb. + 7½%
TOYS—17½%
TRUFFLES—Free
VEGETABLES, prepared—17½%
WATCHES, on $100 watch, duty varies from $6 to $13
WEARING APPAREL
    Embroidered or ornamented—21% to 42½%
    Not embroidered, not ornamented
        Cotton, knit—21%
        Cotton, not knit—8% to 21%
        Linen, not knit—7½%
        Man-made fiber, knit—25¢ lb. + 32½%
        Man-made fiber, not knit—25¢ lb. + 27½%
        Silk, knit—10%
        Silk, not knit—16%
        Wool, knit—37½¢ lb. + 15½% to 32%
        Wool, not knit—25¢ to 37½¢ lb. + 21%
WOOD
    Carvings—8%
    Manufactures of—8%

4. How does the duty-free exemption affect us if we are traveling as a family?
—You may pool your exemptions (for instance: a family of four is entitled to 4 times $300 or $1200 in articles duty-free) as long as you are returning home together and reside in the same household in the United States.
—This regulation is inherently beneficial and potentially economical for families since it is unlikely that any of your kids will use his or her entire duty-free allowance; by pooling family

purchases, you can use what the little devil doesn't.

5. *Are gift items I bring home for others subject to duty?*
—Absolutely, and so are gifts you buy for yourself, wearing apparel purchased overseas and worn on the trip, and any repairs you have done overseas (on clothing, luggage, etc.).

6. *Will items I mail home from overseas be included in my duty-free exemption?*
—No; only those items accompanying you home as you go through U.S. Customs can be included in your duty-free allowance.

—All articles purchased abroad and *mailed* home are subject to duty (if applicable).

—"Unsolicited gifts—value under $25": articles whose value does not exceed $25 each may be sent home as often as you wish while traveling so long as you don't send more than one such gift to the same person in the same day; be sure to mark the package, "unsolicited gift—value under $25" (a shipped item whose value *exceeds* $25 is subject to duty).

7. *I already own a Swiss watch, a Japanese camera, and Italian luggage. How can I prove to a U.S. Customs inspector that these items were purchased in the United States and not during my overseas travels?*
—You can either preregister these foreign-made items with U.S. Customs *prior* to your departure at the airport, or you can present the customs inspector with your sales receipt for the item which will serve as proof that your purchase was made in the United States.

8. *What can't I bring home under any circumstances?*
—Fresh meats, meat products, fresh fruit, plants, and seeds.
—Endangered species (such as certain skins, furs, ivory, etc).
—Obscene materials (pornographic books, films, etc.).
—Treasonous or seditious items.
—Narcotics and dangerous drugs.
—Hazardous products (firecrackers, dangerous toys, etc.).
—Certain trademarked or copyrighted items.

9. *Are customs inspectors really able to distinguish between items bought overseas and those purchased at home?*
—Chances are that they can: don't forget that, from their

training and experience, they know what items are made in which countries and how much they cost (if you spent eight hours a day rummaging through tourists' luggage, you'd have a fairly perceptive radar system, too, for distinguishing between a dress made in St. Louis and one made in Saint-Tropez).

10. What will happen to me if I lie about purchases to the customs inspector?

—If you underestimate the value of an article purchased abroad and the inspector catches you in this lie (tsk, tsk), the item could be seized and forfeited, *and* you still have to pay the duty involved.

—If you fail to declare an article acquired abroad, the item is seized and forfeited, you must pay a fine equal to the value of the item in the United States, *and* you may—in addition—be subject to criminal prosecution (aren't you crazy to take this risk?).

11. Suppose I am given gifts overseas . . . how do I declare them?

—Simple: obtain, or estimate as accurately as possible, the fair retail value of the item(s) in question in the country where they were acquired.

12. Can't I avoid paying duty by sewing an American label in my new French dress?

—Only if you and your French dress want to wind up in an American court.

13. How can I speed up my way through customs?

—Keep sales receipts (showing actual and *not* bogus amounts) for all items purchased overseas; these receipts will help you both to prepare your customs declaration and to respond to any questions raised by the inspector.

—Pack all items acquired abroad in the top layer of your luggage; better yet, carry along a duffel bag or inexpensive collapsible suitcase in which you can separately pack your purchases; these simple procedures will save you and your inspector considerable time in the line.

14. How do I register a complaint concerning my experience going through U.S. Customs?

—If your complaint deals with mishandling or even damage to your property by a Customs Inspector, pick up a form #SF9-5 at any government office and your claim for compensation will be duly processed.

—If you feel you have been harassed by a customs inspector, or if you are contending that an unfair duty has been levied against you, send full details (including photocopies of receipts) of the incident to the District Director, U.S. Customs Office, in the appropriate city listed below:

Anchorage, AL 99501
Baltimore, MD 21202
Boston, MA 02109
Bridgeport, CT 06609
Buffalo, NY 14202
Charleston, SC 24902
Chicago, IL 60607
Cleveland, OH 44114
Detroit, MI 48226
Duluth, MN 55802
El Paso, TX 79985
Galveston, TX 77550
Great Falls, MT 59401
Honolulu, HI 96806
Houston, TX 77052
Laredo, TX 78040
Los Angeles, CA (see San Pedro)
Miami, FL 33131
Milwaukee, WI 53202
Minneapolis, MN 55401
Mobile, AL 36602
New Orleans, LA 70130

*New York, NY 10048
Nogales, AZ 85621
Norfolk, VA 23510
Ogdensburg, NY 13669
Pembina, ND 58271
Philadelphia, PA 19106
Port Arthur, TX 77640
Portland, ME 04111
Portland, OR 97209
Providence, RI 02903
St. Albans, VT 05478
St. Louis, MO 63105
St. Thomas, VI 00801
San Diego, CA 92188
San Francisco, CA 94126
San Juan, PR 00903
San Pedro, CA 90731
Savannah, GA 31401
Seattle, WA 98174
Tampa, FL 33602
Washington, DC 20018
Wilmington, NC 28401

*For New York, write to Regional Commissioner of Customs.

15. Are there any places in the world where you can buy items that are not subject to any duty whatsoever?
—Sure. Thanks to a U.S. Customs program called, "Generalized System of Preferences," 2700 different items in 101 countries and 36 dependent territories have been designated as duty-free. In any of these so-called "beneficiary developing

nations," you may shop to your heart's content knowing that the items *so designated* won't cost you a cent in duty as long as you acquired the eligible article in the same beneficiary country where it was grown, manufactured, or produced.

—Among the items excluded from the 2700 in this group are most clothes, textiles, footwear, and watches—so be careful when making your selections.

—You'd be surprised, I think, to learn which nations have been given this special export privilege; among the GSP beneficiaries you'll find Mexico, Israel, Egypt, Morocco, Argentina, Brazil, Portugal, Hong Kong, and Singapore.

—Since countries and products are reviewed each year, you are well advised to ask your local Customs Office for their brochure, *GSP and the Traveler*.

GSP: BENEFICIARY COUNTRIES AND TERRITORIES

INDEPENDENT COUNTRIES

Afghanistan	Djibouti
Angola	Dominican Republic
Argentina	Egypt
Bahamas	El Salvador
Bahrain	Equatorial Guinea
Bangladesh	Ethiopia
Barbados	Fiji
Benim	Gambia
Bhutan	Ghana
Bolivia	Grenada
Botswana	Guatemala
Brazil	Guinea
Burma	Guinea-Bissau
Burundi	Guyana
Cameroon	Haiti
Cape Verde	Honduras
Central African Empire	India
Chad	Israel
Chile	Ivory Coast
Colombia	Jamaica
Comoros	Jordan
Congo	Kenya
Costa Rica	Korea, Republic of
Cyprus	Lebanon

INDEPENDENT COUNTRIES—*Continued*

Lesotho
Liberia
Malagasy Republic
Malawi
Malaysia
Maldives
Mali
Malta
Mauritania
Mauritius
Mexico
Morocco
Mozambique
Nauru
Nepal
Nicaragua
Niger
Oman
Pakistan
Panama
Papua New Guinea
Paraguay
Peru
Philippines
Portugal
Romania
Rwanda

São Tomé and Principe
Senegal
Seychelles
Sierra Leone
Singapore
Somalia
Sri Lanka
Sudan
Surinam
Swaziland
Syria
Taiwan
Tanzania
Thailand
Togo
Tonga
Trinidad and Tobago
Tunisia
Turkey
Upper Volta
Uruguay
Western Samoa
Yemen Arab Republic
Yugoslavia
Zaire
Zambia

NON-INDEPENDENT COUNTRIES AND TERRITORIES

Antigua
Belize
Bermuda
British Indian Ocean
   Territory
British Solomon Islands
Brunei
Cayman Islands
Christmas Island (Australia)
Cocos (Keeling) Islands
Cook Islands
Dominica

Falkland Islands (Islas
   Malvinas)
French Polynesia
Gibraltar
Gilbert Island
Heard Island and
   McDonald Islands
Hong Kong
Macao
Montserrat
Netherlands Antilles
New Caledonia

GSP: BENEFICIARY COUNTRIES AND TERRITORIES
NON-INDEPENDENT COUNTRIES AND TERRITORIES—*Continued*

New Hebrides Condominium
Niue
Norfolk Island
Pitcairn Islands
St. Christopher-Nevis-
    Anguilla
St. Helena
St. Lucia
St. Vincent

Tokelau Islands
Trust Territory of the
    Pacific Islands
Turks and Caicos Islands
Tuvula
Virgin Islands, British
Wallis and Futuna Islands
Western Sahara

SOME ELIGIBLE DUTY-FREE ITEMS UNDER GSP

BAMBOO, manufactures of; furniture not included

BINOCULARS, prism; opera and field glasses

CAMERAS, motion-picture and still, lenses, and other photographic equipment. (Except certain film viewers, titlers and editors from Hong Kong.)

CANDY

CHINAWARE, bone and nonbone; tableware not included

CIGARETTE LIGHTERS, pocket and table

CORK, manufactures of (except from Portugal)

EARTHEN TABLEWARE or STONEWARE, available in 77-piece sets and valued not over $12 per set (except from Romania)

FIGURINES, china

FLOWERS, artificial:
    Plastic
    Man-made fibers (except from Hong Kong)
    Feathers (except from Republic of Korea)

FURS, wearing apparel, gloves, and other manufactures
    (Except other manufactures of silver, black, or platinum fox from Argentina)

FURNITURE, wood or plastic (except folding director's chairs of wood from Korea)

GAMES, played on boards: chess, backgammon, darts, Mah-Jongg

GOLF BALLS and EQUIPMENT (except golf balls from Korea)

IVORY, beads and other manufactures of ivory (except from Hong Kong)

JADE, cut but not set for use in jewelry (except from Hong Kong); other articles of jade

JEWELRY, of precious metal or stones
  Silver, chief value, valued not over $18 per dozen
  Other (except from Hong Kong)
JEWELRY BOXES, unlined
MOTORCYCLES
MUSICAL INSTRUMENTS, pianos not included (drums from Taiwan are
  excluded)
MUSIC BOXES
PAPER, manufactures of
PEARLS, cultured or imitation, loose or temporarily strung and without
  clasp
PERFUME
PRINTED MATTER
RADIO RECEIVERS, solid state (not for motor vehicles) (except from
  Hong Kong, Taiwan, Singapore, and Republic of Korea)
RATTAN, manufactures other than furniture
RECORDS, phonograph and tapes
RUBBER, natural, manufactures of
SHAVERS, electric
SHELL, manufactures of (except from the Philippine Republic)
SILVER, tableware and flatware
SKIS and SKI EQUIPMENT, ski boots not included
STONES, cut but not set, suitable for use in jewelry (emeralds and diamonds
  not included)
  Sapphires and rubies (except from Thailand)
  Semi-precious stones
  Coral and cameos (except from Taiwan)
TAPE RECORDERS (except from Republic of Korea)
TOILET PREPARATIONS (except bay rum or bay water from Bermuda)
TOYS, dolls not included (toys, including dolls from Hong Kong and
  Taiwan, are excluded)
WIGS (except from Republic of Korea)
WOOD, carvings

*16. Is there anything else I need to know about customs
procedures and regulations?*
—The critical highlights covered here are probably enough to
keep you on the straight and narrow; in addition, you should
certainly read *Customs Hints—Know Before You Go*, a
concise, readable brochure available from the U.S. Customs
Office in your area.
   It may seem superfluous to deal in such detail with the

nuances of shopping overseas and the formalities associated with clearing customs—but I have seen deliriously happy travelers devastated when inspectors seized and confiscated tortoise handbags, canned hams, and baskets of fruit. And then, too, I imagine the disappointed reactions at home when the African dashiki is so small that it won't clear your teenager's head—yet alone drape his or her shoulders; or the look of horror on your neighbor's face when she discovers that instead of the blue shawl she hoped for, she is getting a purple caftan; or the smiling anguish of your mother-in-law as she gamely tries on one Mexican huarache while desperately clinging to her sensible oxford.

Finally, there are those travelers who indulge in a highly specialized kind of buying which results in their acquiring a "collection." A collection normally consists of lots of things that no one else wants or can make room for. In my experience, most collections are very old, comprehensive, eclectic, and dusty.

A good friend of mine, who manifests a vengeance for hoarding, collects antique inkwells. Throughout her travels, she investigates libraries, shops, antique stores, and serendipitous out-of-the-way places in hopes that she will find one more inkwell to add to her collection. Since there is no duty on antiquities, collectors of authentic vintage stuff tend to look for articles which are *at least a hundred years old*, thus officially qualifying as antiques that can be imported duty-free to the United States. If you aspire to collect ancient statuary, medieval tapestries, or Renaissance paintings, always secure certificates of antiquity and authenticity from the local authorities. And, while you're at it, be sure your documentation includes permission from the authorities to export the object in the first place. Based upon some of the antiquities I've seen, you're probably doing them a favor.

Whether you are buying a gift for yourself or for others, or if you are selecting Irish soda bread for brunch or a sapphire for a lifetime, enjoy every moment your purchase brings you... in it, you have a living diary of your trip.

10

WHAT NOT TO LET DRIVE YOU CRAZY

However systematically you organize, no matter how thorough your preparations, whatever lengths you go to in pursuit of a perfect trip—something will probably pop up and be a pain in the passport. Friends of mine who celebrate each wedding anniversary by taking a spectacular trip have lost three sets of matched luggage in ten years. (Well, at least they know what to give each other as a gift.) A fanatically well-organized professor I know has more preliminary in-depth meetings with his travel agent than he does with his doctoral candidates, and yet he returns from each trip with depositions from Bavarian hotel owners who claim they never had his room reservations. A friend of my mother's, who fancies herself a cross between Stella Dallas and Tatum O'Neal, shops all year for cruisewear and then returns from the voyage complaining that her clothes were great but her cabin wasn't. Experiences such as these, and countless others of the unexpected-frustrating-costly variety, threaten to ruin your trip and will *if you let them.*

I haven't commissioned a Harris Poll to catalog a trip's most craze-producing problems, but I have a hunch that some of the following topics are worth a sip or two of Pepto-Bismol.

OVERBOOKING: BY AIRLINES AND HOTELS

Because so many of our thoughtless fellow passengers make multiple flight reservations, or make a reservation and fail to show up for the flight, airlines are obliged to overbook or sell more seats than the airplane has. This procedure, which is perfectly legal, usually works out fine but—in some instances—potential no-shows all show up and someone has to get bumped. Even if you have a confirmed reservation for a flight and have presented yourself at the gate at the specified check-in time, you may not get on the airplane. If there are more bodies than there are seats, the airline normally will ask for volunteers to take a later flight; this failing, it will bump passengers in accordance with a priority seating plan. If you are bumped, you are entitled to "denied boarding compensation" which reimburses you with the full value of your ticket coupon up to your destination (minimum = $37.50; maximum = $200). This monetary compensation is doubled if the airline fails to get you to your destination within two hours of the originally scheduled arrival time (within four hours of scheduled arrival on international flights). And your airline ticket is returned to you from the bumped flight, of course, so that you may use it on your rescheduled, later flight. If worst comes to worst and you are bumped, denied boarding compensation reimburses and placates you for any inconvenience you may experience—an inconvenience suffered last year by 150,000 air travelers. If bumped, do not become paranoid, don't demand to see the president of the airline, and do not threaten to sue (though you may sue, of course, if you've experienced costly "damages" as a result of the delay). Take a deep breath, accept your compensation, carry your ticket and go to the gate for the next flight, and pledge that you will never make multiple reservations or become a no-show yourself.

Overbooking by hotels is a generally accepted policy designed to reduce the effect of last-minute cancelations and no-shows. Arrive at your hotel with your confirmed room reservation in hand, and be certain that specifications regarding room price (minimum, standard, deluxe, etc.), location (high floor, oceanfront, etc.), and accommodations (king-size bed, twin, etc.) are clearly indicated on the voucher. If the room is not available at the confirmed rate, you are entitled to be upgraded to a higher-priced room at no extra charge. If this option is not offered to you, drink the appropriate potion, become "The Incredible Hulk," and raise hell.

Alas, you may arrive at your hotel with a confirmed reservation only to discover that there are no rooms available at all. In this case, the manager should offer to find you equivalent accommodations nearby and to arrange for your transportation to "this lovely little place down the road." Some major hotel chains will pay for the first night's lodging at the substitute hotel while absolving you of any expense for your confirmed (but unavailable) room as well. You will want to write a testy letter to the president of the hotel or motel chain as soon as you return home; when you do so, be certain to name names and give specific details outlining your experience. If you are in doubt as to where to vent your wrath, simply go to the top.

BAD WEATHER

Let's face it, whoever wrote "Autumn in New York" was not next to me on Fifth Avenue last September when the temperature casually dipped to 8 degrees; the inspired devil who craved "April in Paris" didn't watch my new shoes get soaked on the Champs-Elysées by a storm that could have drowned Toulouse-Lautrec; and though I, too, adore "A Foggy Day in London Town," I prefer it when the fog is not joined by snowflakes the size of hockey pucks. While it is true that inclement weather can hurt a vacation, chances are it can't ruin one—unless, of course, you are going to a sun-soaked resort where the success of the trip is measured by whether or not you get second-degree burns. Limited insurance protection against inclement weather is available from travel agents and some airlines; these policies are designed to compensate the traveler for each day of promised sunshine that disintegrates into pelting rain. Obviously, such policies are usually sold in conjunction with sun resort packages since these are the destinations that suffer most when travelers begin to sing,

"Here's That Rainy Day, Again." Think seasons when you plan your trip and make every effort to go when the weather where you are going is traditionally good; beyond that, simply pack an umbrella and pray.

EMERGENCY HELP OVERSEAS

There is some confusion among travelers concerning the help they can expect to receive from United States embassies and consulates abroad. Relieved to find an official local representative—whether in Marrakesh, Madrid, or Manila—American travelers sometimes make outrageous, totally unrealistic demands of the "My taxes pay your salary so you'd better find me a hotel room, fella" variety. Our embassies and consulates abroad provide specifically defined emergency services for American travelers; you can count upon them:

—To help locate medical assistance for you, and to inform your next of kin, if you are injured or become seriously ill.

—To advise you (and protect your rights) if you become involved in a legal or police action, or if you are detained by the police or local authorities.

—To provide, in appropriate cases, a "repatriation loan" consisting of the sum of money necessary to get you *directly* home, and repayable shortly thereafter.

—To provide aid and evacuation, if necessary, during local civil unrest or in the event of a natural disaster (floods, earthquakes, etc.).

—To provide assistance in replacing a lost or stolen passport.

Our State Department representatives throughout the world are not intended to function as interpreters, concierges, travel agents, couriers, or flunkies. Be forewarned that you *cannot* depend upon an American embassy or consulate to cash personal checks, lend money, recommend specific doctors or arrange for free medical service, provide bail, organize sight-seeing trips, arbitrate in disputes with hotels and shopkeepers, receive and hold mail, or search for missing luggage. Our diplomatic representatives abroad serve to ensure the traveler's safe conduct in the host country; if you understand this role, you will call upon them only in emergency situations for which they are authorized to provide help. Don't become an "ugly American" to other Americans.

U.S. EMBASSIES AND CONSULATES ABROAD

An embassy is indicated by an asterisk (*)

Country/City	Address	Telephone
Afghanistan		
*Kabul	Wazir Akbar Khan Mina	24230-9
Algeria		
*Algiers	4 Chemin Cheikh Bachir Brahimi	601425/601255 601186/601716 601828
Argentina		
*Buenos Aires	4300 Colombia, 1425; APO Miami 34034	774-8811 774-7611 774-9911
Australia		
*Canberra	Moonah Pl. Canberra, A.C.T. 2600	(062)73-3711
Melbourne	24 Albert Rd. South Melbourne, Victoria 3205	699-2244
Perth	264 St. George's Terr.	322-4466
Sydney	T & G Tower 36th Floor, Hyde Park Square Sydney 2000, N.S.W. APO San Francisco 96209	235-7044
Brisbane	141 Queen St. Brisbane, 4000	(07) 221-1338
Austria		
*Vienna	IX Boltzmangasse 16 A-1091	(222) 346611 347511

U.S. EMBASSIES AND CONSULATES ABROAD—
Continued

Country/City	Address	Telephone
Salzburg	1 Franz Josefs Kai, Room 302	46461
Bahamas *Nassau	Mosmar Bldg. Queen St.	(809) 322-1700 322-1181
Bahrain *Manama	Shaikh Isa Rd. P.O. Box 26431 FPO NY 09526	714151
Bangladesh *Dacca	Adamjee Court Bldg., 5th Floor Montijheel	244220 through 244229
Barbados *Bridgetown	P.O. Box 302, Box B FPO Miami 34054	63574-7
Belgium *Brussels	27 Boulevard du Regent APO NY 09667	513-3830
Antwerp	64-68 Frankrijklei APO NY 09667	(031) 321800
Belize Belize City	Gabourel Lane and Hutson St.	3261
Benin *Cotonou	Rue Caporal Anani Bernard Boite Postale 2012	31-26-92/50
Bermuda Hamilton	Vallis Bldg. Front St. FPO NY 09560	295-1342

Bolivia
*La Paz

Banco Popular Del   50251
Peru Bldg.
Corner of Calles
Mercado y Colon
APO Miami 34032

Botswana
*Gaborone   P.O. Box 90   2944/7

Brazil
*Brasilia   Lote No. 3   (0612) 223-0120
Avenida das Nocoes
APO Miami 34030

Belém   Avenida Oswaldo   (0912) 223-0800
Cruz 165

Pôrto Alegre   Rua Uruguai 155,   (0512) 31-1888/
11th Floor   32-1046/32-2046
APO Miami 34030

Recife   Rua Goncalves   (0812) 221-14-12/
Maia 163   222-66-12
222-65-77

Salvador   Edificio Ferreirinha   (071) 245-6691/92
(1st Floor)
Avenida Presidente
Vargas 1892

Rio de Janeiro   Avenida Presidente   (021) 252-8055/
Wilson 147,   252-8056/252-8057
APO Miami 34030

São Paulo   Edificio Padre   (011) 64-4688
Joao Manuel   853-2011
927 Rua Padre
Joao Manuel
APO Miami 34030

Bulgaria
*Sofia   1 Stamboliiski   88-48-01 to 05
Blvd.

U.S. EMBASSIES AND CONSULATES ABROAD—
Continued

Country/City	Address	Telephone
Burma		
*Rangoon	581 Merchant St.	18055
Mandalay	71st St. & S. Moat Rd.	555
Burundi		
*Bujumbura	Chaussee Prince Louise Rwagasore Boite Postale 1720	34-54
Cameroon		
*Yaoundé	Rue Nachtigal Boite Postale 817	221633/220512
Douala	21 Avenue du Gen. de Gaulle Boite Postale 4006	423434/425331
Canada		
*Ottawa	100 Wellington St. K1P 5T1	(613) 238-5335
Calgary, Alberta	Room 1050 615 Macleod Trail S.E. Calgary Alberta, Canada T2G 4T8	(403) 266-8962
Halifax, Nova Scotia	Suite 910, Cogswell Tower, Scotia Sq. Halifax, NS, Canada B3J 3K1	(902) 429-2480-1
Montreal, Quebec	Suite 1122 South Tower Place Desjardins P.O. Box 65, Montreal H5B 1G1, Canada	(514) 281-1886
Quebec, Quebec	1 Avenue Ste-Genevieve G1R 4A7	(418) 692-2095

Toronto, Ontario	360 University Ave.	(416) 595-1700
Vancouver, British Columbia	1199 W. Hastings St. V6E 2Y4	(604) 685-4311
Winnipeg, Manitoba	6 Donald St. R3L OK7	(204) 475-3344/8 284-3039
Cape Verde, Republic of *Praia	Rua Hoji Ya Yendi 81	553
Central African Empire *Bangui	Avenue du 1er Janvier, 1966 B.P. 924	610-200 610-205
Ceylon (see Sri Lanka)		
Chad *Ndjamena	Rue du Lt. Col. Colonna D'Oranano B.P. 413	30-91/2/3/4
Chile *Santiago	Codina Bldg. 1343 Agustinas	710133/90 710326/75
China, People's Republic of *Peking (Beijing)	Guang Hua Lu Department of State Washington, DC 20520	522-033
Colombia *Bogotá	Calle 37, 8-40 APO Miami 34038	285-1300
Barranquilla	Edificio Seguros Tequendama Calle 34, No. 44-63, 10th Floor Apartado Aereo 2306 APO Miami 34038	56599

U.S. EMBASSIES AND CONSULATES ABROAD—
Continued

Country/City	Address	Telephone
Cali	Edificio Pielroja Carrera 3, No. 11-55 APO Miami 34038	88-11-36/7
Medellín	Edificio Santa Helena Calle 52, No. 49-27 Mailing Address: Apartado Aereo 980	313-188
People's Republic of the Congo *Brazzaville	B.P. 1015	
Democratic Republic of the Congo (See Zaire)		
Costa Rica *San José	Avenida 3 and Calle 1 APO Miami 34020	22-55-66
Cuba Havana	c/o Swiss Embassy	320551
Cyprus *Nicosia	Therissos St. and Dositheos St. FPO NY 09530	65151/5
Czechoslovakia *Prague	Trziste 15-12548 Praha Amembassy, Prague, c/o Amcongen APO NY 09757	53 66 41/8
Dahomey (See Benin)		

Denmark
*Copenhagen

Dag Hammarskjöld
Alle 24
APO NY 09170

(01) 42 31 44

Republic
of Djibouti
*Djibouti

Villa Plateau du
Serpent Blvd.
Marechal Joffre
Boite Postale 185

35-38-49
35-39-95

Dominican
Republic
*Santo Domingo

Corner of Calle
Cesar Nicolas
Penson & Calle
Leopoldo Navarro
APO Miami 34041

682-2171

Ecuador
*Quito

120 Avenida Patria

584-000

Guayaquil

9 de Octubre y Garcia
Moreno

511570

Egypt, Arab Republic
of
*Cairo

5 Sharia Latin
America, Box 10
FPO NY 09527

28211/9

Alexandria

110 Avenue Horreya

801911, 25607,
28458

Port Said

Apt. 4, 8 Sharia
Aby El Feda
Metarch El Baher

8000, 8586, 8622

El Salvador
*San Salvador

1230, 25 Avenida
Norte
APO Miami 34023

26-7100

Equatorial
Guinea
*Malabo
(Embassy closed)

U.S. EMBASSIES AND CONSULATES ABROAD—
Continued

Country/City	Address	Telephone
Ethiopia		
*Addis Ababa	Entoto St. P.O. Box 1014 APO NY 09319	110666
Fiji		
*Suva	31 Loftus St. P.O. Box 218	23031
Finland		
*Helsinki	Itainen Puistotie 14A APO NY 09664	171931
France		
*Paris	2 Avenue Gabriel 75382 Paris Cedex 08 APO NY 09777	296-1202 261-8075
Bordeaux	No. 4 Rue Esprit des Lois	56/52-65-95
Lyon	7 Quai Général Sarrail 69454 Lyon Cedex 3	24-68-49
Marseille	No. 9 Rue Armeny 13006	54-92-00
Nice	No. 3 Rue Dr. Barety	88-89-55
Strasbourg	15 Avenue d'Alsace 67082 Strasbourg Cedex or APO NY 09777	(88) 35-31-04, 05, 06

*French West
Indies*
Martinique

14 Rue Blenac, Boite   71.93.01, 71.93.03
Postale 561
Fort de France 97206

Gabon
*Libreville

Boulevard de la Mer   72-20-03/04
Boite Postale 4000   72-13-37, 72-13-48

Gambia, The
*Banjul

16 Buckle St.   526-7
P.O. Box 596

*Federal
Republic
of Germany*
*Bonn

Deichmannsaue,   (02221) 89 55
  5300, Bonn
APO NY 09080

Berlin

Clayallee 170   (030) 832 40 87
D-1000 Berlin 33
(Dahlem) APO
NY 09742

Bremen

President-Kennedy-   (0421) 32 00 01
  Platz 1
2800 Bremen 1, Box 1
APO NY 09069

Düsseldorf

Cecilienallee 5   (0211) 49 00 81
4000 Düsseldorf 30
Box 515
APO NY 09080

Frankfurt am
  Main
Hamburg

Siesmayerstrasse 21   (0611) 74 0071
APO NY 09757
Alsterufer 27/28   (040) 44 10 61
2000 Hamburg 36
Box 2, APO NY 09069

U.S. EMBASSIES AND CONSULATES ABROAD—
Continued

Country/City	Address	Telephone
Munich	Koeniginstrasse 5 8000 München 22 APO NY 09108	(089) 2 30 11
Stuttgart	Urbanstrasse 7 7000 Stuttgart APO NY 09154	(0711) 21 02 21
German Democratic Republic *Berlin	108 Berlin Neustaedtische Kirchstrasse 4-5	2202741
Ghana *Accra	Liberia & Kinbu Rds. P.O. Box 194	66811
Greece *Athens	91Vasilissis Sophias Blvd. or APO NY 09253	712951 or 718401
Thessaloniki	59 Vasileos Constantinou St. APO NY 09693	273-941
Guatemala *Guatemala City	7-01 Avenida de la Reforma, Zone 10 APO Miami 34024	31-15-41
Guinea *Conakry	Second Blvd. and Ninth Ave. Boite Postale 603	415-20 through 24
Guinea-Bissau *Bissau	Avenida Domingos Ramos, C.P. 297	28-16/7
Guyana *Georgetown	31 Main St.	62687, Ext. 26

Haiti
*Port-au-Prince   Harry Truman Blvd.   20200

Honduras
*Tegucigalpa   Avenida La Paz   22-3121/22/23/24/27
                       APO Miami 34022
Hong Kong
Hong Kong   26 Garden Rd.   239011
                       FPO San Francisco
                       96659
Hungary
*Budapest   V. Szabadsag Ter 12   329-375
                       Am Embassy
                       APO NY 09757
Iceland
*Reykjavik   Laufasvegur 21   29100
                       FPO NY 09571
India
*New Delhi   Shanti Path   690351
                       Chanakyapuri 21

Bombay   Lincoln House   363611-363618
                       78 Bhulabhai Desai Rd.

Calcutta   5/1 Ho Chi Minh   44-3611/44-3616
                         Sarani
                       Calcutta 700071

Madras   Mount Rd.-6   83041

Indonesia
*Jakarta   Medan Merdeka   340001-9
                         Selatan 5
                       APO San Francisco
                       96356

Medan   Djalan Imam Bondjol   322200
                         13

Surabaya   Jalan Raya Dr.   67545
                       Sutomo 33
Iran
*Tehran
(Embassy Closed)

U.S. EMBASSIES AND CONSULATES ABROAD—
Continued

Country/City	Address	Telephone
Iraq *Baghdad (Embassy Closed)		
Ireland *Dublin	42 Elgin Rd. Ballsbridge	Dublin 688777
Israel *Tel Aviv Jerusalem	71 Hayarkon St. 18 Agron Rd. Nablus Rd.	54338 226312 282231/272681 (both offices via Israel)
Italy *Rome	Via V. Veneto 119/A 00187-Rome APO NY 09794	(06) 4674
Florence	Lungarmo Amerigo Vespucci 38 APO NY 09019	(055) 298-276
Genoa	Banca d'America e d'Italia Bldg. Piazza Portello 6 Box G APO NY 09794	(010) 282-741 through 282-745
Milan	Piazza della Republica 32 APO NY 09689	(02) 652-841/5
Naples	Piazza della Republica 80122 Naples, Box 18 FPO NY 09521	(081) 660966
Palermo	Via Vaccarini 1 90143 APO NY 09794 (c/o Am Embassy Rome-P)	291532-35

Trieste	Via Valdirivo 19, 4th Floor APO NY 09293	(040) 68728/29
Turin	Via Alfieri 17 10121 Torino Box T APO NY 09794	(011) 543-600, 543-610, 513-367
Ivory Coast		
*Abidjan	5, Rue Jesse Owens Boite Postale 1712	32-09-79
Jamaica		
*Kingston	Jamaica Mutual Life Center 2 Oxford Rd., 3rd Floor	(809) 929-4850
Japan		
*Tokyo	10-1, Akasaka 1-chome Minato-Ku APO San Francisco 96503	583-7141
Fukuoka	5-26 Ohori 2-chome Chuo-ku, Fukuoka 810, or Box 10, FPO Seattle 98766	(092) 751-9331/4
Naha, Okinawa	No. 2129, Gusukuma Urasoe City APO San Francisco 96248	0988-77-8142 0988-77-8627
Osaka-Kobe	Sankei Bldg., 9th Floor 4-9, Umeda-chome, Kita Ku, Osaka (503) APO San Francisco 96503	(06) 341-2754/7

U.S. EMBASSIES AND CONSULATES ABROAD—
Continued

Country/City	Address	Telephone
Sapporo	Kita 1-Jyo Nishi 28-Chome, Chuo-Ku APO San Francisco 96821	(011) 641-1115/7
Jordan		
*Amman	Jebel Amman P.O. Box 354	44371-6 38930/38724
Kenya		
*Nairobi	Cotts House Wabera St. P.O. Box 30137	334141
Korea		
*Seoul	Sejong-Ro APO San Francisco 96301	72-2601 through 72-2619
Kuwait		
*Kuwait	P.O. Box 77 SAFAT	424-151
Laos		
*Vientiane	Rue Bartholonie Boite Postale 114 Box V, APO San Francisco 96346	3126, 3570
Lebanon		
*Beirut	Corniche at Rue Ain Mreisseh	361-964/800
Lesotho		
*Maseru	P.O. Box MS 333 Maseru 100	22666/7
Liberia		
*Monrovia	111 United Nations Dr. APO NY 09155	22991, 22992-3-4
Libya		
*Tripoli	Shari Mohammad Thabit P.O. Box 289	34021/6

Luxembourg
| *Luxembourg | 22 Boulevard Emmanuel Servais APO NY 09132 | 40123-4-5-6-7 |

Madagascar
| *Antananarivo | 14 and 16 rue Rainitovo Antsohavola Boite Postale 620 | 212-57 |

Malawi
| *Lilongwe | P.O. Box 30016 | 30396/30166 |

Malaysia
| *Kuala Lumpur | A.I.A. Bldg. Jalan Ampang P.O. Box No. 35 | 26321 |

Mali
| *Bamako | Rue Testard and Rue Mohamed V | 224835, 225834 |

Malta
| *Valletta | Development House, 2nd Floor St. Anne St. Floriana, Malta APO NY 09535 | 623653, 620424, 623216 |

Mauritania
| *Nouakchott | Boite Postale 222 | 52660/52663 |

Mauritius
| *Port Louis | Anglo-Mauritius House, 6th Floor Intendance St. | 2-3218/9 |

Mexico
| *Mexico City | Paseo de la Reforma 305 Mexico 5, D.F. | (905) 553-3333 |

| Cuidad Juárez | 2286 Avenida 16 de Septiembre | 34048 |

U.S. EMBASSIES AND CONSULATES ABROAD— Continued

Country/City	Address	Telephone
Guadalajara	Progreso 175	25-29-98, 25-27-00
Hermosillo	Isseteson Bldg., 3rd Floor Miguel Hidalgo y Costilla No. 15	3-89-22/23/24/25
Matamoros	Avenida Primera No. 232	2-52-50/1/2
Mazatlán	6 Circunvalacion No. 6 (at Venustiana Carranza)	1-26-85, 1-26-87
Mérida	Paseo Montejo 453, Apartado Postal 1301	2-70-11, 2-70-78
Monterey	Avenida Constitucion 411 Poniente	4306 50/59
Nuevo Laredo	Avenida Allende 3330, Col. Jardin	2-00-05
Tijuana	Tapachula 96	6-1001
Morocco *Rabat	2 Avenue de Marrakech Box 99, FPO NY 09544	30361, 30362
Casablanca	8 Boulevard Moulay Youssef or Box 80, FPO 09544	22-41-49
Tangier	Chemin des Amoureux	(09) 359-04

Mozambique		
*Maputo	35 Rua Da Mesquita, 3rd Floor	26051, 2, 3
Nepal		
*Kathmandu	Pani Pokhari	11199, 12718, 11603, 11604
Netherlands		
*The Hague	102 Lange Voorhout APO NY 09159	(070) 62-49-11
Amsterdam	Museumplein 19 APO NY 09159	(020) 790321
Rotterdam	Vilasmarkt 1 APO NY 09159	(010) 11.75.60
Netherlands Antilles		
Curaçao	St. Anna Blvd. 19 P.O. Box 158 Willemstad	13066
New Zealand		
*Wellington	29 Fitzherbert Terrace, Thorndon P.O. Box 1190	722-068
Auckland	Old Northern Society Bldg., 5th Floor Queen & Wellesley Sts. or P.O. Box 7140 Wellesley St. P.O.	375-102, 30-992
Nicaragua		
*Managua	Km. 4½ Carretera Sur. APO Miami 34021	23061-8, 23881-7
Niger		
*Niamey	Boite Postale 201	72-26-61/62/63/64, 72-26-70
Nigeria		
*Lagos	15 Eleke Crescent P.O. Box 554	610097
Kaduna	5 Ahmadu Bello Way	213020

U.S. EMBASSIES AND CONSULATES ABROAD—
Continued

Country/City	Address	Telephone

Norway
*Oslo   Drammensveien 18   56-68-80
                 Oslo 1
                 or
                 APO NY 09085

Oman
*Muscat   P.O. Box 966   722021

Pakistan
*Islamabad   Diplomatic Enclave   26161-26179
                 Ramna 4

Karachi   8 Abdullah Haroon   515081
                 Rd.

Lahore   50 Zafar Ali Rd.   870221/5
                 Gulberg 5

Peshawar   11 Hospital Rd.   73061/73405

Panama
*Panama City   Avenida Balboa y   25-3600
                 Calle 38
                 Apartado 6959, R.P. 5

Papua
New Guinea
*Port Moresby   Armit St.   211455, 211594,
                 P.O. Box 3492   211654

Paraguay
*Asunción   1776 Mariscal Lopez   201-040
                 Ave.
                 APO Miami 34036

Peru
*Lima   Corner Avenidas Inca 286000
                 Garcilaso de la
                 Vega & Espana
                 P.O. Box 1995

Philippines *Manila	1201 Roxas Blvd. APO San Francisco 96528	598-011
Cebu	Philippine American Life Insurance Bldg., 3rd Floor Jones Ave., APO San Francisco 96528	7-95-10/24
Poland *Warsaw	Aleje Ujazdowskie 29/31 American Embassy Warsaw, c/o AmConGen APO NY 09757	283041-9
Crakow	Ulica Stolarska 9 31043 Crakow or AmConsul Crakow c/o AmConGen APO NY 09757	29764, 21400
Poznan	Ulica Chopina 4 or c/o AmConGen APO NY 09757	595-86, 598-74
Portugal *Lisbon	Avenida Duque de Loule No. 39 APO NY 09678	570102
Oporto	Apartado No. 88 Rua Julio Dinis 826-30	6-3094, 6-3095, 6-3096
Ponta Delgada, São Miguel, Azores	Avenida D. Henrique APO NY 09406	22216, 22217
Qatar *Doha	Farig Bin Omran P.O. Box 2399	87701, 87702, 87703

U.S. EMBASSIES AND CONSULATES ABROAD—
Continued

Country/City	Address	Telephone
Romania *Bucharest	Strada Tudor Arghezi 7-9 or AmConGen (Buch), APO NY 09757	12-40-40
Rwanda *Kigali	Blvd. de la Revolution B.P. 28	5601
Saudi Arabia *Jidda	Palestine Rd. Ruwais, APO NY 09697	670080
Dhahran	Between Aramco HQ and Dhahran International Airport P.O. Box 81 or APO NY 09616	43200, 43452 43613
Senegal *Dakar	Boite Postale 49 Avenue Jean XXIII	21-41-96
Seychelles *Victoria	Box 148 APO NY 09030	23921/2
Sierra Leone *Freetown	Corner Walpole and Siaka Stevens Sts.	26481
Singapore *Singapore	30 Hill St. FPO San Francisco 96699	30251
Somalia *Mogadishu	Corso Primo Luglio	28011

South Africa
*Pretoria   Thibault House   48-4266
                            225 Pretorius St.

Cape Town   Broadway Industries   021-471280
                              Center
                            Heerengracht
                            Foreshore

Durban   Durban Bay House   324-737
                            333 Smith St., 29th Floor
                            Durban 4001

Johannesburg   Kine Ctr., 11th Floor   (011) 21-1684/7
                            Commissioner and
                              Kruis Sts.
                            P.O. Box 2155

Spain
*Madrid   Serrano 75   276-3400, 276-3600
                            APO NY 09285

Barcelona   Via Layetana 33   319-9550
                            APO NY 09285

Bilbao   Avenida del   435-8308, 9
                              Ejercito, 11-3d
                              Floor
                            Deusto-Bilbao L2
                            APO NY 09285

Seville   Paseo de las   23-18-85
                              Delicias No. 7
                            APO NY 09285

Sri Lanka
*Colombo   44 Galle Rd.   26211 through
                            Colombo 3   26218
                            P.O. Box 106

Sudan
*Khartoum   Gamhouria Ave.   74611 and
                            P.O. Box 699   74700

Surinam
*Paramaribo   Dr. Sophie   73024, 75620
                              Redmondstraat
                            P.O. Box 1821

U.S. EMBASSIES AND CONSULATES ABROAD— *Continued*

Country/City	Address	Telephone
Swaziland		
*Mbabane	Embassy House P.O. Box 199 Allister Miller St.	2272-3-4
Sweden		
*Stockholm	Strandvagen 101	(08) 63-05-20
Göteborg	Sodra Hamngatan 53 Box 428	(031) 80-38-60
Switzerland		
*Bern	Jubilaeumstrasse 93 3005 Bern	(031) 437011
Zurich	Zollikerstrasse 141	(01) 55-25-66
Geneva	80 Rue du Lausanne	(022) 32-70-20
Syria		
*Damascus	Abu Rumaneh Al Monsur St. No. 2 P.O. Box 29	332315, 332814
Taiwan		
*Taipei (Embassy Closed)		
Tanzania		
*Dar es Salaam	National Bank of Commerce Bldg., City Dr. P.O. Box 9123	22775
Zanzibar	83A Tuzungumzeni Sq. P.O. Box 4	2118, 2119

Thailand

*Bangkok	95 Wireless Rd. APO San Francisco 96346	252-5040
	Com. Off.: "R" Floor Shell Bldg. 140 Wireless Rd.	251-9160
Chiang Mai	Vidhayanond Rd. APO San Francisco 96272	234566-7
Songkhla	9 Sadao Rd.	311-589
Udorn	35/6 Supakitjanya Rd.	221548

Togo

*Lomé	Rue Pelletier Caventou & Rue Vouban Boite Postale 852	29-91

Trinidad and Tobago

*Port of Spain	15, Queen's Park W. P.O. Box 752	62-26371

Tunisia

*Tunis	144 Avenue de al Liberte	282.566

Turkey

*Ankara	110 Ataturk Blvd. APO NY 09254	26 54 70
Adana	Ataturk Caddesi	14702/3, 14818
Istanbul	104 Mesrutiyet Caddesi Tepebasi	43-62-00/09
Izmir	386 Ataturk Caddesi APO NY 09224	132135/7

Uganda

*Kampala	P.O. Box 7007 Embassy House 9-11 Parliament Ave.	54451

U.S. EMBASSIES AND CONSULATES ABROAD— *Continued*

Country/City	Address	Telephone
Union of Soviet Socialist Republics		
*Moscow	Ulitsa Chaykovskogo 19/21/23 or APO NY 09862	252-00-11/19
	Com. Off.: Ulitsa Chaykovskogo, 15	255-48-48/255-46-60
Leningrad	Ul. Petra Lavrova 15, Box L APO NY 09664	274-8235
United Arab Emirates		
*Abu Dhabi	Shaikh Khalid Bldg. Corniche Rd. P.O. Box 4009	61534/35
Dubai	Al Futtaim Bldg. Creek Rd., Deira P.O. Box 5343	29003
United Kingdom		
*London, England	24/31 Grosvenor Sq. W. 1A 1AE or Box 40, FPO NY 09510	(01) 499-9000
Belfast, Northern Ireland	Queen's House 14 Queen St., BT1, 6EQ	(0232) 28239
Edinburgh, Scotland	3 Regent Terr. EH7 5BW	031-556-8315
Upper Volta		
*Ouagadougou	Boite Postale 35	35442/4/6
Uruguay		
*Montevideo	Calle Lauro Muller 1776 APO Miami 34035	40-90-51, 40-91-26

Venezuela		
*Caracas	Avenida Francisco de Miranda and Avenida Principal de la Floresta APO Miami 34037	284-7111
Maracaibo	Edificio Matema, 1 Piso, Avenida 15 Calle 78 or APO Miami 34037	(061) 51-65-06/7
Yemen Arab Republic		
*San'a	Box 33 FPO NY 09545	2790, 5826
Yugoslavia		
*Belgrade	Kneza Milosa 50	645655
Zagreb	Brace Kavurica 2	444-800
Zaire		
*Kinshasa	310 Avenue des Aviateurs APO NY 09662	25881-2-3-4-5-6
Bukavu	Mobutu Ave. Boite Postale 3037 APO NY 09662	2594
Lubumbashi	1029 Boulevard Kamanyola Boite Postale 1196 APO NY 09662	2324, 2325
Zambia		
*Lusaka	P.O. Box 1617	50222

TIPPING

Some time ago, my English host took four of us to dinner at a
much heralded, multistarred restaurant in London. The setting
was elegant, the food was a symphony of taste treats, and the

service was a scene from *I Love Lucy*. Apparently unprepared for the tourist boom in business, the restaurant's attention to service deteriorated at the same speed as our patience. Our normally unflappable English host flapped plenty about the constant reminders to serve more wine, the failure to clear used plates, and the need to ask for certain utensils in order to eat. As we got ready to leave, our host signed the bill and left just a few coins for the surly waiter. The waiter, outrage duly noted, asked if that was to be his entire tip. "No," my host said, "my real tip is that you should stop being a waiter." So much for vocational guidance in England.

This was admittedly an extreme situation, though there are many instances in which a restaurant or hotel permits shoddy service and a customer tolerates it. I subscribe to the theory that—local customs notwithstanding—the amount of the tip should be in direct proportion to the quality of the service. Presuming I have received at least satisfactory service, I usually apply the same standard for tipping abroad as I do at home, to wit:

Waiter—15%
Sommelier (or wine steward)—10% of wine bill
Bartender—10% to 15%
Porter—.50¢ to $1 per bag (depending upon distance carried)
Concierge—$1 per significant service rendered (i.e., arranging for a car, confirming airline tickets, etc.) or $10 per week whichever is less
Maid—.50¢ to $1 for each day of stay (tip dependent upon special services, i.e., turning down bed, extra towels and soap, etc.)
Barber or beautician—10%
Taxi driver—10% to 15%

There is a tendency for travelers to overtip because of our lack of understanding as to the actual value of foreign bills and coins (once, confused by lire in Rome, I tipped a taxi driver $4 on a $3 fare). Since local customs, foreign currencies, and our own embarrassment conspire to confuse the tipping situation, at least be guided by several suggestions:

1. Always ask the waiter or maître d' if a service charge is included. If such a charge has already been added to your restaurant bill and if service has been satisfactory or better, you need only leave a few additional coins to convey your pleasure.

2. Tipping is an expression of satisfaction with service; as such, your generosity (or lack of it) should reflect the extent to which you were pleased by the service you received. Do not leave a 15 percent tip to a lousy waiter and the same percentage for service which has been truly exceptional. And, although the size of your bill may be smaller at lunch than it is at dinner, the same tipping percentages apply to both meals.

3. When traveling overseas, it is usually preferable for you to give tips in the local currency. This practice will be appreciated by the locals who frequently have a difficult time converting foreign currencies; as a matter of fact, some governments actually forbid their citizens to engage in foreign currency exchange.

4. Believe it or not, there are actually some places in the world (Fiji, Tahiti, Japan, and some Communist countries to name a few) where tipping is not expected. Yet.

5. Various service personnel—by virtue of their employment contract, governmental affiliation, or tradition—do not accept gratuities. As a rule, you should never tip airline personnel (in-flight or on the ground), ships' captains and pursers, customs inspectors, immigration officials, and policemen.

It is absolutely unnecessary for you to become intimidated by, or self-conscious about, tipping. Local tipping expectations, coupled with your own common sense, will provide valuable guidance for each occasion when you need to grease palms. To determine just how much local service personnel will expect from you, your best bet is to consult the appropriate regional travel guide, airline destination brochures (for the countries you plan to visit), or your travel agent. Though there is no universally prescribed (yet alone accepted) tipping formula to simplify how much you tip whom and where, the following chart is about as practical as anything you are likely to find.

WHAT TO TIP WHOM, WHERE*

	Waiters	Chambermaids	Bellhops and Baggage Porters
AUSTRIA	5% over usual service charge	5 shillings a day	5 schillings
EGYPT	10% over the 10% service charge	25 piastres a day	25 piastres
FRANCE	12% to 15% service charge usually included on check	10 francs for stay of more than week or for special service	3 to 5 francs for a load of luggage; 2 francs per bag or service
WEST GERMANY	5% of check over usual service charge	1 mark for 1 night's stay; 5 marks a week	1 mark per bag or service
GREAT BRITAIN	10% to 15% of check	10 pence a day or 40 to 50 pence a week	20 pence per bag
GREECE	15% service charge included on check; leave 5% to 10% more	100 drachmas a week	10 drachmas per bag
ISRAEL	10% over the 10% service charge	50 to 75 pounds a week	5 to 10 pounds per bag
ITALY	10% of check over service charge	300 lire a day or 1500 lire a week	200 lire per bag or service
PORTUGAL	10% to 15% service charge included on check; leave 5% more	100 escudos a week	10 escudos per bag
SPAIN	25 pesetas minimum over 15% service charge; 5% to 10% over check	25 pesetas a day or 100 pesetas a week	25 pesetas per bag or a service in room; 10 pesetas to bellhops
UNITED STATES	15% to 20% of the check	Up to $5 per week based on service received	50¢ per bag (more for heavy items)

*This information is taken from TWA's *Tipping in Europe, the Middle East, and the United States*, an excellent brochure available from that airline.

Doorman	Concierge	Taxicab Driver	Airport and Station Porter
5 schillings	20 schillings for a special service	10% of the meter	Fixed rate of 5 schillings
10 piastres	50 piastres for a special service	10% of the meter	10 piastres per bag but not less than 25 piastres
2 francs for calling a cab	2 francs a service 10 francs a week, even if no services are performed	10% to 15% of the meter	2 francs per bag at airport or railroad station
1 mark for calling a cab	1 to 2 marks for a special service	10% of the meter	Fixed rates
20 pence for calling a cab	50 pence for a special service	10p on fares up to 50p; 15p on fares up to 75p; 10% to 15% if higher	20 pence per bag
drachmas for calling a cab	30 to 50 drachmas for a special service	10% of the fare	10 drachmas per bag
0 pounds for special service	15 pounds for a special service	10% to 15% of the charge	5 pounds per bag
) to 200 lire for calling a cab	15% of his bill for cables, phone calls, etc.	15% of the meter. 150 lire minimum	200 lire per bag
0 escudos for calling a cab	20 escudos a service	15% of the price registered	10 escudos per bag
to 25 pesetas for calling a cab	No tip if not much service; 50 pesetas a day or more for service	5 pesetas if fare is under 50 pesetas 10% if higher	25 pesetas per bag
25¢ to $1 for calling a cab	$1 to $5 to bell captain, only for special assistance	15% of the meter, plus tolls when applicable	50¢ per bag

WHAT TO TIP WHOM, WHERE—*Continued*

	Ladies' Room Attendant	Hairdresser	Theater Usher
AUSTRIA	1 to 2 schillings	10% of the bill	Nothing
EGYPT	10 piastres	100 piastres	25 piastres
FRANCE	1 franc	15% to 20% usually included in bill. 5F to 10F for hairdresser; 2F to 5F for shampoo girl and manicurist	2F if alone. 1F per person for a group at cinema 2F per person at a play or concert
WEST GERMANY	50 pfennigs	2 marks	Nothing
GREAT BRITAIN	10 pence	20% of the bill	Nothing
GREECE	5 to 10 drachmas	50 drachmas	10 drachmas
ISRAEL	Nothing	15% of the bill	Nothing
ITALY	50 to 100 lire	10% of the bill	200 lire
PORTUGAL	5 escudos	10 escudos	5 escudos
SPAIN	10 pesetas	25 pesetas or 10% of the bill	10 pesetas per person (bullfights, football) matches, etc.)
UNITED STATES	25 cents	15% of the bill	Nothing

PROTECTING VALUABLES: THE MATTER OF SECURITY

Wherever you go in your travels, chances are some items of value are making the trip with you. Even if your cash, traveler's checks, clothing, luggage, and jewelry are protected against loss, there are a number of simple precautions that may help ensure that you will never use your insurance.

To me, it is simply foolhardy to travel with lots of cash or good jewelry, either of which is virtually impossible to retrieve if lost or stolen. Thus forewarned, you should know that hotel thefts are common throughout the world without apparent regard for the quality of the establishment or security systems in effect. Chances are your hotel stay will be more secure if you:

1. Place all valuables in a hotel safe-deposit box (this is the place for your jewelry, *not* the top of the night table).

2. Don't flash bills and credit cards in such public places as the hotel's lobby and restaurants.

3. Watch your luggage as it sits on curbsides or in the hotel lobby as you await check-in.

4. Place the Please Make Up Room sign on your door as you leave for breakfast; after breakfast, return to your room and place the Do Not Disturb sign on your door (this practice should dramatically reduce the flow of any traffic in and out of your room while you're away).

5. Use the dead-bolt lock on your hotel room door, *especially when you're asleep.*

6. Consider buying a "safe hanger" which looks like a large clothes hanger but contains a compartment, secured with a combination lock, in which you can store valuables (once you hang a coat or dress over the safe hanger, it looks like any other hanger in your closet).

7. Buy a money belt or bra cache in which to conceal cash or valuables you wish to carry on your person.

8. Buy a safety travel lock which can be affixed to your hotel room door when you go to sleep; such locks probably provide better protection on doors than on dresser drawers

where their very presence is likely to call attention to the valuables you wish to hide.

9. Keep your hotel key with you at all times. No matter what the management says, this practice will reduce the likelihood that your key will fall into the wrong hands while you're out.

If you are traveling to your destination by car, it's equally important that you take certain measures which will protect the clothes and valuables riding along with you. If an empty car is enticing to a burglar, a packed one is downright irresistible.

1. Install an alarm system in your car (keep in mind that 72 percent of all car thieves are under twenty-one years old; the alarm itself should prove sufficiently discouraging).

2. Lock the luggage in your car trunk (not in the more visible back seat); better yet, take the luggage with you.

3. Lock the doors of your car and take the keys with you.

4. Keep your car key on a separate chain (handing over *all* your keys to an especially crafty parking or hotel attendant can be very dangerous).

5. Park close to well-lit areas (this precaution will not only dissuade burglars on the prowl for your car and its contents, it might also prove safer for *you*).

Most trips have their full share of hectic scheduling and continuous moving about, and it is precisely these elements which combine to make us more negligent about our possessions. Secure the necessary insurance, use common sense precautions, and enjoy your possessions during the trip since it is far more likely you will still own them when it is over.

EXHAUSTING ITINERARIES

Chances are that your body needs this vacation as much as your mind does; you do both a serious disservice if you fail to pay attention to aching arches, throbbing migraines, and a generalized feeling of fatigue. You can anticipate such symptoms if you plan a trip that has you racing from city to city without the requisite time for rest and rehabilitation. Ask yourself how much you can see and do in a given period of time without destroying your endurance and your body's resistance to illness. If you are feeling tired and weak, indulge yourself and spend a spontaneously relaxing day seeing less and—because you are feeling better—enjoying it more. If you are weary, skip the city tour early in the morning and do it on your own that afternoon; forget the 7:00 A.M. wake-up, and luxuriate instead with a late breakfast on the hotel's stunning patio.

Sometimes we allow our packed itineraries to dictate to us instead of vice versa, and this tendency to become a schedule's slave can easily produce exhaustion, resentment, irritability, and even rage. Make adjustments to your itinerary en route if necessary in order to see and do everything you'd like, while feeling fine doing it. Even the hypnotizing tranquillity of a cruise ship can generate a peculiar kind of exhaustion if, for instance, most of your days consist of sight-seeing onshore as opposed to cruising at sea. With the guidance of your travel agent, maintain a reasonable ratio of days to race and days to rest.

OVERWEIGHT LUGGAGE

Because it is the universal bane of travelers, the problem of overweight luggage deserves this additional caution: take only what you can comfortably carry yourself. I have seen panting husbands flirt with coronaries as they valiantly struggle with bulging garment bags. Airports are packed with holiday travelers stranded in the baggage claim area waiting expectantly for the appearance of a porter who does not appear. And who among us has missed the experience of checking into a foreign hotel after midnight, only to discover that the bellhops were no longer on duty?

The yawning monstrosity being juggled precariously under your aching arm is probably unnecessary (who needs all those clothes?), and it is potentially expensive as well. If your suitcase is packed to the brim, you will have to ship all acquired purchases home (expense #1), and there is the strong likelihood that you are courting overweight payments to those foreign airlines which still levy such surcharges (expense #2). Pack only what you need, leave room for what you might buy, and take only what you can carry.

FOREIGN LANGUAGES

To avoid a feeling of total helplessness (known to give way to paranoia) that comes from being surrounded by a language you cannot understand, arm yourself with a few basic phrases in the native tongue of each country you plan to visit. You'll be surprised at how much can be communicated if you have grasped the traveler's basic vocabulary of a foreign language; occasionally, you may even be delighted with the personal experiences that such an effort can produce. You learn nothing by bursting into a shop and asking, "Does anyone here speak English?", or flashing fingers in a merchant's face instead of asking the price in the native language, or insisting upon starting each day in the hotel dining room with "good morning" rather than the appropriate "bonjour" or "buenos dias."

Linguists estimate that it takes two hundred hours to learn to speak a language at good conversational level. Since few of us would be willing to make that commitment in time or money (at about $9 an hour), it is reassuring to discover that there are an endless variety of minicourses offered by many language schools. These courses, normally involving study with audio-lingual tapes and an instructor, are taught either on a one-to-one basis or in small groups. At an approximate cost of $300 to $500 (or $7 to $15 per hour of instruction), these courses teach basic mechanics and usage. For the traveler, grasp of a foreign language could make the difference between simply seeing a country and truly experiencing it.

In dealing with foreign languages, you also have the option of buying and using one of the new language translators manufactured by Craig or Lexicon. These clever little computerized gadgets, which are the size of a paperback, come equipped with memory cassettes which store 1500 words in each language (French, German, Spanish, Italian, etc.). For a mere $200 or so (plus the cost of the respective language cassettes), you get to type in "the check, please," access the Spanish key, and watch in wonder as "la cuenta, por favor" flashes on the translator's "screen." If you think you'll be incredulous, wait till you see your waiter's face in Madrid.

Finally, it is worth noting the availability of numerous pocket handbooks of handy foreign phrases ($1.95 to $4.95). In selecting such a companion for your trip, scan the book first to be sure it provides typical phrases which you will need in shops, restaurants, airports, hotels, and in your travels around the country. Some phrase books are difficult to use or, worse, badly outdated. As evidence to support this claim, I need only mention a French-language phrase book which recently presumed to teach me to say, "My harlot desires an apricot." Whose doesn't?

GUILT

Nothing has greater potential for making you crazy on a trip than the peculiar collection of anxieties which produce guilt. Why am I here when there is so much work to do at the office? How am I going to make up the money I'm losing by taking this vacation? How can I be away when the kids are in school? And for many of us, the guilt which makes us most unhappy is the one that hammers away at the theme that we don't deserve to be this happy at all. Sun-drenched beaches, snow-banked mountains, and fish-filled lakes can be reduced to cardboard cutouts if somehow you feel you don't deserve them. Go on the trip with a *positive* feeling and a genuine appreciation of your *right to enjoy*.

I'm sure there are many other misbegotten causes which conspire to make us crazy on trips, but I've provided these few in case you have none of your own. As for myself, long years of soul-searching and diligent self-analysis have taught me that I am most likely to be done in by great expectations and bad advice; the following epilogue proves I have had my fair share of both.

EPILOGUE: ON THINGS THAT DON'T WORK OVERSEAS...INCLUDING MY BODY

My most recent trip abroad was a revelation—not because I ate fabulous pirogi or drifted shamelessly to the strains of a polonaise; the revelation was simply that the able-bodied traveler simply can't depend on anything to work . . . least of all his or her body. Think back on your last foray into the mystical world of croissants and bidets; reexamine your misadventures with wake-ups and weather forecasts and ask yourself (as I do now) if anything *really* worked.

Bathrooms. Let's face it, this admittedly necessary facility was conceived by a high-school dropout who meant to build the Cuisinart. A bidet, it seems to me, is good for only one thing: to exclaim as one descends for dinner, "You know, Frieda, my bathroom has one of those short things with water." So does Frieda's. A bidet would better serve as a wading pool for beginning swimmers or as a summer camp for turtles. At a hotel I recently imposed upon in Paris, there was of course a bidet . . . and a shower. There was, however, pas de shower curtain. But the gifted schizophrenic who designed the enclosure put a duct on the floor with a superpowerful vacuum that inhaled the excess water, together with two pairs of my underwear and a half a kimono. I was lucky to get out with my life.

Mini Bars. As a concession both to the mechanization of hotel services and possibly to the problem drinker, newer hotels have installed mini bars completely stocked with small bottles of alcoholic beverages, requisite mixes, juices, and bags of pretzels. Guests simply check off their needs as they blissfully bomb their way through the inventory. My first night in Warsaw, I drank a mineral water and dutifully checked off Mineral Water—1. The next day my mineral water was replaced, and I got a new inventory checklist. I also got charged for two bottles of vodka, one orange juice, and six bags of pretzels. I cannot explain the accounting snafu, but I can explain my chambermaid who looked very, very happy (and decidedly plotzed) as she turned down my bed that night.

Nightclubs. Nightclub tours of any city in the world should be taken only by theatrical agents, vampires, and an occasional werewolf. Recently, against my better judgment (but anxious to spend the evening entertained by something more than a bidet or mini bar), I visited a nightclub in Lima. It could as easily have been in Lusaka or London because the scenario is inscribed in marble. Most nightclubs have a production singer who has an indistinguishable accent of questionable origin which somehow allows him to bring a new gusto to "Zee Most Bootiful Girl in Zee Vorld." This assault on the arts usually is followed by an adagio team who seem to derive great pleasure from beating each other up while a harpist tries to find her foot pedals in the dark. As a sort of duress de resistance, a faded soprano walks into the spotlight (shocked to be discovered) and launches into a song whose only distinction is that she is unable to sing it. In Tahiti recently, one such charmer dramatically attacked "Zend in Da Clones"... double proof that nightclubs anywhere in the world do not work.

Stomachs. This physiological appurtenance was not meant to eat ravioli, kielbasi, truffles, and soda bread, or to drink sake and aquavit. My stomach barely copes with cornflakes, so travel abroad presents several problematic options. On my last trip to happy Yugoslavia, I went to bed at midnight (local time) and awakened at 7:00 A.M. My stomach, however, arose at 4:00 A.M. with an unmanageable desire for butter pecan ice cream and Fritos—neither of which is easy to come by in Dubrovnik. Doctors and airline health advisers suggest that it takes two full days for the body's time clock to regulate and acclimate to the new time zone. My body is still acclimating to a trip it took in 1973 and, as far as I can tell, it will never be regulated. As delicately as possible, I want to add that the inoperability of my stomach and its associates has caused me to be dubbed "King Kaopectate" and "Lord Lomotil." But then my stomach hardly works in Los Angeles; why should it prosper in Peru?

Drip-Dry. According to ancient Egyptian mythology, Cleopatra used drip-dry fabrics when she traveled. But then what did Cleopatra know from laundry? I recently purchased some drip-dry underwear for a trip to Poland and, at last report, my shorts (which dripped all through Warsaw) were still drying in Cracow. To add insult to injury, in South America I experimented with a new clothesline made of interwoven surgical rubber which clenched the garments— thus cleverly eliminating the need for clothespins. I attached one end of the line to the bathroom doorknob; the other end was secured around the shower faucet. All of my clothes dripped and dried gloriously on the line and I thought I had at last discovered something that worked. Alas, the maid came in to clean the bathroom before I took down the clothesline. The elasticity of the surgical rubber is a force to be reckoned with and, when last charted, the maid from Bogotá was being catapulted to Cartagena. Not to worry—at least she would get there before my shorts dried.

High School Command of the Language. I'm a firm believer in making every effort to spread my "Buenos diases," "Bongiornos," and "Dzien Dobrys" around, but beyond the barest amenities I find that one's high-school French or Spanish can cause international incidents. Two examples. In Sri Lanka I was encouraged at one particularly elegant restaurant to struggle along with my high-school French. Gallantly, I snapped my fingers and signaled for "l'addition, s'il vous plait." When the check came, I perused it much too quickly, muttered several "Très Biens" and one "Merveilleux," jotted down some figures, and then discovered that the total was incredibly inflated because I had inadvertently added the date. Somehow I know David Niven would have handled it better. Much more recently, during a sun-baked vacation in La Paz, I was having dinner with a charming señorita who accidentally spilled some wine. Anxious to calm her embarrassment *and* to impress her with my Spanish, I said, "No embarazada," only to find out I had told her not to become pregnant. As I recall, she spilled more wine.

Advice. Nothing, not a talk show with starlets, not a winter in Chicago, not a traffic jam in Manhattan, *nothing* is fraught with greater potential for disaster than advice given to a traveler. Advice to a traveler is like admiring a woman in a bikini: you get a lot of promising information, but somehow fail to find out exactly what you need to know. I am speaking here of the travel advice that does not work. Advice like, "Don't take an umbrella to the South Pacific," "Forget the sweaters—our summers in Prague are hot," "Don't worry, it won't snow in Greece," "Certainly you can change money at the border," "You will find a better selection of rugs in the next village," "Don't bring toilet paper; ours is soft," and, "You absolutely will not have to pay duty on that item." All of this well-intentioned counseling is offered by people who give weather forecasts as if they had studied meteorology with Copernicus and merchandising at Montgomery Ward. I urge you to resist their counsel: take raincoats and umbrellas everywhere, buy the rug where you first see it, and clutch soft, serviceable toilet paper as if you were carrying the Mona Lisa.

Mind you, it is possible that you might be fortunate and receive excellent advice, the gadgets in your hotel room may work inexplainably with a magic all their own, and your stomach might adapt to Machu Picchu and Minsk as if it were still at home. If all of that comes to pass, *please*, I don't want to hear about it.

INDEX